KU-236-505

LIVING THE GLOBAL CITY

CITY

Globalization as a local process

Edited by John Eade

London and New York

KING ALFRED'S COLLEGE
WINCHESTER

337 EAD | 0239 3972

First published 1997
by Routledge
11 New Fetter Lane, London, EC4P 4EE

Simultaneously published in the USA and Canada
by Routledge
29 West 35th Street, New York, NY 10001

© 1997 John Eade selection and editorial matter;
individual chapters, the contributors.

Typeset in Garamond by
J&L Composition Ltd, Filey, North Yorkshire
Printed and bound in Great Britain by
Biddles Ltd, Guildford and King's Lynn

All rights reserved. No part of this book may be reprinted or
reproduced or utilized in any form or by any electronic,
mechanical, or other means, now known or hereafter
invented, including photocopying and recording, or in any
information storage or retrieval system, without permission in
writing from the publishers.

British Library Cataloguing in Publication Data
A catalogue record for this book is available from the British Library

Library of Congress Cataloging in Publication Data
Living the global city/edited by John Eade.
p.   cm.
Includes bibliographical references and index.
ISBN 0–415–13886–8.—ISBN 0–415–13887–6 (pbk.)
1. International economic relations.   2. International trade.
3. International division of labor.   I. Eade, John, 1946–
HF1359.L587   1996   96–7921
337—dc20   CIP

CONTENTS

CONTENTS

FIGURES

TABLES

NOTES ON CONTRIBUTORS

Martin Albrow has held chairs in sociology in Wales and Munich and is currently Research Professor in the Social Sciences at the Roehampton Institute, London. He is Founding Editor of *International Sociology*, the journal of the International Sociological Association, and an Honorary Vice-President of the British Sociological Association. His books include *Max Weber's Construction of Social Theory* (Macmillan, 1990) and *The Global Age* (Polity, forthcoming).

Patricia Alleyne-Dettmers was educated in Trinidad, the USA and the Federal Republic of Germany. She recently received her PhD from the University of Pennsylvania, Philadelphia, USA. Currently she is a Senior Research Officer in the Department of Sociology and Social Policy at Roehampton Institute. In partnership with the Institute and the Arts Council of England she has been commissioned to set up a national database for British carnivalists.

Laura Buffoni has a degree in political science from the University of Genoa, Italy. Her research interest is concerned with globalization, development and poverty. She is currently a post-graduate student at the University of Pisa where she is working on the impact of globalization on poverty in both industrialized and developing countries. She is also a member of Globalization Research Cluster at the Roehampton Institute.

Jörg Dürrschmidt is a Lecturer in Sociology at the University of the West of England. He has a background in phenomenological philosophy and his research interests lie within the phenomenology of everyday life and current processes of microglobalization in global cities. He is currently completing his PhD, an examination of the challenges presented for the concept of 'milieu' by processes of microglobalization in the sociocultural environment of the world city, London.

John Eade is a Principal Lecturer in the Department of Sociology and Social Policy at the Roehampton Institute. He has published numerous articles and chapters in books concerning the Bangladeshi community in

Tower Hamlets where he undertook his doctoral research as well as writing on Bengali Muslims in Calcutta. He has also written about pilgrimage and tourism and co-edited with Michael Sallnow *Contesting the Sacred: The Anthropology of Christian Pilgrimage* (Routledge, 1991).

Graham Fennell is a Professor and Head of the Department of Sociology and Social Policy at the Roehampton Institute. Previously he was Lecturer in Sociology at the University of East Anglia. His research includes survey studies of housing for elderly people, observational studies in day centres and large-scale statistical analysis of demographic trends in sheltered housing. He has co-authored with Chris Phillipson and Helen Evers *The Sociology of Old Age* (Open University Press, 1988).

Darren O'Byrne graduated in sociology from the University of Sheffield and is currently carrying out research at the Roehampton Institute, London, on the meanings of national citizenship under globalized conditions. His other areas of interest include sociological theory, human rights and the death penalty.

Neil Washbourne is an Academic Assistant in the Department of Sociology and Social Policy at the Roehampton Institute. He is currently researching the use of networked information technology in organizations of the Global Green Movement.

ACKNOWLEDGEMENTS

This volume emerged from lively debates within both the Department of Sociology and Social Policy and the Globalization Research Cluster at the Roehampton Institute. Contributors to this volume have also been assisted by comments made at various conferences and workshops both in Britain and overseas. We were also grateful for the welcome advice provided by the two referees for our proposal. In preparing the manuscript the patient assistance of Linda Wilson was crucial.

1

INTRODUCTION

John Eade

INTELLECTUAL AND POLITICAL MOVEMENTS

This is an exciting time to produce a volume on living the global city. There is a widespread sense that the world is changing rapidly and drastically. While an awareness of change is nothing new contemporary debates about *specific* changes raise novel issues. These issues are debated not only in the mass media but in academic institutions where popular discourses concerning an emerging new world both inform and become the objects of analysis.

Sociologists have inevitably played a key role in this public debate about a 'changing world'. They have engaged in a continuing process of discursive revision during the last twenty years as different structural paradigms have been challenged by the deconstructionist critique of those who have announced the 'end of the social' and, therefore, of conventional sociology. A rich diversity has emerged where different constituencies position themselves tangentially to others as locality, particularism, hybridity and heterogeneity are celebrated in opposition to the 'grand narratives' of the sociological Masters (sic). Usually described as 'post-modern', these critiques have sought to provide intellectual space where various minorities could speak, i.e. gays, lesbians, black people, refugees, migrants, residents of the 'Third World'. Advocates of a 'third space' inhabited by these minorities have also challenged the traditional methods of Western analysis such as the preoccupation with binary oppositions.

As the twentieth century draws to a close an intellectual and political challenge has emerged from the diverse post-modern celebrations of a highly localized, heterogeneous, fragmented world: how to reveal the possibility of strategic alliances across such divisions as gender, sexuality, race, ethnicity and nation? This crucial question lies behind public debates about the resurgence of 'ethnic violence' in former Yugoslavia and USSR as the Cold War gave way to what the opponents of communism hailed as the 'new world order'. At the more specific level of British politics the increasing popularity of single-issue campaigns has raised the question of

1

how these different interest groups can find common ground in challenging central government.

During this period of rapid fragmentation and heterogeneity attention has been drawn by politicians, business leaders and journalists to a contradictory process of globalization. References by George Bush to a homogeneous new world order following the collapse of communist regimes are an example of a political attempt to anticipate and determine what that order might be. The deficiencies of United Nations missions in Somalia and Bosnia-Herzegovina have strengthened the position of those who question the reality of such a world order or the feasibility of a world order emerging. Attention is drawn to the abiding significance of the United States as the dominant partner in any global political arrangement and the continuing importance of nation-states. These reservations have also informed popular debates about the economic dimensions of globalization. Sceptics contend that the emergence of global markets where capital and information flow freely and instantaneously across time zones and geopolitical space is related to the continuing dominance of the United States or Western industrial nations. They also argue that globalization refers to a free enterprise project which is far more limited in its extent than its exponents would like to think.

The social and cultural dimensions of globalization are also popularly associated with debates concerning the extent to which differences between nation-states are diminished or eliminated by the global flow of ideas, information, capital and labour. The advocates of national and sub-national differences inevitably hail the continued vitality of those heterogeneous practices as a witness to the very limited impact of globalization or what some would prefer to call Americanization.

These popular debates have been paralleled by an academic discourse which has drawn on the homogeneity/heterogeneity opposition in an attempt to go beyond the formulations of politicians, journalists, business leaders and non-governmental organizations. They have have also tried to move away from two academic paradigms which dominated the sociological analysis of international social and cultural change during the 1960s and 1970s – modernization and world systems theories. The drive to replace these two theoretical perspectives can be partially attributed to the very developments which the exponents of globalization wished to investigate, i.e. the decline of traditional class solidarities, the proliferation of de-centred social and cultural worlds and of third spaces between 'insiders' and 'outsiders', the end of the Cold War and the expansion of allegiances which referred to both supra-national and sub-national 'imagined communities'.

At the Roehampton Institute we have debated the theoretical and substantive issues raised by the burgeoning academic interest in globalization. Our Research Cluster has brought together those undertaking research projects as well as colleagues from different departments who are generally interested in the topic. Given the highly generalized nature of the globalization debate our research strategy has focused on how people's everyday lives are caught up in the globalization process. Our location within London has provided us with an opportunity to investigate locales within one of the world cities where it is widely accepted that the inter-weaving of global and local developments is intense. Through our discus-sions and substantive research we have produced a volume which is intended to: (a) engage in the theoretical issues raised by the globalization literature; and (b) relate those debates to an analysis of the engagement between global and local processes within London. As far as we are aware our project is the first of its kind to be undertaken within the UK and we believe that it could provide a model for new and appropriate research on globalization anywhere in the world.

Before we consider the particular arguments proposed by this volume's contributors more light needs to be shed upon the key concepts with which we engage in our respective chapters.

KEY CONCEPTS

Globalization, glocalization and globality

Although Roland Robertson (1992) has noted the considerable disagree-ment over definitions of globalization, a prime concern among commen-tators has been the compression of both time and space. Anthony Giddens (1990), for example, analyses the ways in which space and time have become compressed in terms of two processes – 'distanciation' and 'disembedding'. Distanciation refers to 'the conditions under which time and space are organised so as to connect presence and absence' (Giddens 1990: 14), while disembedding concerns the ways in which social relations are lifted out of their local contexts and restructured 'across indefinite spans of time–space' (ibid.: 21). The significance of nation-state bound-aries and institutions declines as global and local social relations interweave and worldwide social relations intensify. Globalization does not necessarily lead to increasing social homogenization according to Giddens because distanciated relations are frequently engaged in a dialectical transformation. For Giddens '[l]ocal transformation is as much a part of globalization as the lateral extension of social connections across time and space' (ibid.: 64, emphasis in the original).

While the analysis of globalization provided by Giddens focuses on social relations, Roland Robertson chooses to emphasize 'the scope and depth of consciousness of the world as single place'. Globalization, therefore, involves not just 'the objectiveness of increasing connectedness' but also 'subjective and cultural matters'. Robertson draws attention to the growth

3

of 'globe talk' – 'the discourse of globality' – which 'consists largely in the shifting and contested terms in which the world as a whole is "defined"' and which is 'a vital component of contemporary global culture' (Robertson 1992: 113).

The implications of globalization for notions of locality are developed by Robertson in a more recent discussion where he claims that globalization entails the reconstruction and 'the production of "home", "community" and "locality"' (Robertson 1995: 30). Rather than the local and the global constituting analytical opposites locality 'can be regarded, with certain reservations, as *an aspect* of globalization' (ibid., emphasis in the original). Through global compression localities are both brought together and invented (ibid.: 35). While globalization is useful as an analytical concept referring to the 'simultaneity and the interpenetration of what are conventionally called the global and the local, or – in more abstract vein the universal and the particular', Robertson suggests that 'glocalization' might be a more accurate term to describe the global/local relationship. Glocalization refers, in the subjective and personal sphere, to the construction and invention of diverse localities through global flows of ideas and information.

Although Giddens and Robertson share a mutual interest in the interweaving of global and local processes, Robertson's discussion of globality leads him to criticize Giddens for failing to appreciate 'the significance of culture' (Robertson 1992: 144) and, therefore, being unable to theorize 'the issue of "other cultures"' (ibid.). Giddens is further taken to task for not realizing that:

> The whole idea that one can sensibly interpret the contemporary world
> without addressing the issues that arise from current debates about the
> politics of culture, cultural capital, cultural difference, cultural homo-
> geneity and heterogeneity, ethnicity, race and gender, and so on, is
> implausible.
>
> (ibid.: 145)

Despite their differences in approach towards globalization Giddens and Robertson have both emphasized the importance of reflexivity in their understanding of global/local relations. In the process they have drawn on a sociological heritage which includes such 'masters' as Weber, Simmel, Durkheim and Parsons. Against post-modern attempts to deconstruct the social their discussion of globalization presents a case for the continuing relevance of academic sociology and its intellectual heritage.

Martin Albrow also rejects the post-modern deconstruction of the social but claims that globalization presents sociology with a novel challenge. The coming of what he calls the 'global age' (cf. Albrow 1996) requires a new sociological framework as sociology is itself globalized as individual sociologists enjoy the freedom of collaborating with their colleagues 'anywhere on the globe' and appreciate 'the worldwide processes within which and on which they work' (Albrow 1990: 7). He detects, therefore, the emergence of a 'universal discourse' which embraces 'multiple interlocutors based on different regions and cultures' (ibid.: 8). An illustration of the way in which traditional sociological concepts can be reconstituted is provided in Chapter 2 of this volume where we explore community, culture and milieu. We suggest that globalization entails, for example, the deterritorialization of traditional concepts, their disaggregation and resynthesis, their extension 'to embrace new realities' and their global operationalization as well as 'the generalization of local concepts to the level of global relevance and their assimilation into a transnational discourse'.

Scapes and spheres

The issues raised by Robertson's examination of cultural homogeneity and heterogenity can be further explored through a seminal treatment by Arjun Appadurai of what he describes as a disjunctured 'global cultural economy' (Appadurai 1990: 296). The relative autonomy of this global culture is sustained by the disjunctures between cultural, political and economic processes (ibid.). Appadurai outlines 'an elementary framework' for analysing the disjunctured global culture consisting of 'the relationship between five dimensions of global cultural flow which can be termed: (a) ethnoscapes; (b) mediascapes; (c) technoscapes; (d) finanscapes; and (e) ideoscapes' (ibid.). These scapes are 'deeply perspectival constructs' and comprise a 'set of landscapes' which are 'navigated' by individual social actors 'who both experience and constitute larger formations, in part by their sense of what these landscapes offer' (ibid.).

One of the advantages of the term 'scapes' lies in its reference to 'the fluid, irregular shapes of these landscapes' (ibid.: 297). From these scapes are built 'imagined worlds' – 'multiple worlds which are constituted by the historically situated imaginations of persons and groups spread around the globe' (ibid.: 296–7). For Appadurai these scapes are engaged in processes of inequality and power. People across the world can challenge and perhaps undermine the 'imagined worlds' of state officials and entrepreneurs (ibid.: 297). The fluidity of these different components of global cultural flow is contrasted with the 'relatively stable communities and networks' through which people move (ibid.).

Appadurai's model is attractively sensitive to the asymmetric flows of ideas, information, people and capital and it complements Robertson's cultural perspective through its rejection of the highly economistic approach adopted by Wallerstein in world systems theory. Yet a question is raised by Appadurai's assumption concerning the stability of the communities and networks through which people move. As Martin Albrow, for example, writes in Chapter 3 of this volume: 'from the perspective of participants are they not equally "-scapes"?' and suggests that Appadurai's model needs to incorporate the concept of 'socioscape' – 'the vision of social formations which are more than the people who occupy them at any one time'. Conventional descriptions of local socioscapes in terms of 'community' and 'neighbourhood' are made redundant by globalization. In an extension of the argument introduced in the previous section, Albrow detects a 'growing indeterminacy' in people's application of both old and new categories as social formations become delocalized. He suggests both that 'sociosphere' might describe 'the sense of varying but overlapping spatial scope' as local attachments are dis-embedded and that 'socioscapes' emerge where these sociospheres intersect.

Collective solidarities and individual meanings, the universal and the particular

The formulations devised by Giddens, Robertson and Albrow in particular reveal a persistent engagement in the relationship between the universal and the particular and between collective solidarities and individual understandings. Integral to Giddens' model of globalization and reflexive modernity, for example, is his understanding of risk and trust where individuals can sustain physical and psychological security in a rapidly changing world where local social relations are disembedded. In a recent discussion Giddens refers to the ways in which 'the most intimate connections between gender, sexuality and self-identity, are publicly placed in question', as people disengage from traditional relations (1994: 106). Violence and dialogue are possibilities at both the level of the personal and the global and he detects 'a real and clear symmetry between the possibility of a "democracy of the emotions" on the level of the personal life and the potential for democracy on the level of the global order' (ibid.).

It appears that individual meanings for Giddens are the outcomes of the structural process of distanciation, disembedding and reflexivity. As Waters notes each of these three 'main dynamics of modernization implies universalizing tendencies which render social relations ever more inclusive' so that individual understandings of self and society increasingly extend across the globe (Waters 1995: 50).

At the core of Robertson's model of globalization is 'the relationship between the universal and the particular (Robertson 1992: 97). This relationship is analysed in the contemporary context of 'a massive, twofold process involving the interpenetration of the universalization of particularism and the particularization of universalism' (ibid.: 100). The universalization of particularism entails 'the idea of the universal being given global-human concreteness' (ibid.: 102) through 'increasingly fine-grained modes of identity presentation' (ibid.: 178). Particularization of universalism, on the other hand, involves 'the search for *global* fundamentals' where move-ments and individuals look for 'the meaning of the world as a whole' (ibid.).

Interestingly, Robertson welcomes Appadurai's exploration of the dis-junctures between different cultural 'scapes' at the global level but claims that Appadurai's '*chaos*–theoretic approach' rejects the 'massive, twofold process' described above (ibid.: 103, emphasis in the original). For Appa-durai the prime characteristic of contemporary global culture is: 'the politics of the mutual effort of sameness and difference to cannibalize one another and thus to proclaim their successful hijacking of the twin Enlightenment ideas of the triumphantly universal and the resiliently particular' (ibid.: 308). Individuals have to navigate a world 'characterized by radical disjunctures between different sorts of global flows and the uncertain landscapes created in and through these disjunctures' (ibid.).

Albrow implicitly endorses Appadurai's model of a disjunctive order in his development of the socioscape. The structure of a socioscape is produced by the intersection of individual sociospheres through routine procedures and pragmatic accommodations about which Goffman's writ-ings and the phenomenological discussion of milieu have much to teach us. Albrow also establishes a link with Giddens' discussion of time and space and claims that the relationship between social relations and individual perceptions in globalized conditions should be understood in terms of time–space social stratification – the unequal distribution among indivi-duals of control over temporal and spatial resources.

These diverse explorations of the collective/individual and universal/particular have engaged, implicitly and explicitly, with neo-Marxist perspec-tives. Robertson, for example, acknowledges the contribution of Waller-stein's writings on the 'modern world-system' to the '"global shift" in sociological theory' (Robertson 1992: 65). Appadurai acknowledges his debt to Jameson's discussion of 'the relationship between postmodernism and late capitalism' while admitting that his attempt to restructure 'the Marxist narrative (by stressing lags and disjunctures)' may be abhorrent to many Marxists (Appadurai 1990: 308). Since those who have drawn even more explicitly on Marxist discourses engage in rather different models of the relationship between individual meanings and structural processes this discussion will be continued later in the next section after a close con-sideration of the issues of power, inequality and conflict.

Power, inequality and conflict

The various accounts of globalization so far introduced have already referred to the issues of power, inequality and conflict. Their formulations are devised with contemporary struggles around economic, social and political resources very much in mind. Here I want to explore further the ways in which these struggles have been placed within a global perspective through certain direct engagements with Marxist discourses. I will focus on the following contributors in particular – Harvey, Lash and Urry, Hall and Massey.

David Harvey (1989) attempts to make sense of post-modernist ideas in the context of capitalism's 'political–economic background' where 'the experience of space and time [is] one singularly important mediating link between the dynamism of capitalism's historical–geographical development and complex processes of cultural production and ideological transformation' (ibid.: viii). While Giddens differentiates space from time, Harvey understands 'time–space compression' as the annihilation of space by time (cf. Waters 1995: 55). He delivers an analysis which firmly locates global compression within long-established Marxist concerns with the contradictions of capitalism and crises both in economic overaccumulation and cultural and political formations (cf. Waters 1995: 258). Accepting the transition from Fordism to flexible accumulation in recent capitalist developments (cf. Gregory and Urry 1985) he suggests:

> that we have been experiencing, these last two decades, an intense phase of time–space compression that has led to a disorienting and disruptive impact upon political–economic practices, the balance of class power, as well as upon cultural and social life.
>
> (Harvey 1989: 284)

Depthlessness, ephemerality, the production and marketing of images, the move from the production of goods to the production and consumption of services are intimately associated with post-modern discourses but these cultural and political shifts are nothing new to those who, like him, wish to pursue a 'historical materialist enquiry' (ibid.: 328). Such an enquiry entails the formulation of a counter-narrative based on a 'project of Becoming rather than Being' and a 'search for unity within difference' (ibid.: 359).

In a more recent deliberation, Harvey emphasizes the way in which time–space compression has 'undermined older material and territorial definitions of place'. The 'collapse of spatial boundaries' has crucial consequences for the relationship between general processes and individual understandings since there is a 'renewed emphasis upon the interrogation of metaphorical and psychological meanings' leading to 'new material definitions of place by way of exclusionary territorial behaviour' (Harvey 1993: 4).

As we have already seen, Harvey builds on models of flexible accumulation and disorganized capitalism proposed by Urry and Gregory. More recently John Urry has joined Scott Lash in an analysis of subjectivity, especially 'an increasingly significant *reflexive* human subjectivity' (Lash and Urry 1994: 3). They claim that this form of human subjectivity' is caught up in a process of 'reflexive modernisation' (ibid.: 3) which affects 'not just the subjects, but the *objects* involved in mobility' (ibid.: 4, emphasis in

8

the original). In a globalizing world of post-Fordist production 'what is increasingly produced are not material objects but *signs*' which take the form of post-industrial, informational or post-modern, aesthetic goods (ibid.). Organized capitalism has been replaced, therefore, by an 'economy of signs and space' located within a global order or disorder which consists of both 'a structure of flows' and an opposing process of reflexivity. The 'institutions of the new information society' can, therefore, be challenged by a 'large number of men and women who are taking an increasingly critical and *reflexive* distance' concerning those institutions (ibid.).

In their application of this framework to what they see as 'a complex dialectic of global *and* local processes' (ibid.: 284) Lash and Urry draw on Harvey's analysis of globalization and localization. They approvingly quote Harvey's (1989) assertion that the 'collapse of spatial barriers does not mean that the significance of place is decreasing' and as 'spatial barriers diminish so we become more sensitized to what the world's spaces contain' (ibid.: 303). Lash and Urry proceed to relate Harvey's interpretation of time–space compression to their understanding of reflexive modernization and the aestheticization of the world in which we live. They appear to suggest that human beings can use their reflexive capacity to resist, at a local level, the collapse of spatial boundaries which globalization entails. The flows of capital, information, images and people across the globe can lead to new formulations of place at the local level as people pursue a critical stance towards the global economy of signs and space. Yet, as they also note, these reformulations of locality may be undertaken in order to attract global capital and those working within the new information society and the new service class in particular (ibid.: 319).

The implications of the global flow of people from former colonial territories to metropolitan centres is developed further by Stuart Hall, who relates global cultural movements to national discourses and the emergence of hybrid identities and diasporic communities. In criticizing those who would present globalization as a homogenizing process he detects 'a new articulation between "the global" and "the local" . . . where it seems unlikely that globalization will simply destroy national identities' (Hall 1992b: 304). Globalization is described as being 'an uneven process' and despite the survival of 'some aspects of Western global domination . . . cultural identities everywhere are being relativized by the impact of time–space compression' (ibid.: 306). Globalization can 'lead to a *strengthening* of local identities, or to the production of *new identities*' (ibid.: 308, emphasis in the original).

The dialectical character of identity formation means that globalization's 'general impact remains contradictory' (ibid.: 309). Identities can move towards Tradition or Translation and for our purposes Hall now proceeds to the most useful part of his analysis. Translation refers to 'those identity formations which cut across and intersect natural frontiers and which are composed of people who have been dispersed forever from their home-lands' (ibid.: 310). They construct hybrid cultures and through the process of global migration they create 'new diasporas' where they 'must learn to inhabit at least two identities, to speak two cultural languages, to translate and negotiate between them' (ibid.: 310). In opposition to these identities are 'equally powerful attempts to reconstruct purified identities, to restore coherence, closure and "Tradition"' (ibid.: 311) and Hall cites 'the resurgence of nationalism in Eastern Europe and the rise of fundamentalism' as two examples of these new traditional identities (ibid.).

The issues of power and inequality are even more explicitly addressed by Doreen Massey. She wants to relate time–space compression to 'the possibility of developing a politics of mobility and access'. She reminds us that 'it is not simply a question of unequal distribution' but that 'the mobility and control of some groups can actively weaken other people' and that the 'time–compression of some groups can undermine the power of others' (Massey 1993: 62). A progressive politics can build on a notion of places as social relations rather than bounded enclosures and an understanding of centre–periphery relations and migrant settlers as well as the longer-established 'alien others – women' (ibid.: 67).

Recurrent themes

A number of questions recur during the accounts which I have very briefly introduced.

- How is contemporary society changing as globalization proceeds?
- What are the consequences for traditional sociological interpretations which have focused on issues of class, ethnic, racial or gender formations?
- What new political, social and economic strategies should be devised to respond to the global flows of capital, information, images and people?
- How can traditional discussions of power, resistance and inequality be reinterpreted in the light of globalization?

The answers to these questions are shaped by the different commentators' theoretical perspectives, of course. Giddens focuses largely on the consequences of globalization for understandings of the individual and formulations of ontological security. The advance of global consciousness for Robertson shapes local understandings so that the local cannot be seen as 'a counterpoint to the global'. Albrow speaks of both 'delocalization' and 'a growing indeterminacy' in applying social categories among people in particular localities.

In Appadurai's treatment of the 'global cultural economy' we move more closely towards an appreciation of inequality and power – issues which also concern Harvey, Lash and Urry, and Hall whose writing bears the impress of Marxist revisionist attempts to respond to radical changes in global capitalism and the social formation of nation-states. For Harvey, and Lash and Urry spatial changes and reinterpretations of place offer both progressive and reactionary possibilities. Harvey believes that 'territorial place-based identity' is a basis for 'both progressive political mobilization and reactionary exclusionary politics' (Harvey 1993: 4) while Lash and Urry contend that 'the growth of information can be seen as liberating or as repressive' (Lash and Urry 1994: 324). Similar contradictory processes are possible in the context of the nation-state, while placelessness may be opposed by reimagined places intended 'often to attract flows of tourists or entrepreneurs (a tame zone), or to repel migrants or low-wage capital (to a wild zone)' (ibid.: 326).

Both Hall and Massey refer to the 'power-geometry' of globalization in discussions which refer to the boundaries of nation, race, ethnicity and gender. Hall (1992a, 1992b) is particularly interested in the progressive possibilities of hybrid, translated identities and diasporic communities while Massey (1993), in acknowledging the global movement of migrant workers to metropolitan centres, also notes the potential contribution of other aliens – women – to a progressive politics of place.

We draw in different ways on these varying responses to the questions outlined above and in the process we want to demonstrate how the contested arena which surrounds globalization can be related more specifically to the everyday life of people in a world city. Our intention is not to suggest that people's lives are shaped by the global city: rather they are participating in diverse global processes which are occurring throughout the world but can be analysed in specific contexts – in this case, London. Before introducing our different perspectives on those contexts I want to outline very briefly why London can be described as a 'global city' and the general scope of our research within that city.

LONDON: A GLOBAL CITY

Although Anthony King has produced an important study of London's role as a 'command and control centre' in the 'capitalist world-economy' (1990), the location of his discussion of the 'world city' within a world systems theory perspective is less useful for our purposes than the work of Saskia Sassen (1991, 1994). She has mounted the most impressive case for describing London among others (notably New York and Tokyo) as a global city. She describes global cities as:

sites for (1) the production of specialized services needed by complex organizations for running a spatially dispersed network of factories,

11

offices, and service outlets; and (2) the production of financial innovations and the making of markets, both central to the internationaliz-
ation and expansion of the financial industry.

(Sassen 1991: 5)

For our purposes the most interesting aspect of her analysis is her
delineation of the political challenge which is created by the growing
spatial and class polarization and migrant settlements which she records
(Sassen 1991: 245 *passim*). She contends that global cities are confronted
with a key political question: 'what happens to accountability when the
leading economic sectors are oriented to a world market and to firms rather
than to individuals' (ibid.: 334). Increases in homelessness, poverty, badly
paid jobs and homework 'are linked to the growth of an industrial complex
oriented to the world market' rather than to local economies and to 'the
growth of what amounts to an ideology of globalism, whereby localities are
seeen as powerless in an era of global economic forces' (ibid.).

While acknowledging the significance of the economic and political
issues explored by Sassen and others (cf. King 1990; Budd and Whimster
1992; Fainstein, Gordon and Harloe 1992; Keith and Pile 1993) in this
volume we want to focus on the meanings which these structural developments hold for individuals and how these meanings relate – if at all – to
traditional collective categories such as 'classes' and minority (ethnic or
racial) 'communities'. A strong case has been made for the impact of global
economic forces on urban life. However, the disjunctures between the
various scapes described by Appadurai and Albrow prevent any straightfor-
ward determinacy of people's understandings by the processes of economic
and geographical separation and inequality associated with those global
forces.

Our research has focused, therefore, on social, cultural and political
issues which have largely been ignored in the expanding literature on the
global or world city. These issues are associated with certain key developments which took place during the 1980s. In that decade London's role as a
major centre for global capital transactions became more transparent and
significant as industrial production in the capital declined as the service
sector expanded (see Budd and Whimster 1992). Alternative economic
strategies were devised by political opponents of the central (Conservative) government's 'free market' approach. However, Conservative electoral
success under the leadership of Margaret Thatcher during the 1980s led to
the demise of political resistance at the metropolitan level through the
elimination of the Greater London Council and the Inner London Education Authority. Vigorous attempts were made to rein in central government spending on public resources such as housing, social and welfare
services and both political and financial support was provided to local
borough councils such as Wandsworth who pioneered the implementation

of central government policy. The derelict dock area of east London – a symbol of Britain's industrial past and class confrontation – was redeveloped as a demonstration of the free market philosophy, the freedom from interfering local authorities and the effectiveness of global investment (see Brownhill 1990; Keith and Rogers 1991; Budd and Whimster 1992; Bird 1993; Fainstein 1994).

These developments provide the background to our decision in 1993 to launch a pioneering study of local/global relations in Wandsworth. Certain areas of the borough had changed considerably during the 1980s as middle-class settlers moved into privatized council stock where they joined many working-class residents who had taken the opportunity of becoming owner-occupiers of council flats. Given the increasing social and cultural diversity of the borough we decided to concentrate on four areas for our analysis of the ways in which people communicated with the outside world and the meanings which these connections held for them. Two of these areas have provided the setting for chapters by Martin Albrow and Darren O'Byrne in this volume. After the completion of the largely qualitative study of local–global relations which serves as the empirical basis for the chapters by Albrow and O'Byrne, a borough-wide quantitative survey was undertaken and is also reported in this volume.

The social and cultural issues examined in the Wandsworth globalization studies were not simply reflections of the political and economic developments outlined above. This broad assertion was supported by parallel research undertaken by members of the Globalization Cluster elsewhere in the city. Jörg Dürrschmidt operated in Streatham, which was located in the neighbouring borough of Lambeth. Here was a borough with a very different (left-wing) political strategy towards public spending and economic development. However, the issues covered by Dürrschmidt do not fit neatly within these conventional political boundaries – a phenomenon encountered by other contributors to this volume who consider other areas of London, i.e. Docklands and Spitalfields in east London and Ladbroke Grove/Notting Hill which extends across another 'inner city' locale. Let us now look in more detail at the issues which these chapters cover.

INTRODUCING THE CHAPTERS

We begin in Chapter 2 with an exploration of the implications which the discussion by Robertson and Giddens of globalization holds for conventional sociological discourses. A social transformation has been detected which requires 'changes in basic sociological concepts as research strives to keep pace with the changing world'. This argument is pursued through a consideration of three key traditional concepts – community, culture and milieu – and two conclusions are developed. At the substantive level they claim to 'have identified the persistent pressure on older concepts to accommodate shifting and deterritorialized forms of social relationships'. Appadurai's work is adapted through the concept of the socioscape which is related to 'the relative, even momentary stabilities of social relationship, networks, groups and organisations under globalized conditions'. At a procedural level the conclusion also suggests that 'at least eight possible creative conceptual strategies are at work', viz. the operationalization of older abstract concepts for a managed world; the assimilation of local concepts to a transnational, global discourse; the abstraction of older concepts from territorial reference; the idealization of older concepts; the disaggregation of older concepts into analytical components; the extension of old concepts to embrace new realities; the synthesis of new concepts and the reflexive reconstruction of the social.

Martin Albrow notes in Chapter 3 that one of the implications of the argument outlined above is 'that globalization is much more than an extension of longer standing processes of modernization'. A sociological framework is required which dispenses with those staple concerns of modernization debates – community, nation and culture. He draws on the Wandsworth local/global research to substantiate his claim that we must reconsider 'the way social relations are tied to place' as well as our assumptions about the intimate bond between locality and culture.

To make sense of the new social relations and meanings apparent within the global city Albrow turns again to the notion of the socioscape and, a related concept, sociosphere. Even from the limited number of interviews undertaken by the Wandsworth project there is sufficient evidence to indicate a globalized locality where the diverse sociospheres produce an experience of the local which is like a 'cavalcade where passing actors find minimal levels of tolerable co-existence with varying intimations of the scope of other people's lives'. New conflicts involve 'locals and cosmopolitans and all gradations in between, where the local may be newcomers and the cosmopolitans may be long-term residents'. The realities of class are concealed as poor residents lose even the 'sight of their exploiters' with the dissolution of local culture 'into the generalized facilities of a convenient place to live'.

Jörg Dürrschmidt approaches, in Chapter 4, some of the points made by Albrow from a different intellectual tradition. He draws on German phenomenological discourses concerning milieux and situatedness to investigate what he calls a process of microglobalization, i.e. 'the integration of global difference(s) and variety into a distinctive social environment'. Milieux are defined 'as relatively stable and situated configurations of action and experience, in which individuals actively generate a distinctive degree of familiarity and practical competence'. Through the processes of disembedding and physical mobility individuals can succeed in negotiating the 'changing variety of "microglobalization"'. An individual's milieu is no

14

longer embedded in a particular locality but becomes extended with the result that '"here" and "there" do not equal "near" and "far"', that is "familiar" and "unfamiliar"'. A person's milieu, therefore, is situated not in a particular locality but through the individual 'determination to hold together the different fragments of an extended milieu'. These milieux can be understood as 'one concrete realization of "sociospheres"' where people 'inhabit a shrinking world, co-existing, overlapping, and intermingling with other people's "milieux", and thus negotiating the relevant spaces of "their" world'.

Darren O'Byrne places class – and specifically the 'working class' – in the foreground of his contribution in Chapter 5. Drawing on an eclectic range of writers (for example, Mannheim, Willis and Bourdieu, as well as Harvey, Robertson and Giddens) he examines the way in which globalization entails both the break-up of communities and the survival of localism. Starting with the assertion that 'working-class communities have always been political constructs based on issues of conflict' he draws on interviews conducted in Roehampton to challenge any assumption that class identity can be reduced to 'a reactive adaptation to global processes'. Adopting a hermeneutic perspective of 'working-class culture as a way of life' O'Byrne outlines an alternative interpretation which emphasizes 'the relative autonomy of both "globalization" and class culture'.

Like the other contributors, Darren O'Byrne stresses the creativity of social actors. He also notes a growing social diversity even within this traditional working-class area which suggests the existence of different groups existing at different 'spheres', 'scapes' and 'horizons'. Co-existence of these groups can entail conflict where individuals draw on such collective concepts as 'working class', 'locality', 'white' and 'black' to distinguish between 'insiders' and 'outsiders' in the context of structural factors, i.e. the economy and 'the transmission of cultural capital'. The locality 'divorced from any practical significance for its residents or the state, retains its ideological significance as the site for these struggles'.

In Chapter 6 we consider the quantitative data which complemented the initial research discussed by Albrow and O'Byrne above. Graham Fennell reveals the extent to which a random sample of 221 Wandsworth residents was linked to the wider world. Fennell develops his chapter by setting the quantitative data generated by the random sample against five ways in which methodological bias may have distorted earlier studies of 'the relationship between locality, living, connectedness, belonging, family and community'. These biases are revealed in the following procedures: (i) looking in but not out; (ii) finding the sample; (iii) imposing a length of residence test; (iv) asking questions which may exclude important social relationships which stretch beyond the locality; and (v) focusing on the local community. These biases have played a key role in ensuring 'that the relevant questions had not been asked, the data not collected or not thought worthy to record'.

Graham Fennell concludes his chapter by briefly discussing another methodological problem – the tendency for random samples to cover the white majority and, therefore, to leave out ethnic minorities. Sixteen per cent of the respondents in the Wandsworth random sample located themselves outside of the white majority. While one might expect this minority of the sample to be highly aware of the wider world the survey also investigated the degree to which people in general were involved in the world beyond this nation's borders. Significantly, almost half the respondents 'claim to speak at least one language other than English' and 68 per cent '*felt* that their lives were affected by people, events and organizations in other countries'.

In Chapter 7 we move away from a particular locality in south London to an exploration of individual perceptions of poverty in globalized conditions. Laura Buffoni defines poverty both as 'the lack of material and cultural resources which restricts one's ability to socialize' and 'a "trajectory" of progressive decline and of reduced availability of options in everyday life' and relates this definition to her concern with what Dürrschmidt calls 'microglobalization' through a study of globality, time/space compression and the relationship between global and local forces. She then proceeds to a discussion of individual meanings which supports the provocative call for a rethinking of traditional sociological perspectives towards poverty through the use of A. Sen's capability approach.

Buffoni concludes that, for some people at least, 'the possibility of maintaining social relations across the world and knowing about poverty in the world transforms the perception of their own relative poverty'. While people may lack material resources they can acquire *social* resources through their ability to exploit the 'technology, communications, cultural and social opportunities' of the global city. At the same time 'the dislocation brought about by globalization may be an element of additional disadvantage for those who are worse off and have no access to "global networking"'. Furthermore, a 'reduced set of capabilities due to age, material resources, technological illiteracy makes life in globalized conditions even more difficult'. She returns to the concept of sociosphere and socioscape to describe a situation of uneven access to resources where the 'various social worlds are not closed, but draw resources, meanings and knowledge from the outer, global social setting, thus dissociating the boundaries of access and non-access'.

The increasing complexity in social, cultural and economic conditions caused by globalization appears, from Laura Buffoni's account, to exacerbate the position of those who lack the cultural and economic means to take advantage of global networks. Debates concerning poverty have conventionally centred on issues of class inequality but in the chapters so far introduced class has frequently been placed in the background and associated with 'traditional' sociological perspectives.

Class is one of several themes which emerge in Chapter 8 where John Eade considers the diverse reconstructions of locality in Docklands and Spitalfields. Migration into this area has been dominated by two groups whose economic and social positions are radically different: (i) overseas investors and a predominantly white new service class; and (ii) a largely Muslim Bangladeshi working class employed in small businesses and low-paid jobs in the public sector. Those concerned with 'redeveloping' Docklands and Spitalfields produce interpretations of these localities' past which are designed to appeal to global and national investors and the new service class. These nostalgic visions of an urban landscape co-exist with alternative interpretations by young highly educated Bangladeshis who develop diverse new understandings of place which also look to a world beyond the locality but in terms of a clear awareness of a racialized, unequal and fragmented society.

These different constructions of place are analysed with reference to the models of scapes proposed by Appadurai and Albrow. The disjunctures between the different types of scope are related to the equally important separation between the local traditional political arena and the new institutions, especially the London Docklands Development Corporation, established by the central government. These disjunctures between political institutions are reinforced by global flows of people, capital, images and ideas which encourage Bangladeshis to look beyond the national political structure to political and ideological developments taking place across the world and which they can discursively construct in terms of various imagined, global communities. Those encouraging the global flow of capital and wealthy residents into the locality reinforce the disjunctures between scapes and relegate the 'working class' to the margins of their urban landscape. Young Bangladeshis also develop their own visions of the world around them in ways which 'indicate the kind of detachment from a nostalgic, essentialized notion of locality which is required for the development of a politics of resistance which can actually confront the forces beyond the existing political arena'.

John Eade again draws on the interviews with the young Bangladeshis in the following chapter to explore further the diverse ways in which individuals construct social identities through imagined communities. He concentrates here on national and Muslim constructions of belonging to a particular place. For some people national boundaries need to be transgressed in order to identify with a superordinate Islamic community (*umma*). While individuals pursue a strategy of accommodating these different constructions within a hierarchy of significance these 'ideoscapes' can claim rival primacies which cannot be so easily circumvented. National discourses can become embroiled in racialized constructions which exclude Bangladeshis and other 'outsiders' from a primordial community of white 'insiders'.

The young Bangladeshis can challenge these exclusivist constructions by developing individual, hybrid identities where diverse cultural resources can be utilized through global connections. However, their highly versatile intepretations of the globalized world in which they lived do not exclude 'anxious moments of self-doubt and ambiguity' where 'home' is not firmly located. Translation across political and ideological boundaries places global migrants and their offspring in an uneasy situation where essentialized traditions could exclude them from Britain or offer them an alternative home beyond the British nation-state. Bangladeshis in higher education show versatility in reflexively ordering this complex, fragmented world. They indicate the existence of perspectives 'which reveal the tensions, hierarchical claims and ambiguities involved in identity construction and relations with others across the global city and national frontiers'.

In Chapter 10 the themes of diasporic communities, hybrid identities and new ethnicities are taken further through Patricia Alleyne-Dettmers' exploration of global compression in the context of the Notting Hill carnival. She detects globalizing influences which 'impact on carnival *mas* art providing it with an 'easy compressed world . . . and an evolving aesthetic repertoire that violates all fixed ethnic, geographical and national boundaries'. Masquerade designers play a pivotal role in moving 'powerful cultural symbols around the world' through reconstituting and reinterpreting 'different histories and identities in the local, global city'. Consequently, 'national hegemonies are publicly dislocated and open, public arenas are constructed, whereby a variety of these national modes are being contested'.

In support of her argument she provides a case study of a particular designer and band leader's presentation – 'Tribal Arts' – for the 1993 Notting Hill Carnival. Four African regions were recreated in a process whereby Africa becomes 'not an imagined community but an imaginary community' partly for the aesthetic expression of black British identity in relation to a black diaspora which links Africa, the Caribbean and the UK. The success of 'Tribal Arts' in the carnival competitions not only increases the prestige of the individual designer but also involves the band itself in a process of ethnic empowerment. In the context of the Notting Hill carnival, therefore, globalization entails 'a politics of multiple diasporization and the formation of multiple identities'.

In this volume, therefore, we provide a varied discussion of the social and cultural processes involved in globalization across London. These processes are placed in tangential relationship to the political and economic developments which are also taking place within the city. While we share a mutual interest in the expanding sociological literature concerning global/local processes we differ in our selection of the concepts and issues upon which that literature has focused. We hope that the outcome of this diverse strategy is a more nuanced understanding of how people are creating 'new' forms of social belongings and meanings within a globalizing world where, simultaneously, traditional certainties can be even more firmly asserted.

ACKNOWLEDGEMENTS

I would like to thank all the contributors to this volume for their help in preparing this chapter. Darren O'Byrne's advice and patience was especially appreciated. I am also grateful for Caroline Egan-Strang's support as an interested and enthusiastic onlooker.

2

THE IMPACT OF GLOBALIZATION ON SOCIOLOGICAL CONCEPTS

Community, culture and milieu*

Martin Albrow, John Eade, Jörg Dürrschmidt and Neil Washbourne

INTRODUCTION

It is only in the last decade that a number of related processes which combine to increase the interconnectedness of social life at the world level have come to be known as globalization. But major claims have already been made for the social impact and theoretical significance of the phenomenon. For Robertson its discussion 'touches just about every aspect of academic disciplines' (1992: 9). For Giddens the term 'must have a key position in the lexicon of the social sciences' (1990: 52). Robertson construes the concept as referring 'both to the compression of the world and the intensification of consciousness of the world as a whole' (1992: 8). Giddens defines it as 'the intensification of worldwide social relations' (1990: 64). Both agree that its consequence must be a refocusing of sociological work.

That refocusing, if we are to follow the implications of Giddens' and Robertson's accounts, must already have been under way for some time. For both of them stress the essentially reflexive nature of globalization processes, whereby the interaction of the local and global is transformative of social relations. In Robertson's account the global field involves the multiple relativization of phenomena such as societies, selves and citizenship; in Giddens' account the dialectic of global and local is conducted through new trust-generating abstract systems.

In each case then old certainties give way to a dynamized set of relations in which reference points meaningful for people in their everyday lives have constantly to be reconstituted. Giddens' and Robertson's accounts refer to changes in the social world which must put established sociological conceptualizations under strain. The implication is that sociologists need new

20

ways of talking and writing about the world because it has changed, but that these will also be evidenced in that world since they are part of its self-reflexive nature. Concepts which reflected an older order, such as society, class, state, will consequently all bear the strain. Giddens notes the difficulty of operating with society as equated with the nation-state (1990: 64). Robertson sees globalization as stimulating a search for fundamentals which underpin these shifting phenomena (1992: 174–7).

The aim of this chapter is to see whether these large claims for the impact of globalization on sociology are borne out in the trajectory of key sociological concepts hitherto. For it has to be emphasized that the refocusing which Giddens and Robertson allude to must already be a long way along the road if they are also right about the historical depth of the globalization process. It cannot have been waiting for the moment when they have pronounced, even if their pronouncements do in turn have consequences for the process they describe.

We shall then take a connected set of key concepts and consider how far their development over the last decades can be construed as reflecting the impact of globalization, and as we do so we shall seek to distil out the general implications which arise for sociological concept formation. The sequence we follow: community – culture – milieu – flows from the pressure of considerations which globalization raises. The conclusion suggests the need for a much more elaborated re-examination of the development of sociological concepts under globalized conditions.

COMMUNITY

If we take the concept of community we can address at the outset the classic features of the embeddedness of the sociological concept in the social realities of a particular historical period. Communities were part of lived life for a multitude of people, 'community' became the talisman of a comprehensive theorization of modern social change, in which certain attributes were invested by sociologists with primordial significance for the conduct of living.

Nineteenth-century analysts of social and economic change – De Tocqueville, Comte, Tönnies, Durkheim and Marx – began their projects with an examination of what was causing the demise of 'community' (see Bell and Newby 1971: 22). They generally valued 'community' positively and frequently shared 'a pervading posture of nostalgia – of praising the past to blame the present – and the two themes combined when the present "society" was criticised with reference to past "community"' (ibid.). Despite the wide variety of definitions of 'community' which have since been proposed, with the social sciences the influence of these early writers appears to have encouraged assumptions that community involves 'particularism and ascription and diffuseness and affectivity – as a consequence,

21

for example, of kinship being important and of stability and "knowing" everyone' (ibid.: 27). Even though these features potentially could be disaggregated and analysed separately from each other, they were constantly referred back to the bounded entity of the small local community.

The influence of these assumptions can be detected in the plethora of American and British empirical studies of localities undertaken between 1920 and the early 1960s. Classic studies by R.E. Park and other members of the 'Chicago school' (Anderson 1923; Park and Burgess 1925; Thrasher 1927; Wirth 1928; Zorbaugh 1929), by the Lynds in 'Middletown' (Lynd and Lynd 1937) and Lloyd Warner in 'Yankee City' (Warner 1941, 1945, 1947) provided substantive data for sociological debates concerning local communities in northern US urban settings while small-town life in the 'Deep South' was explored in pioneering research undertaken by Davis, Gardner and Gardner (1941) and Dollard (1957). In post-war Britain the themes of community and locality were examined in similar detailed studies which encompassed both urban and rural settlements (Rees 1950; Brennan, Cooney and Pollins 1954; Williams 1956; Young and Willmott 1957; Stacey 1960) and extended to other parts of Europe (Keur and Keur 1955; Banfield 1956; Wylie 1957).

During the 1960s and 1970s assumptions concerning locality and community and the sociological models of society to which they were related were extensively criticized as the impact of wider social, economic and political forces on local communities came to be appreciated and the issues of internal cleavages and conflicts were highlighted (see Bell and Newby 1971: 154–62, 218–52). In Britain sociological interest in local community studies has waned, probably because those wider forces appear to relocate the attributes of community elsewhere, for instance in ethnic minorities and peasant society within Western Europe on which anthropological research has gathered pace (Jeffery 1976; Davis 1977; Watson 1977; Saifullah Khan 1979; Werbner 1985, 1990, 1991; Cohen 1986; MacDonald 1989; Bouquet and Winter 1987; Mandel 1990). While this research has added considerably to our knowledge about specific groups of people in certain localities the assumptions and theoretical problems which dogged sociological writing on community do not appear to have been resolved.

The expanding literature on Britain's ethnic minorities, for example, has usually focused on the social, cultural, economic and political content of local communities and the ethnic boundaries which these groups maintain between themselves and outsiders (primarily the 'indigenous' majority). The fundamental institutions of these groups are assumed to be the family, kinship networks, religious and cultural organizations (see, for example, Wallman 1979, Bhachu 1985, Shaw 1988, Werbner 1990). While these writings do not challenge the conventions established by the community studies tradition some recent discussions of ethnicity and 'race' in

Britain and the USA indicate a growing awareness of the need for new approaches towards community and locality. Appadurai (1990, 1993), Bhabha (1990), Hall (1991a, 1991b) and Gilroy (1987, 1993) have analysed in different ways the construction of imagined, diasporic communities, 'new ethnicities' and a third, hybrid space between 'insiders' and 'outsiders' in the context of global processes. In their accounts they have emphasized the central role played by migrant workers, refugees and tourists, for example, in the changing definitions of belonging where nation-state boundaries and loyalties are challenged or bypassed by global/local dynamics. Appadurai is particularly persuasive in his analysis of the ways by which the production of locality takes place within the context of global technological communications and the emergence of 'virtual communities' which span the globe.

The shift to seeing the imagined community as the guiding principle for lived social relations represents an important step towards the disembedding of community, for it opens the possibility of representing the absent and distant as being integral to the local. At the same time the process of globalization, if acknowledged at all by those concerned with community, is usually understood as having only limited relevance to the communities studied and, where relevant, leading to the homogenization of culture (see Albrow 1993a). In adopting such a suspicious or limited view of globalization the discussion of changes taking place within Britain and other Western nations fails to appreciate the manifold ways in which the orderings and imaginings of community are determined by not only more global levels (metropolitan, national and international) but by globalization as a process, *sui generis*.

As we have noted earlier, Giddens has emphasized the ways by which modern technology enables people to maintain social relationships across the globe (disembedding) and the implications of this process for the maintenance of national boundaries and loyalties. While accepting that the concept of disembedding is illuminating in the specific context of 'symbolic tokens' and 'expert systems' Robertson notes that Giddens neglects 'the fact that social *and cultural* differentiation and the tensions and conflicts often occasioned by such, including "fundamentalistic" attempts to dedifferentiate sociocultural systems, have been pivotal circumstances of recent world history' (Robertson 1992: 144).

Robertson's argument is particularly powerful when ethnic movements are considered across the globe, i.e. ethnic groups in the USA and Britain, ethnic conflict in Northern Ireland or the former Yugoslavia and ethnic revivalism in the former USSR. In Britain the production of local communities by ethnic minorities is shaped by global processes which extend far beyond national boundaries and imaginings and involve 'fundamentalist' rhetorics of belonging which can establish among British Muslims, for example, an identification with a worldwide Islamic community (*umma*) where national boundaries have no place. Britain's 'white' majority is also caught up in this global process of identity formation where the 'future for Britain in a rapidly changing world' is a constant theme in the media and other forums for public debate. National elites play a key role in this public debate and extend their rival interpretations across the globe through their privileged access to the means of information production and distribution.

The construction of 'community' in a specific locality, therefore, cannot be analysed on the assumption that the local is prior, primordial, more 'real'. Local solidarities and imaginings may also be produced by global processes – a process which is most dramatically illustrated in the lives of migrant workers and their descendants but includes others within the nation-state. Second-generation Bangladeshis in the East End of London, for instance, engage in lively, diverse commentaries on belonging which range across numerous boundaries of space and time (Eade 1989, 1990, 1993). Their sense of being British/Bengali/Bangladeshi/Muslim is informed by the links they maintain with others across the UK, other Western countries, their country of origin, other territories and co-religionists (Eade 1990, Gardner 1992). Their stories of where they have come from engage dynamically with interpretations of their present situation in East London. The knowledge which is used in these constructions of belonging is produced and transmitted through telephone conversations, religious ceremonies, newspaper accounts, television and radio programmes and videos and music recordings, through a global network of social and technological linkages. Visits to friends and relatives, interaction with colleagues at work and other forms of 'community' involvement employ this global network to produce 'locality'. Their productivity runs parallel with the activity of other 'locals' such as 'white' residents whose narratives of the past and present may exclude them as 'foreigners' in some instances but which also draw on global networks to establish the knowledge of who belongs to the locality and the nation.

To understand community, therefore, a break has to be made with an intellectual tradition which was shaped by our nineteenth-century forebears and which associated community with a disappearing world of traditional solidarities and values. The current ignorance or suspicion of debates concerning globalization among those who undertake detailed studies of ethnic minorities in Britain, for example, parallels those earlier celebrations of community in opposition to modern society. At the same time the shift in the focus of community studies to the abstract, imagined community requires more careful attention to the issue of disembedding in particular than the discussion of diasporic communities, hybridity and 'new ethnicities' has so far allowed. At the same time the analysis of globalization needs to be located in a deeper empirical investigation of specific situations – one of the undoubted strengths of local community studies and ethnic minority group reports.

24

Community is in the process of being disembedded, therefore, to the extent that we identify its reconstitution on a non-local, non-spatially bounded basis. The potential was already there in the early formulations of Tönnies, but those attributes of community were persistently referred back to the bounded locality. In large part this was because community was idealized and associated with a disappearing past which was represented as more clearly delimited and where people knew where they stood. It was a potent myth to reinforce efforts to shape the everchanging contemporary reality, to stabilize the state, contain disorder and limit the consequences of seemingly uncheckable forces of modernity. As such it was intimately connected with the myth of cultural integration.

CULTURE:
FROM INTEGRATION TO DISINTEGRATION

The same kind of emphasis on boundedness and coherence traditionally dominated the sociological treatment of the idea of culture, even though this was potentially, and indeed has become, the idea through which the transitory nature of social arrangements can most easily be represented. Indeed 'culture' has become something of a watchword for those who document the decline of recognizable social entities and the disintegration of society itself.

The source of the shift in the sociological interpretation of culture can be found in the inherent tension which was at the heart of Raymond Williams' project, namely 'to reconcile the meanings of culture as "creative activity" and "a whole way of life"' (Williams [1961] 1984: 56). In the functionalist paradigm of sociology 'the way of life' tracked the course of community and became its ideal counterpart.

This paradigm was reinforced by its incorporation in a dichotomy which was celebrated in German social theory, namely between *Kultur* and *Zivilisation*. The latter paralleled the development of *Gesellschaft* and was associated with technical progress. As one much read theorist of the 1920s put it when commenting on Oswald Spengler: 'civilisation is a gift which may pass to unworthy generations, culture is a realisation which none can share but those to whom it really belongs' (MacIver 1928: 437). The creative aspect of culture was thus linked with the essential characteristics of a group, embedded in a group, separating it from the wider world, where rationality held sway. Even an iconoclast like McLuhan (1962) could not resist exploiting the parallelism of community and culture when he invoked the 'Global Village'.

Margaret Archer (1988) argues that culture has been, and still is, one of the vaguest and most vacillating of concepts in sociological analysis. None the less the 'myth of cultural integration' (to be seen in an archetype of culture as perfectly woven, all-enmeshing web) she states has: 'Projected an

25

image of culture which proved so powerful that it scored the retina, leaving a perceptual after-image, which distorted subsequent perception' (Archer 1988: 2). The myth was nurtured above all by the assimilation of anthropological perspectives into the functionalist paradigm for modern societies. The result was that where instances of minority detachment from mainstream culture were manifest, the paradigm was preserved by engaging in the ethnography of the 'sub-culture' in which the assumptions of separateness, boundaries and essential nature were reproduced. Integration remained the core issue as this definition of sub-culture suggests:

> a sub-division of a national culture, composed of a combination of factorable social situations such as class status, ethnic background, regional and rural or urban residence, and religious affiliation, *but forming in their combination a functioning unit which has an integrated impact on the participating individuals.*
>
> (Gordon [1944] in Gould and Kolb 1964: 167–8)

In other words 'sub-culture' is offered as a device to recognize diversity, whilst reducing the pluralism of its possibilities, by making it an integrated part of an integrated whole (cf. Boudon and Bourricaud 1989: 95–6).

In the post-war period the myth of 'cultural integration' has in effect been challenged from the outside by the development of the field known as cultural studies. Raymond Williams was one of the key figures in its growth. He argued that there were three dominant uses of 'culture' – culture as the process of human perfection through intellectual, spiritual and aesthetic development; culture as high culture; and culture as a way of life. More than once in his work he reflected upon the 'genuine complexity' of the various meanings and use of the term (Williams [1961] 1984: 59; 1976: 80–1), and this notion of complexity as a good thing, rather than a bad thing or a simply irreducible facticity, can also be seen in other work in the cultural studies mode (Jackson 1992: xi). In itself this has provided a positive route into the exploration of alternative sources of culture and of challenges to the hegemony of high culture. This became the main concern of the Birmingham Centre for Contemporary Cultural Studies, made famous in the work of Richard Hoggart and Stuart Hall.

More recent work in the cultural studies tradition has tended to focus upon 'popular culture' defined not (just) by what sells, but by a sense of the oppositional, which can easily be coded, for example, into the street style of sub-cultural groups. In the much more 'mobile' streetwise world of Dick Hebdige (1988) we are offered a definition of culture that challenges the myth of cultural integration. In part of an essay devoted to an analysis of the rapid turnover of consumption of musical styles and forms he argues that:

> It no longer appears adequate to confine the appeal of these forms . . . to the ghetto of discrete, numerically small subcultures. For they

permeate and help organise a much broader, less bounded territory
where cultures, subjectivities, identities impinge on each other.

(Hebdige 1988: 212)

This is an important break away from the notion of culture as a way of life.
Hebdige criticizes the use of the idea of mass culture and is more likely to
use notions of youth cultures or (more especially) popular culture. But a
recent article shows how difficult it is to avoid introducing the idea of
cultural integration by default. Frow has thoroughly criticized the concept
of popular culture as conceived by practitioners in the cultural studies field.
He argues that the concept of 'the popular' actively elides the distinction
between three different senses of the popular. The first being the 'market
notion' of what we might call capitalist common sense, the second a
'descriptive notion' being all the things that 'the people' do or have
done, the third is the sense favoured by cultural studies. Frow describes
the essential features of this favoured notion as 'the relations which define
"popular culture" in a continuing tension (relationship, influence, antagon-
ism) to the dominant culture' (Frow 1992: 26–7).

That 'continuing tension' is still defined in relation to a dominant culture.
But the other two notions Frow mentions potentially escape this context.
The development of the market and modern media technology partake of
the creative, disruptive connotations of the old notion of culture. Linked
with the idea of the active initiatives of ordinary people, culture takes on an
unbounded quality in which media, rather than essence, shapes the object
of intellectual interest. The way is open for new, non-integrative formulations of the idea of culture. We have an example in John Thompson's
Ideology and Modern Culture (1990): 'Cultural phenomena, according to this
conception, may be understood as symbolic forms in structured contexts;
and cultural analysis may be construed as the study of the meaningful
constitution and social contextualisation of symbolic forms' (Thompson
1990: 123). By recognizing the mobility of symbolic forms Thompson has
started to articulate a critique of the integration myth, as he had earlier done
of the 'fallacy of internalism' in relation to ideology (ibid.: 24). Effectively
he is reducing the meaning of 'culture' to an empty label since it adds
nothing to an analysis which is entirely adequately conducted in terms of
the ideas of meaning, symbolism, symbolic form, and by relating those
concepts to the social contexts in which meaning is encountered, produced
and so on. At the same time Thompson recognizes that such an analysis
must be seen in relation to the history of the production and circulation of
symbolic forms, by now a global operation. This disaggregation of the
concept of culture means that its elements can be separable components in
a commercialized media production process on a world scale.

Globalization or globalizing practices mean changes in social and material
existences of the modern world such that new connections between places

are forged and the world as a whole is articulated as the appropriate arena in which to pursue marketing, intellectual, environmental and other practices. There are profound implications for the notion of culture.

Mike Featherstone in his introduction to the collection *Global Culture* (1990) speculates about the possibility of a global culture, the existence of 'third cultures', and trans-societal cultural processes, all of which challenge lazy associations of culture and national identity and simple associations of culture and territoriality. Globalizing processes have raised to the forefront of our thought experiences of borders, 'multi-culturalism' within a locality, and hybrids as products of post-coloniality (Gupta and Ferguson 1992: 7–8).

These changes in social and material existences demand new forms and modes of analysis, and to some extent this is being achieved. When Ulf Hannerz assents to there being a world culture he means that it has become 'one network of social relationships' (Hannerz 1990: 237). This world culture is created, he argues, 'through the increasing connectedness of varied local cultures, as well as through . . . cultures without a clear anchorage in any one territory' (ibid.). These are all, he asserts, 'becoming subcultures . . . within the wider whole; cultures which are . . . better understood in the context of their cultural surroundings than in isolation' (ibid.).

But we can still see the problem here that these 'cultures' seem to remain untouched by an internal problem, any recognition of the pluralism within a 'culture'. Rather, they merely respond to a wider cultural framework, within which they have their operation and gain their meanings. In the same volume Appadurai (1990) is more successful in moving us away from the realm of cultures *qua* culture by exploring a framework for the disjunctures between economy, culture and politics. He analyses global cultural flows in terms of five perspectival dimensions called ethno-scapes, mediascapes, technoscapes, finanscapes and ideoscapes and develops ideas whereby the speed and hallucinatory quality of some aspects of modern societies may be articulated. Near the end of his essay he argues that the central feature of global culture today is: 'the politics of the mutual effort of sameness and difference to cannibalize one another and thus proclaim their successful hijacking of the twin Enlightenment ideas of the triumphantly universal and the resiliently particular (Appadurai 1990: 307–8). What is most interesting about this is that, what John B. Thompson (1990) called the classical conception of culture is the origin of our modern senses of culture and has set the agenda for all discussions of and 'in' culture. As Darcy has argued of the Enlightenment origins of the concept of culture:

> the individuals' world was expanding along the axes of both space and time; the environment was becoming more complex, and larger portions of this man-made environment were becoming relevant to the individual's being. . . . 'Culture' became the term applied by the western

philosophical and intellectual traditions to the matrix of these changes to space, time and human environment.

(Darcy 1987: 7)

The relationship between the plurality and diversity of particular groups and the psychic unity of humanity entered into the definition of culture which was supposed to negotiate those very relations, to solve their problematic 'relationship'. Every successive solution to the problem re-iterated the relation in specific kinds of ways. Since the modern concept of culture worked in a constant tension between particularity and universality, it could be used to articulate antithetical viewpoints and has resisted operationalization – at least simply for intellectual purposes (see Boyne 1990: 58–9).

But globalization has dramatic effects on that tension in the old concept. The media which make worldwide communication possible are disengaged from any primordial base. Communications technology itself promotes the disembedding of community, detaches culture from historical roots and becomes the bearer of commercialized symbolic forms so that any 'cultural integration' is more to be sought in media organizations themselves.

Paradoxically the means whereby culture has been globalized themselves militate against anything which could be called a unitary global culture. The locus of culture is disembedded from either high or low culture locations and its new site is in a phase of mass production. The universality of culture is achieved, equally destroyed, through the particularity of mega-stars and global media events and images. Culture can no longer potentially simply encapsulate the historic experience of a people. In that sense it may not be exaggerated to speak of the end of culture.

This is entirely consistent with the fact that culture is now a key concept for social units which have long had minimal territorial associations, namely the large-scale corporation. It is valued by the modern business consultant for the essentialist, boundary defining, deep motivating factors that the idea has evoked in the past, with the added factor of imparting a primary elemental force to organizational structure, thus effectively conferring charisma on the dark-suited executive. It is a pure case of a concept disembedded from its territorial base and re-embedded in a communications media frame. But its new locus makes it ephemeral and manipulable, its dimensions altered at will by the modern magician. It is just as alien and external to the individual as 'high culture' was to an illiterate peasantry.

GENERALIZED AND EXTENDED MILIEUX

The alienation of individuals from a global culture serves to highlight those concepts which focus on the individual's active efforts to create and maintain his or her own world. The phenomenology of the milieu in a globalized world can thus emerge as an explicit testing ground for new sociological conceptualization and with the formulation of the idea of globalization we are now in a better position to appreciate the significance of the phenomenological project as the reappropriation of meaning by individuals in a world escaping their control.

If we take the concept of the milieu in Schützean fashion – how to make 'our' world from our 'world' – we are bound to take account of the individual's intersubjective experience of the processes of globalization. We are bound to emphasize the interplay of an increasingly global, often anonymous, structure of society and the attempt of individuals to organize their surroundings in a self-determined and familiar way.

By 'the milieu' we refer to our ability, but also the necessity, of creating our own environment according to our intentions and always in co-operation and conflict with our fellow-beings. Although for a time it attracted the Chicago School, and C. Wright Mills once named the distinction between social structure and personal milieux as one 'of the most important available' (1956: 321), it is this emphasis on the willed activity of the individual which has probably made the concept resistant to incorporation within the sociological paradigm which gave community and culture such prominence.

Max Scheler developed the conception of milieu within the context of Philosophical Anthropology. He sees us committed to a relatively stable set of intentions, which spur on, navigate and control our acting in the world. Those intentions refer to our respective systems of values, which 'evaluate' the world as 'our' world and determine our attitude towards the world by selecting a 'practical world' fitting our intentions. Therefore activity in life already meets a world arranged and structured according to the predispositions of the actor, to an (unconscious) 'selection', making the 'world' to 'our' world. Thus the milieu is the limiting of the pre-given world as the framework for all our practical actions.

Here it is important to appreciate Scheler's distinction between the milieu as 'milieu-structure' and 'actual milieu' as the current 'practical world'. The first refers to an attitude towards the world. As living individuals we see 'milieu-things' as they are relevant to our acting, but not however as scientifically measurable things (as a scientist would see) or 'things-in-themselves' (as a philosopher would see). Scheler (1966) refers to this first aspect, using the term 'relatively natural world view', 'natural' referring to the attitude towards the world, 'relative' referring to certain groups of people with similar settings of intentions (cultures, occupations, etc.). The actual milieu, however, is linked to the current and transitory contents of the milieu. The milieu-structure remains stable, whereas the actual milieu can completely change (Scheler 1966: 148–72).

It was the notion of the 'relatively natural world view' which Aron Gurwitsch then developed to take in the view of the 'fellow-being'. We see our fellow-beings in the milieu, neither as complete strangers nor as whole individuals but as people who fit somehow. The fellow-being enters my milieu as a concrete other in a function which is defined by the 'situation' or a 'horizon' which defines the concrete other in the milieu and predetermines our relationship. Without knowing the concrete other as an individual, the situation in the milieu gives us an 'implicit knowledge' of how to deal with him/her. Since Gurwitsch is mainly concerned with concrete types of 'milieu-situations' and their impact on intersubjectivity, especially the notion of 'near' and 'far', his analysis provides an entry into encounters in the context of globalization, in, for instance, global cities or social networks based on computer networks, etc. (Gurwitsch [1931] 1977).

The current sociology of milieu is mainly concerned with the mainte-nance of 'normality' between fellow-beings. It is important to understand that this version is embedded in the theory of Everyday-Life. In Everyday-Life we see the world through relatively abstract types of perception ('the' dog, 'the' house) and act according to standardized situations ('the' stu-dent/'the' teacher). But there are relationships which cannot be kept up in that way (mother and son, neighbour and neighbour). These kinds of relationships are so intimate (mother and son) or difficult (neighbour) that they require a special kind of attitude and ways of approaching the other. So special attention is given to the shared borderlines of individual milieux. Accordingly it lays emphasis on a type of intersubjectivity which defines the borders of the milieu – the 'neighbour as the nearest stranger'. Since the world comes increasingly together in processes of globalization (migration, travellers, transnational cultures) this concept is important in helping to redefine 'acquaintances' and 'strangers' in terms of relative proximity (Grathoff 1989).

What kind of links are there between global processes and the milieu? We can start with one of the very obvious results of globalization – 'the voluntary and involuntary cosmopolitans' (labour migrants, refugees, businessmen, athletes, intellectuals). They all must develop the ability to make themselves at home in various places in the world. As we know with Scheler, our milieu-structure is not influenced by a local change, since it is just our actual milieu which changes with mobility. Our milieu enables us to be locally mobile. But this advantage seems rather ambiva-lent in terms of globalization. To have a relatively stable milieu means somehow to have a limited access towards the world as well. Moving around the world does not necessarily mean to broaden one's horizon. One can rather remain a 'local at heart' (Hannerz 1990: 241) with the help of the rapidly growing 'culture shock prevention industry' (Hannerz 1990: 245). In Scheler's words a '"bohemian" remains a bohemian, a "philistine" remains a philistine' (Scheler 1966: 156ff). We can extend our actual milieu in a global dimension without broadening the contents of the milieu-structure at all.

31

But there are people who really try to transcend their milieu. The 'transnational milieu' of intellectuals views phenomena from different perspectives to create something like a 'decontextualised knowledge' (Hannerz 1990: 246) without commitments to local or cultural boundaries. But scientific knowledge by definition is no longer 'milieu-knowledge' – as taken for granted in the attitude of the 'relatively natural world view'.

Tendencies to transcend the milieu or to give it a cosmopolitan or even global dimension bring with them a basic problem. Even the 'global individual' needs a place to sleep, to rest and recover. Sleep needs to be protected and organized, like anything else. The way of dealing with this problem and related problems of everyday needs is through the worldwide creation and maintenance of 'generalized milieux', by which we mean those places which provide or serve the basic needs of the global individual in an organized and standardized manner. Hotels, fast-food outlets, petrol stations and car rental firms are organized in chains which operate to the same standard anywhere. McDonald's is the classic example where experience of one in a particular town allows us to use others anywhere in the world. These places save the global individual from the need to organize, possibly every day, another actual milieu to serve his or her basic needs at a different location.

There is an obverse side to this transcendence of the local. Those who remain tied to a locality feel the impact of globalization as local milieux become sites for other people's generalized milieux. Again McDonald's is a good example for this interplay between the local and the global. Although designed for the global traveller rather than for the needs of local residents, their generalized nature equally allows locals to enter. The local 'character' takes her place in the nearest McDonald's, finds the discarded newspaper, someone to talk to, and, if she is lucky, a free coffee. She develops her actual milieu within the generalized milieu and brings the global and the local together.

But the spread of generalized milieux results in an increasingly standardized Everyday-Life adapted to global needs. We can ask whether it is only the 'character' who is individual enough to create a local milieu out of a McDonald's. For local residents these settings are largely associated with the kind of flow of 'voluntary and involuntary Cosmopolitans' which led to 'all of Greater London's thirty-two boroughs becoming more cosmopolitan between 1971 and 1981' (King 1990: 141).

The conception of milieu never had a notion of strict borderlines or culture-bounded contents. Its territoriality was a function of the individual's values. In that sense it was never embedded in the way 'culture' and 'community' were. The inherent relativizing of space and time which it involves thus opens up critical access to problems of internationalization and multi-cultural communication. The relationship between two concrete others is determined by the horizon in which they interact rather than by

32

some arbitrary borderline. The borders and barriers between milieux are always a relatively fluid product of shared effort, work and conflict instead of abstract commitment to a closed culture or community or adherence to state commands. It is the 'neighbour as nearest stranger' (Grathoff 1989) who is a necessary determination of our milieu and at the same time conditions the scope of my acting in my milieu. With the internationaliz-ation of the local milieu it is very likely to be the cultural stranger who becomes my neighbour with whom I have to interact to maintain the common boundaries of our milieux. At the same time there are many people who consider their local milieu as a 'stopover'. In that sense a 'danger' to the local milieu is not the cultural stranger as neighbour but the neighbour who does not want to be engaged in the maintenance of the milieu.

The converse is that the nearest and dearest persons by birth or by choice live elsewhere in the world or one has moved far from them. Families may be extended around the world and with modern communication that dispersal may no longer mean broken contact. The telephoned news of a birth in Washington raises cheers in London and the new grandmother makes hasty arrangements for a transatlantic flight.

That raises the question of the range or extension of the milieu. Presence is no longer required in the different local extensions of our milieu because we can use global media of communication like telephone, fax or computer. They become familiar parts of our milieu, with its extension over space limited, as any other aspect of the milieu, by the personal determination to hold the different 'fragments' of his/her milieu together. The extension of the milieu in this sense means an extension of the concept itself, an increased scope, a refinement of its contents and a differentiation of its varieties. It also raises questions about the contents of other closely related concepts.

The possibility of such extended milieux, which are not limited to family or friendship relations, but may be the basis for work and leisure activities too, raises a crucial question of the degree to which the notions of 'familiarity' and 'normality' can be produced and reproduced without face-to-face interaction. Globalization effectively brings the nature of human social relationships under new critical scrutiny.

CONCLUSION

The problematics of conceptual shifts and historical change are not new. They have been recognized explicitly at least since J.G. Herder in the eighteenth century (Cohen 1962: 10). Nor has this recognition been confined to idealist accounts.

John Stuart Mill described what he called the natural history of the variations in the meaning of terms. He recounted how terms might be narrowed or expanded in their application in response to changes in the world around, or as a result of travel and conquest. He instanced the application of English concepts of landed proprietorship to Bengal as producing social disorganization greater than any produced by ruthless barbarians (Mill [1843] 1872: 239). But the processes of expansion and contraction of concepts which he described did not allow for a fundamental shift in the relationship between concept and reality, simply a variation between known limits.

Globalization, in its aspects of disembedding and re-embedding, appears to involve the reorganization of social life around processes of conceptual generation and analysis. Ideas which took shape in reflection on the concrete processes of historic, geographically situated nation-states are given new concrete representations as foci for individual and collective action in settings detached from those historic locations. Community and culture are detribalized, acquire an abstract quality and are then resited in new locations like organizations, or disaggregated with their components like affectivity or symbolic form re-emerging as elements of commercial production processes.

Far from a breakdown of the social we see a reconstitution of it in which individuals can both disembed themselves by moving through generalized milieux, or alternatively embed themselves by attachment to local placements of global phenomena. In such a context the social relationship becomes a fabricatable guide for interaction, reconstituted afresh in widely differing contexts and no longer an elementary particle of an all-embracing historic social system.

The globalized world presents the relation between concept and reality differently from Mill's account because the conceptualization of reality has become an active aspect of its transformation. The boundaries of objects are no longer simply expanding and contracting, like the fortunes of imperial powers. They are constantly being redrawn, transcended or simply ignored. Globalization does not merely have impact on sociological concepts, it is a process in which sociological thought is an element in the overall transformation of people's lives.

However, the disembedded abstract concepts which arise out of the historical trajectories we have examined bear highly contested relationships with the realities of the globalized world. They certainly do not purport to capture its phenomenal reality. Social descriptions of the globalized world would describe megalopolises, computer dating, video link-ups, interactive art, virtual reality, data banks, backyard sales, new age travellers. In some respects we may feel that our sociological conceptual changes take us away from rather than closer to these. But our assessment suggests a more complex outcome. Briefly and tentatively, since the subject must bear far more extensive analysis, we would identify the following broad impacts of globalization on sociological concept formation:

1 *The abstraction of older concepts from territorial reference.* This means the boundaries of the concept no longer have an intrinsic territorial reference, as in the case of community, and the very notion of boundedness itself becomes questionable as with culture.

2 *The disaggregation of older concepts into analytical components and their resynthesis.* Taking the example of culture, its analysis into meaning, symbolic form, social context (and their further analysis) permits conceptual reformulation which equally elides old boundaries and allows for new realities to emerge.

3 *The extension of old concepts to embrace new realities.* We found that the re-embedding of the milieu under globalized conditions prompted new formulations: the generalized and extended milieu.

4 *The idealization of older concepts.* The pursuit of the 'pure relationship' is the attempt to reappropriate reflexively the abstract development of the concept into everyday life, even though its abstractness makes its realization elusive.

These four modes of conceptual change are highlighted in the course of our enquiry. Our examples do not exhaust the possibilities, even of all those changes to which we have alluded here. The list would undoubtedly be extended if we were to take, say, state, society and class, but that must be reserved to another occasion.

However, we should draw attention to two crucial features of globalization which have scarcely figured in this enquiry since our starting point has consciously arisen out of essentially Western history and sociology. Two further modes of conceptual change would be highlighted if we had taken a different starting point (fully globalized):

5 *The generalization of local concepts to the level of global relevance and their assimilation into a transnational discourse.* This has in the past been seen as purely a phenomenon of Western conceptual imperialism (e.g. the example of Bengal cited by Mill). But we may cite as an example the Islamic *jihad*, or holy war, which may well highlight Western phenomena in a way concealed to the West's self-understanding. Western social science has long involved the cross-cultural modification of concepts embedded originally in national languages. Global relations multiply the sources from which conceptual inputs can be made into a fully internationalized sociology.

6 *The global operationalization of older abstract concepts as the world becomes a managed social entity.* There is a new concreteness about the use of concepts like human rights, health, communication, even humanity in the context of the work of world organizations.

It is scarcely surprising that the the sheer variety of sources of conceptual change in the globalized world should have occasioned concern for the enterprise of sociology as a discipline with a coherent conceptual framework. Fragmentation appears to be the feature of discourse about society as much as of society itself. We share the concern. Globalization theory is itself an indicator of the active response sociology can make to the new conditions. There is no reason on our account to think that it is inherently inadequate for the task.

NOTE

* This chapter is a slightly revised version of an article of the same title which was published in *Innovation* 7 (4): 371–89, 1994.

3

TRAVELLING BEYOND LOCAL CULTURES[1]

Socioscapes in a global city

Martin Albrow

INTRODUCTION

The argument of the last chapter suggests that globalization is much more than an extension of longer-standing processes of modernization. If it were simply that we would be able to accommodate it easily in the conceptual frame which was forged in the heat of the social change of the industrial revolution. Increasingly we can recognize that this was the perspective of nation-state sociology, employing ideas of community, nation and culture which reflected social conditions which have passed away. Modernity is now already 'classic', old, often outworn.

This is not a perspective peculiar to sociology. The economic geographer Peter Dickens (1992) has stressed that the 'global shift' is not simply an extension of the processes of internationalization. The transformation of the world economy is much more than increased trade across national borders. It involves manifold possibilities of integrating production on a global scale which dramatically limit the scope for government economic management. It shifts the parameters of national economies and forces governments to attend to intangible 'supply side' factors like skills, motivation and national culture.

The global shift similarly affects the frame for the state management of society. Migration no longer carries the same meaning when residence and work away from home or abroad is a way of maintaining social relations at a distance. But if social relations are regularly maintained at a distance then concepts of locality, community and even citizenship are strained to accommodate them. This is not just a problem for social scientists; it equally affects all administrators who use these basic conceptual tools of the welfare state.

One of the key aspects of the classic conceptual framework was the acceptance that place was linked to community through local culture. Migrants ultimately had to be assimilated into local culture to become part of the community. Multi-culturalism put considerable strain on this framework without offering effective alternatives to older concepts of community. The proposal in this chapter is that we seek through globalization theory to provide conceptualizations which are more sensitive to the new conditions of local living.

In doing so we may have to be irreverent about older notions of social structure. In this respect Arjun Appadurai has provided a useful precedent in his suggestion that the suffix 'scape' is a better reflection of the fluidity of social formations under conditions of global cultural flow. It also has the advantage of suggesting the participants' perspectival vision. So he uses 'ethnoscape' for the landscape of persons and moving groups like tourists and refugees who constitute a shifting world. He contrasts this with the relatively stable communities and networks through which these people and groups move (Appadurai 1990: 297).

But how stable are these 'relative stabilities' and from the perspective of participants are they not equally 'scapes'? The missing term here surely has to be 'socioscape', the vision of social formations which are more than the people who occupy them at any one time. Under globalized conditions people are increasingly uncomfortable when referring to them in old structural terms like 'community' or 'neighbourhood'.

In this chapter, then, we will explore living in a locality in London, almost the archetypal global city where geographical mobility is an accepted fact of life.[2] We do this using the idea of the socioscape and other concepts like 'sociospheres' and 'time–space stratification' to avoid forcing the account into the classic conceptual framework. But, to reinforce the argument that we need to escape from that framework. Let us first deconstruct the idea of local culture in some classic studies of community life.

THE CLASSIC PARADIGM

In a brief classification of the stages of the history of sociology (Albrow 1990) I spoke of the time after the establishment of professional sociology and before the internationalism of post-1945 as the period of national sociologies. The topic of local culture and migrations occupied a central place in it. The classic exemplification is in the work of the Chicago School, which adapted Simmel's insights and applied them to the process of Americanization.

There is a tendency to forget, when we emphasize the way structural-functionalism represented American values and reified the United States, that, prior to it, a major aspect of the work of the Chicago School was directed towards nation-building. Within that framework historically situated concepts like nation-state and community took on categorical status, that is to say they were treated as parameters for data collection and frameworks within which social processes were located. If we consider, for instance, the conceptual framework for analysing migration processes which students imbibed from Park and Burgess' textbook (1921) – assimilation, accommodation, adaptation, conflict – whichever one of these predominates the analysis begins and returns to the old-established community occupying a definite territory.

The Lynds' studies in the 1920s and 1930s are the classic statement of community analysis for the period (Lynd and Lynd 1926, 1937). They saw Middletown as a stable reference point throughout the Great Depression and they reported on its inhabitants as seeing it in the same way. In spite of a recorded near 30 per cent rise in its population between 1925 and 1935, of which only perhaps one-third was accounted for by natural increase and the rest reflected 'relatively heavy migration into and out of the city' (Lynd and Lynd, 1937: 516), the impact of this movement goes virtually unrecorded.[3]

Small-town America succeeded in weathering the Depression by denying the outside world, but that in itself had repercussions. As the Lynds put it:

> One of the problems of the Middletowns of the country, organized centripetally about the major concern with making their living, is resistance to new ideas from without that interfere with the smoothly gliding processes of their own living, an in-turned concentration on the local, the familiar, the habitual in an era when the larger national culture is confronted with new issues and is restating some of its fundamental assumptions.
>
> (ibid.: 217)

The problem restated is the meaningful articulation of local with national culture, for while the Lynds depict Middletown as quintessentially American, there is a national level which operates on and through people who do not act on the local stage. It was the same problem which was to exercise American political science as it sought to make sense of a system where the sum of local elites still did not constitute the national ruling class.

The origins of that problem reside in locality and territoriality, both as everyday assumptions and as normally unstated premises of sociological analysis. The community and locality were tied to each other in a one-to-one relationship; so also were the nation and territoriality. But the effect was to leave communities isolated one from another, even though they shared in the national identity. The flows of people between communities, the normal processes of internal migration, even trade and commerce, were treated as extrinsic to their structure, both in social and sociological consciousness.

Against that firm background of place the fluxes of modernity and the pace of urbanism could be framed within an overarching rationality. For some people community has appeared as a relic of a pre-modern era. However, we should properly see the conceptual twinning of *Gemeinschaft* and *Gesellschaft* as characteristically modern. David Harvey has pointed to the architectural mythology of building local space to generate community as a facet of modernism's 'perpetual dialogue with localism and nationalism' (Harvey 1989: 276). The construction of 'heritage' is also part of the same modernist programme.

This inclusiveness of community expressed itself in the idea of local culture. In Britain the classic illustration is a book which exercised an enormous influence on the newly expanding discipline of sociology in the 1960s, Richard Hoggart's *Uses of Literacy* (1957). This account has an urban setting in Leeds, is largely autobiographical and set in the 1930s. The theme is the gradual disappearance of working-class culture under the impact of the mass media. At first this might seem to imply a national consciousness in so far as the working class is a national phenomenon. Yet Hoggart makes it clear that 'the core of working class attitudes . . . is a sense of the personal, the concrete, the local . . . first the family and second the neighbourhood' (ibid.: 32).

So within 'the massed proletarian areas' there are 'small worlds, each as homogeneous and well-defined as a village [where] one knows practically everybody an extremely local life, in which everything is remarkably near' (ibid.: 52–3). The working-class man is going to live in his local area all his life and the family live near. His life centres on a group of known streets and he rarely travels outside them. The group will regard a newcomer from a town forty miles away as 'not one of us' for years (ibid.: 72). It is a culture which, in Hoggart's terms, is much the same anywhere for the working class but is also largely detached from the institutions of the wider society, from patriotism and from politics. Its very localism treats those things as big abstractions, at the same time we can infer it effectively inhibits collaboration across the local divides.

Hoggart had travelled a long way from the childhood in Leeds he depicted (he was to travel much further, eventually to become Deputy Secretary General of UNESCO). His grandmother too had travelled from the country and spent some years in Sheffield. But his type of working class does not travel. They have no time for politics either. We don't know if they vote, since elections have no place in Hoggart's account. Histories of working-class movements are therefore accounts of 'minorities' (ibid.: 17). But then children do not vote and this is an adult's recollection of a child's eye view, with the eye for concrete detail which children display, and without the contact with the world from which children are excluded.

From Hoggart's account we can only see the effects of past fluxes indirectly, in his grandmother's persisting country ways or Oriental influences on ideas of luxury and pleasure. On the other hand, when he considers contemporary influences during the 1950s he laments the lack of a sense of the past and a mass media serving images of a world experiencing incessant change (ibid.: 159). He deplores the shiny barbarism of the teenage gang, imported from America and modified for British tastes (ibid.: 160). The working class is subjected to a barrage of bitty information from all over the world, encouraged to enjoy 'fragmentation' (ibid.: 167).

The culture of the local community, then, in Hoggart's imagery is a repetitive enactment of daily practices by people who know each other and whose rhythm is undisturbed by events or outsiders. It is threatened by the mass media and outside influences. It is an image repeated in dozens of community studies where purposes of analysis bracket out non-resident visitors, travel outside, national events, and even and above all, the inflows and outflows of population.

Those are questions which do not figure in the standard schedule. When they do, as for instance in the study which Williams undertook in Gosforth (1956), where he deliberately chose a remote long-established small farming community, he found that just over half of his population had been born outside the community. The moment migration enters into the frame for community studies a new range of questions arises. Williams indeed sought to draw out the significance of changes like Army service, and the building of the Sellafield nuclear power plant for Gosforth and concluded that community social structure 'was not designed for a world where every individual is conceived of as a highly mobile unit' (ibid.: 203). He noted the way newly formed organizations in the village catered only for parts of its population. His final thought was of the sociologist fifty years hence who would not find it easy to distinguish Gosforth from any other English rural parish (ibid.).

It was the questions of mobility and immigration which Elias and Scotson (1965) addressed in their study of Winston Parva where they counterposed their configurational analysis to the tradition of British community studies. They examined the impact of a new housing estate on an older village, depicting the conflicts and cleavages not only between the two areas, but also the way in which the division between 'nice' and rough families within the estate gave it a bad reputation for the old working-class village – 'foreigners and criminals' as one older resident described them. Equally the village was stratified in terms of its relations with adjacent middle-class housing where many of the residents worked in the neighbouring city.

Communities and neighbourhoods were, in Elias and Scotson's terms, 'configurations' which persisted while individuals came and went (ibid.: 171). They also proposed that the pattern of relationships between those established and outsiders was paradigmatic for a broad range of phenomena in industrializing societies, often classified under headings of prejudice, ethnic minority or social mobility problems (ibid.: 156–9). Indeed they explicitly rejected images of communities as ideal pre-industrial villages with no mobility and called for conceptualizations which fitted the conditions of migratory social mobility as a normal feature of industrial societies.

At the same time their configurational analysis, while emphasizing mobility and conflict, still situated common understandings and a sense of interdependence around a local site. In fact they criticized Bott (1957) on social networks precisely because she was concerned to trace them beyond local areas (ibid.: 185).

Elias and Scotson were concerned to ward off a form of analysis in which individual and society were counterposed. In this they objected in principle to a perspective which allowed the idea of the masses and mass culture to confront an old order, one which Hoggart among others promoted, and where community in industrializing society meant an old integrated order confronted with atomization, fragmentation and homogenization.

Ahead of its time, largely ignored for many years since it was outside the mainstream of British community studies, Elias and Scotson's work now appears a prescient forerunner of globalization research. In treating geographical social mobility as normal it effectively opened the possibility that community itself had to be seen as a contingent feature of social relationships, even an ephemeral configuration. It paved the way for thinking about localities without community and cultures without locality. They transformed the idea of community in order to meet new conditions but at the expense of tying community to locality.

We should mention one other route to the contemporary deconstruction of local culture. In the classic Chicago paradigm the main way in which migration was accommodated in the city was through the famous notion of the urban 'zone of transition', a term which suggested precisely the uneasy relation of the idea to a stable community. The zone of transition was an area with high levels of in- and out-migration and social problems interpreted as the consequence of such mobility. Rex and Moore were still using this concept as their interpretative frame as late as 1967, suggesting that, although the area of Birmingham they examined could never become like any other community, yet community associations could work out accommodations between each other and resolve potential conflicts (1967: 284–5).

But one comment which Rex and Moore made suggested an alternative direction for the future. They noted that organizations in the area were inhibited from working in this way 'by their national and international affiliations and by the universalistic ideas contained in their ideologies and charters' (ibid.: 284). Here was a hint of the future explorations of the inner city and racism where a focus on the political experience of generations, combined with a sense of the imaginary nature of community, linked the trajectory of change to non-local culture, to global forces beyond the control of any local configuration or community associations.

GLOBALIZATION, CULTURE AND LOCALITY

The studies we have just mentioned assumed that communities were located in industrial society and subject to industrialization. To that extent they acknowledged forces transcending the nation-state and crossing its boundaries. Yet the territorial base of community remained and with it the assumed need to stabilize mutual understandings around a local culture.

In the last thirty years transformations of industrial organization in the advanced societies, accompanied by the acceptance of the ideas of post-industrialism and post-modernity, mean that the problem-setting for community analysis has shifted. In the last decade globalization theory has brought issues of time, space and territorial organization into the centre of the frame of argument.[4] We have to look again at the way social relations are tied to place and re-examine issues of locality and culture.

The Wandsworth study illustrates the need to develop globalization theory specifically to grasp the reality of contemporary changes in the configuration of local social relations. Our data about people in one small area suggest that locality has a much less absolute salience for individuals and social relations than older paradigms of research allow. They live in a global city, London, which has already been the focus for much globalization research. However, research has largely focused on links with international finance, on urban development and on the more emphatically international lifestyles of jet-setters and yuppies (King 1990; Budd and Whimster 1992). Scant attention has been paid to everyday life. Thus Knight and Gappert's useful volume on cities in a global society (1989) contains twenty-three papers, but not one considers everyday life in the city. Yet the volume already implies quite different patterns of living for those caught up in global processes and takes us far outside notions of locality as the boundary for meaningful social relations.

Yet the theorization of everyday life under global conditions effectively introduces a range of considerations which takes us beyond ideas of post-modernity and post-industrialism. These ideas evolved out of earlier mass society concerns and the notion of the fragmentation of industrial society. To that extent post-modernity theory lent credence to the idea of a dissolution of concepts without effectively advocating an alternative frame. Indeed very often the claim was implicit that the search for an alternative was a doomed project from the beginning.

Globalization theory, on the other hand, does commit itself to propositions about the trajectory of social change which do not envisage a collapse into chaos or a meaningless juxtaposition of innumerable and incommensurable viewpoints. As we proposed in the last chapter it puts on the agenda a recasting of the whole range of sociological concepts which were forged for the period of nation-state sociology (Albrow *et al.* 1994).

43

We do not have to begin from scratch. For our purposes in this chapter we can draw on a number of core propositions about globalization based on earlier work. In exploring their relevance for local social relations we will find that we develop them further and discover the need to advance additional ones. Our starting points to which we will return are:

1 The values informing daily behaviour for many groups in contemporary society relate to real or imagined material states of the globe and its inhabitants (*globalism*).
2 Images, information and commodities from any part of the earth may be available anywhere and anytime for ever-increasing numbers of people worldwide, while the consequences of worldwide forces and events impinge on local lives at any time (*globality*, Robertson 1992).
3 Information and communication technology now make it possible to maintain social relationships on the basis of direct interaction over any distance across the globe (*time–space compression*, Harvey 1989).
4 Worldwide institutional arrangements now permit mobility of people across national boundaries with the confidence that they can maintain their lifestyles and life routines wherever they are (*disembedding*, Giddens 1991).

We could add to this list but for the moment it is sufficient to permit us to turn to our local studies and identify the patterns of social life which call out for new sociological conceptualizations. Before doing so we ought to add that while these propositions are associated with the general theory of globalization, the extent to which they necessarily implicate the globe as a whole, or require the unicity of the world, is open to an argument which does not have to be resolved here in order to show their relevance for studies of local social relations.

SOCIAL AND CULTURAL SPHERES IN AN INNER LONDON LOCALITY

The transformations of the last sixty years now make it difficult to capture anything in London like the picture of locality you will find in a study such as Hoggart's. The paradigmatic equivalent of his account in empirical research was the work of Willmott and Young at the Institute of Community Studies (1957). But they were capturing a world imminently dissolving. The variety of possibilities now evident extend our conceptual capacities to the extreme. They certainly burst the bounds of nation-state sociology.

Our research on locality and globalization is based in the inner London borough of Wandsworth, south of the river, west of centre, formed from the amalgamation of seven or eight nineteenth-century villages, which give their names to the local areas within what is a largely continuous residential belt. In terms of race politics headlines Wandsworth has led a quiet life in comparison with neighbouring Lambeth. Its press image is mainly associated with the policies of the Conservative-controlled local council which has been known as the 'flagship' authority of the Thatcher years for its advocacy of low local taxation, contracting out of local services and the sale of council houses.

This image of tranquil continuity through change is maintained even for the area of Tooting which has a large Asian immigrant population. Yet even a cursory visit suggests that the concept of local culture is unlikely to fit new conditions. Given that the task of reconceptualization and documenting new realities is long term, I will not attempt to prejudge our findings by a premature characterization of Tooting. However, if we turn to our respondents in Tooting and, instead of seeking to fit them to pre-given sociological categories, listen to their own references to locality, culture and community, we already detect the possibility of new cultural configurations occupying the same territorial area.

Adopting an individualistic methodology as one strategy for penetrating the new social relations, we can identify a range of responses which take us beyond the notion of local culture and community without suggesting any corollary of anomie or social disorganization as the old conceptual frames tended to assume. At this stage we are not offering a holistic account of social relations in this area of London, but we can already say that globalization theory is going to allow us to interpret our respondents in a quite different way from older sociologies which focused on place rather than space.

True we can find old-established 'locals', benchmarks for analysis, but if we let them speak, the nuances of a new age come through. Take 73-year-old Grace Angel,[5] who was born in Wandsworth and has lived in her house in Tooting for over fifty years, who met her husband when they carried stretchers for the injured during the air raids on London in the Second World War. He is now disabled but she benefits from the support of her own age group, mainly white women, who meet at a Day Centre three times a week. She engages in all the traditional activities of a settled life, visiting family, knitting and enjoying crafts. She rarely leaves Wandsworth; she enjoys the sense of community.

At the same time her life is not confined by the locality. She tells how she writes letters to France and the United States. She also wrote 'to Terry Waite all the time he was held hostage and to his wife. I actually got a letter from him, thanking me for my support.' Into her local frame enters a mass media symbol of the conflict between the West and militant Islam. We have to ask where that fits in with the concept of local culture, not simply an ephemeral image cast on a screen as diversion or even information, but a global figure who becomes a personal correspondent.

Mrs Angel would hardly recognize the image of Tooting another resident provides. True, Reginald Scrivens only moved to Tooting seventeen years ago but he has lived in London for thirty-two years and works in a City bank. He reads the broadsheet Conservative newspapers, has a drink with his colleagues after work and watches television with his wife in the evening. They don't socialize locally and he doesn't enjoy living in Tooting any more:

> It's very mixed these days, with the Asians and the blacks, and a lot of the area is quite run down. It's not a nice place to walk through. There isn't any real community either. I still know a few people along my street, but most of the people I used to know moved out, because Tooting got so bad. . . .
>
> Families come and go. Neighbours don't care about each other any more. The foreigners all stick together though. I'll say this about them – they look after their own. That's more than you can say about most of our lot these days.

His wife goes to local shops. He goes to a local church. They are not going to move. It is an easy journey to work in Central London.

Mr Scrivens lives in Tooting but is alienated from it, or rather Tooting falls short of an image of community which he thinks it might have had or ought to have. Yet it still is convenient enough to remain there. Convenience, however, can also combine with indifference. Forty-four-year-old Ted North came to Tooting from Yorkshire ten years ago and has worked as a traffic warden ever since, feels settled, belongs to the local Conservative club, rarely goes out of the area, but doesn't really notice whether there is a community as such.

A Londoner, who moved to Tooting three years ago at the age of 22 and became a postman, Gary Upton, is even more detached:

> Locality isn't all that important to me, but I don't really feel affected by the rest of the world either. I have my life to lead and I'll lead it wherever I am.

Even a much older man, Harry Carter, a 62-year-old taxi driver, who has lived in Tooting for twenty-two years, would move anywhere and feels community spirit has totally disappeared almost everywhere in London. For him globalization is 'common sense' and 'obviously happening'. And if you are a young unemployed man like Dean Garrett, born in Tooting the year Harry arrived, living with your girlfriend and her parents, you are used to the Asians because you were brought up with them but stick with your own. You stay in Tooting and use its library and shops but not because of community feeling.

This indifference to place, however, can be transvalued into a positive desire for constant mobility and into an estimation of locality as a consumer good. Keith Bennett is 25, works in a shop and came to Tooting six months ago. He has travelled through the United States, his mother lives abroad, he has completed a degree, reckons travel has changed his life and would love to go all over the world. He has never had a sense of community but values Tooting:

> because it's got a mixed feel . . . it helps to make people aware of other people . . . it's close enough to fun places like Brixton and Streatham, and it's easy to get into town from here.

He is white but lives with an Asian family and has an Asian friend. His Asian friends tell him 'that they have a good community feel among other Asians but not with the whites'. For an older widow living alone, like 77-year-old Agnes Cooper, the issues of culture and community cannot be transvalued into spectacle as they are with Keith. She responds directly to their messages. The Asians are close-knit 'with no room for outsiders' and she was plainly baffled by a Sikh who could not understand the meaning of hot cross buns at Easter when she tried to explain them to him. She has lived for fourteen years in Tooting and her social network and activity are as local as Grace Angel's, but she notices a lack of true community feeling. She remarked on people buying properties in the area just for resale.

Eight white residents of Tooting, each one with a different orientation to the local area, easily generalized into a different type, potentially raising a series of conceptual distinctions which render the question of the presence or absence of local community simplistic. This question makes more sense in the case of our older respondents, but their answers are quite different. For Grace it is there, Agnes is not sure, for Reginald it has gone and for Harry it went a long time ago everywhere in London. Ted is younger than them and came later. He does not know whether community is there and is unconcerned as he gets on with his local life.

Our three young men have different responses again. As with Ted 'community' has lost salience, and locality has become facility. Globalist Keith finds Tooting a useful point from which to enjoy the world, for Gary its generalizable qualities are what counts, it could be anywhere and that suits him, while for Dean it's a question of necessity rather than values. There is nowhere else to go.

At one time a sociologist might have held that these were all different perspectives on the same phenomenon, partial points of view which could be composited into the social reality of Tooting. Later these views would have been held to justify a sociological relativism – perspectives which simply co-existed without any way of reconciling them. A later post-modernist view would find in them a fragmented, dislocated reality.

There is another (at least one) alternative. The Deans co-exist with the Agneses, the Reginalds with the Keiths. If they do not meet each other at least they encounter many others who are similar. These people inhabit co-existing social spheres, coeval and overlapping in space, but with fundamentally different horizons and time-spans. The reality of Tooting is constituted by the intermeshing and interrelating of these spheres. Grace's community is no more the authentic, original Tooting than is Ted's.

There is an additional vital point. Apart from Grace these white Tooting residents are all immigrants, they all moved into the area, respectively seventeen, ten, three, twenty-two, a half and fourteen years ago. It is an area which is always on the move and in that sense in- and out-migration is normal. Yet this does not preclude a sense of the 'other' in Tooting, namely the Asians, often perceived as holding together, as constituting a community in the sense that the whites are not. To that extent we can see the Asian community acquires in the eyes of the whites the qualities which they consider themselves to have lost. Instead of seeking to assimilate the incoming ethnic group, which in any case has lived there longer than them, whites like Keith, with Asian friends and living in an Asian family, may seek to be assimilated themselves. We may then be tempted to apply the concept of local culture, not to the white residents but to the Asians.

Our oldest Asian respondent, Naranjan, is 65 years old and has lived in Tooting for nineteen years. She came from Tanzania but met her husband in India and nearly all her family live there apart from sons who live just outside London. She is in constant touch with her family in India and a sister in New York, usually by letter, and returns to India every year. Yet she and her husband are fond of Germany and Switzerland and she enjoys travelling. Otherwise she is very busy locally, sings in her temple, attends the elderly day centre and has friends in all ethnic groups.

Here the point which comes through strongly is that Indian culture is as much a family culture as a local one. Religious occasions encourage the maintenance of family ties across space. The disembedding Giddens associates with modernity effectively sustains pre-modern kin relations and permits a form of reverse colonization.[6]

The same is the case with a much younger Pakistani woman, Zubdha, aged 26, born in Bradford, who came to Tooting three years ago. She is married and works in a social agency, maintains constant touch by telephone with family in Pakistan and visited over 120 friends and relatives there earlier in the year. However, she likes Tooting as a place where she is comfortable with her ethnic culture, can buy *halal* meat, has plenty of friends and no wish to leave.

For the white population, looking in from the outside, the Asians in Tooting appear to constitute a community. From the inside the orientations are varied. One thing is clear, racial segregation is apparent to both sides, but its meaning varies from person to person. In some cases it is a matter of feeling safer rather than any deep identification with an ethnic group. Such was the case with a 28-year-old shop owner, born in Birmingham, who moved to Tooting four years ago and who has no contact with aunts and uncles in India. His experience in both Birmingham and Tooting was that Asian youths stuck together for safety but he feels a sense of community in

Tooting, too, which does not extend to cover blacks and whites. He thinks he will stay in Tooting so that his daughter can settle in somewhere. Settling seems a matter of contingent considerations rather than anything deeper.

A much more recent newcomer is Ajit, also 28 years old, who came to Tooting from Delhi three years ago and brought his wife, but has broken off relations with his family in India. He has set up a small business and his contacts are other businessmen. He notices no real community but has no intention of returning to India either. He sees signs of racial barriers breaking down for young people and considers this process as providing hope for the future.

These hopes might be borne out by the experience of 18-year-old Kuldeep, who helps in his parents' shop. He came to Britain from Bombay with them six years ago and says that he could not now return to India because he feels 'too English'. He considers most white people to be very open but his friends are almost all Asian and they spend a lot of time together out in clubs or playing football.

The same questioning of his Indian identity arises for a 35-year-old Asian pharmacist, Kishor, who was born in East Africa and has lived in Tooting for ten years. He finds no real community and strong racial segregation but he appreciates Tooting for its convenient location for work and his sports club. He has distant cousins in the United States whom he occasionally calls and when he has a holiday he usually goes to Portugal.

In sum, our Asian respondents have orientations to community as varied as those of the whites. They all acknowledge the barriers between Asian and white but their orientations to other Asians are not as the whites imagine.[7] For a start the most intense felt identification with the Asian community comes from women and their local involvements are matched by the strength of their ties with the sub-continent. The men have a more instrumental relationship with other Asians, one of mutual protection and business opportunity, but not one which leads them to celebrate cultural difference.

Out of these interviews emerge both real differences in involvement in local culture and quite refined conscious distinctions about the nature of community. Most observant of all is possibly a Jamaican-born black community worker, Michael, who has lived with his parents in Tooting for eighteen years and works in Battersea, the other side of Wandsworth. For him nothing happens in Tooting which could be called community life. He contrasts it with Battersea, but even there what goes on he attributes to boredom rather than real involvement. His own friends are spread across London and everything he does revolves around the telephone. He calls Jamaica and the United States every week, and has been back to Jamaica every year for the last ten years. He sees Britain as just another American state but does not believe that the world is becoming a smaller place.

Somehow for him the very strength of his Caribbean ties and the barriers coming down between people also push other people away.

NEW CONCEPTS FOR LOCAL/GLOBAL CONDITIONS

We have cited individual cases at some length, not to confirm a general picture, nor to find a common thread. Indeed it would be possible to construct a different general type of orientation to living in the global city for each of our respondents. Equally we are not concerned to identify where some are right and others wrong. Our initial hypothesis is that each may be right for his or her own circumstances and social network.

Grace Angel and Naranjan both find active lives in a local community, one white the other Asian, and we have no reason to think that these are not reliable respondents. It is just that their worlds co-exist without impinging on each other.

Similarly the much-travelled Keith Bennett and Michael, the Jamaican community worker, agree that there is no community life in Tooting. Each finds it a convenient base for a London life and links with the rest of the world. But just because they agree there is no reason to take their view to be of more weight than anyone else's.

Let us suppose that this is not a matter of perspectives; rather that our interviews represent different realities, linked by their co-existence in a locality but not thereby creating a local culture or community. If that were the case the local area of Tooting would be characterized by a co-present diversity of lifestyles and social configurations. This diversity would then *constitute* the reality, not some average of a set of dispersed readings of the same phenomenon.

Yet this diversity would not represent chaos. Broadly there is no sense from our interviews of a collapsing world, even if there is regret for a world that is past. Each respondent makes sense of a situation, each relating in a different way to the local area. Certainly there is no sense of a Tooting community which comprises the population of the local area. Nor even is there a configuration in Elias' sense, except in so far as there is substantial agreement on the importance of the ethnic divide between whites and Asians. Yet ethnicity provides only one of the conditions for the lives of our respondents and in no sense creates an overall framework in the way Elias and Scotson's 'established' and 'outsiders' model encapsulates and co-ordinates the lives of the inhabitants of Winston Parva.

In other words our material is suggestive of a different order of things, which requires different conceptualizations from those available even only twenty years ago. Note the word 'suggestive' – we are talking about empirical possibilities. Their realization is not yet demonstrated by these few interviews. Further research will need to adopt a variety of methodologies and take account of contextual factors, such as the possible effects of local state policies, before it can conclude that the globalized locality exists in Tooting. Moreover the impact of any future political mobilization can never be discounted. None the less, we have enough evidence to warrant the close examination of an alternative theoretical framework for future research.

We can make sense of these interviews by drawing on globalization theory. In particular by taking account of the different time horizons and spatial extent of our respondents' social networks we can specify the new elements of regularly constituted social relations in a locality in a global city. Let us now advance four new propositions about locality paralleling the four on globalization we set out above:

1 The locality can sustain as much globalist sentiment as there are sources of information for and partners in making sense of worldwide events.
2 A locality can exhibit the traces of world events (e.g. the expulsion of East African Asians) which remove any feeling of separation from the wider world.
3 The networks of individuals in a locality can extend as far as their resources and will to use the communications at their disposal. Time–space compression allows the maintenance of kin relations with India or Jamaica as much as with Birmingham or Brentford.
4 The resources and facilities of a locality may link it to globally institutionalized practices. It is convenient both to be there if you want to use the products of global culture and as good as anywhere else as a base from which to travel. As such both transients and permanent residents can equally make a life which is open to the world.

Let us now bring these four propositions about a globalized locality together. In sum they suggest the possibility that individuals with very different lifestyles and social networks can live in close proximity without untoward interference with each other. There is an old community for some, for others there is a new site for a community which draws its culture from India. For some Tooting is a setting for peer group leisure activity, for others it provides a place to sleep and access to London. It can be a spectacle for some, for others the anticipation of a better, more multicultural community.

Each of these attitudes our interviews report suggest distinct patterns of social activities belonging to networks of social relations of very different intensity, spanning widely different territorial extents, from a few to many thousands of miles. In the locality they may scarcely touch each other. To convey the sense of varying but overlapping spatial scope, discrete movement and separateness, I am going to call these social formations '*sociospheres*', evoking a common use of the term 'sphere' to mean a field of concern or relevance which does not have in any geometrical sense to be spherical. It leaves open whether older categories like family, community,

51

friendship or newer ones like partnership, enclave and lifestyle group apply to these formations, recognizing that along with delocalization there is also a growing indeterminacy in applying such classifications.

But how, then, do individuals construct locality if their participation in sociospheres is so variable? For each person their place in the locality represents a point where their sociosphere literally touches the earth. But for each person who is viewing other people there can only be a very partial idea of the relevance of the locality for others' sociospheres. What they experience is not, therefore, in general anything like the traditional concept of community based on a shared local culture. Rather they engage in something like a cavalcade where passing actors find minimal levels of tolerable co-existence with varying intimations of the scope of other people's lives.

From this vantage point where the sociospheres intersect we view the socioscape. As sociologists we can put ourselves in the position of observers and construct a composite out of the totality of experiences in a locality and endow that with some objectivity. However, we should be particularly alert to the dangers of reification here. This composite socioscape is not to be equated with a pattern of underlying rules which make everyday life possible for the inhabitants of a locality. It is not this social and cultural diversity *per se* which replaces the old-style community as a basis for everyday social life in a locality, it is the generation of routine procedures and pragmatic accommodations, which Goffman made his special field, and which in this volume is represented by Jörg Dürrschmidt's milieu analysis.

Moreover, on my account if we wish to identify the determinants of socioscapes in a locality we have to turn to the trajectories of the sociospheres. In other words we look for determinants in the course of business firms, ethnic groups, religious conflicts in distant places, family inheritances, in anything which alters the sociosphere in which the individual is involved. This is quite apart from those agencies, public and private, which may control space and facilities.

TIME–SPACE SOCIAL STRATIFICATION

So where is community here? It may be nowhere and it is this new situation which we seek to express through a new vocabulary. It makes for considerable discomfort for political and other interest groups which seek to use old community rhetoric for contemporary causes, especially since the new vocabulary only begins to suggest the complexity of social relations in globalized localities. We know precious little about the ways in which the different sociospheres relate to each other except in stereotypes formed in the stage of nation-state sociologies. So we hear of the young unemployed aggravating senior citizens and of white residents objecting to a mosque and the spheres do not seem to fit together to make a harmonious social machinery. At the same time segregation operates in time and space to obviate the need often to introduce new mechanisms. The streets are occupied by different types of people at different times of day. Civil inattention and avoidance strategies effectively zone the streets to prevent friction between representatives of different lifestyles. The occupancy of both public space and private residence is distributed wildly unevenly across different user groups.

The new socioscape is constituted by sociospheres which have very different extensions in time and space. Disembedding and time–space compression operate very differently for different groups. One of the key effects of globalization on locality – namely that people can reside in one place and have their meaningful social relations almost entirely outside it and across the globe – means that people use the locality as site and resource for social activities in widely differing ways according to the extension of their sociosphere.

The single yuppie with business in Brussels and holidays in the Seychelles can ignore the unemployed lad next door and is unconcerned by the lack of playspace for the Asian family in the next street. They, in turn, may hardly know of their neighbours' existence since their paths may rarely cross. They live stratified existences, just as airliners operate in different air spaces according to the length of their journeys and cross each other's path at different heights in co-ordinated but unconcerned ways. So resources and stratification are as relevant as ever as issues under globalized conditions but the new configurations mean that older class- and welfare-based notions appear inapplicable to the new processes at work. It is this which prompts Laura Buffoni to propose a re-examination of poverty in the global city (see Chapter 7).

The images of socioscapes and sociospheres have their conceptual anticipation in Giddens' use of the idea of regionalization which refers to the zoning of social practices in time and space and which he illustrates with the different uses of rooms in a house at different times of day (1984: 119). He also suggests its application to urban areas and the world economy (ibid.: 130–1) without escaping completely from the earlier territorial ideas of zones of Park and Burgess. The point is that today zoning involves simultaneous multiple uses of spatial areas and the segregation practices depend on social stratification.

The locality is criss-crossed by networks of social relations whose scope and extent range from neighbouring houses over a few weeks, to religious and kin relations spanning generations and continents. They may also be short on time and long in spatial extent, as with an international business deal, or enduring and purely local as with a long-established chapel con-gregation. But broadly the longer the time-span and the more extended the space over which social relations are perpetuated the more resources are required by the parties involved. We therefore need to conceptualize contemporary local social relations in relation to a concept of time–space social stratification.

Giddens has proposed (1991) that the idea of disembedding is as vital a characteristic of late modern societies as differentiation was of early modern ones. Yet with differentiation went class. Globalization theory, by focusing on the lifting of social relations from local contexts, must equally attend to the resources available to the parties to those relations. Time–space social stratification is to disembedding as class was to differentiation.

The new conflicts are not between established and outsiders in the globalized localities but between locals and cosmopolitans and all gradations between, where the local may be newcomers and the cosmopolitans may be long-term residents. The stratification layers are vividly represented by the different modes of transport available, the use of telecommunications and the use made of space. Very frequently the greatest living space is available to those who occupy it least.

All these facets of local/global life, which obviate direct confrontation between the sociospheres, mask the realities of class which in any case are no longer confined by nation-state realities. Time–space social stratification is the frame within which inequalities of access to resources and life chances are contained today which are more acute than any which prevailed during the period of class-based industrial society. Travel and migration become the new circulatory principles and medium through which locality can be converted into a resource and a consumption good. For those who are left as poor locals globalization deprives them even of the sense of deprivation and of a sight of their exploiters, as local culture dissolves with little trace into the generalized facilities of a convenient place to live.

Linking globalization to the new forms of social stratification should dispel an impression that the new theory is in any way a restatement of the harmonious community at the global level. There is no room for false optimism in this respect. At the same time in the European context it should highlight the need not to reify old boundaries or to give priority to claims to primordial identity. We are suggesting that there are processes at work which reduce their significance and give the new migrations a possible future meaning very different from past experiences. Globalization makes co-present enclaves of diverse origins one possible social configuration characterizing a new Europe.

ACKNOWLEDGEMENTS

I am indebted to the work of John Eade, Graham Fennell and Darren O'Byrne on the Roehampton Institute's Wandsworth Local/Global Study and to their and Neil Washbourne's comments on an earlier version of this Chapter.

NOTES

1 This is a revised version of a paper given originally to the Amalfi meetings of the Italian Sociological Association's Sociological Theory and Social Transformation Section in May 1994.

2 The findings reported here are drawn from the Roehampton Institute's Wandsworth Local study (Albrow *et al.* 1994). John Eade directed the study and Darren O'Byrne carried out the interviewing.

3 Occasionally there is a reference to outside links, such as the ruling family taking its leisure in Chicago and New York and even visiting Europe (ibid: 96), General Motors closing its plant and then returning (ibid: 521–2). But only 2 per cent of the families were 'foreign born', there was no foreign quarter (ibid: 165) and the general hostility to international links is epitomized by the local newspaper which warned a teacher who has advocated joining the World Court that schools were supported by taxes.

4 In social theory Anthony Giddens' (1984) linkage of time geography with structuration theory provided the jumping-off point for his own development of globalization theory (1990, 1991).

5 The names of all our respondents in this and subsequent chapters have been changed to prevent identification.

6 This means that earlier assumptions like 'extended kinship is seriously damaged by the fact of migration' (Rex 1986: 132) cannot be taken for granted.

7 This diversity is not a necessary result of the individualistic methodology employed here. John Eade's recent study of politics in the Bangladeshi community in East London, which adopted an institutional and organizational approach, equally discovered a diversity of local sectoral interests which belied any claim by local representatives that they could speak for a cohesive local community (Eade 1989: 189).

4

THE DELINKING OF LOCALE AND MILIEU

On the situatedness of extended milieux in a global environment

Jörg Dürrschmidt

INTRODUCTION

In one of the more recent volumes on the phenomenon of global cities, Gottmann (1989) makes a remarkable statement:

> Modern cities are the pillars of the developing global system. It is a poetic illusion to assume that the world is shrinking because the communication improves. In reality the world of each of us constantly expands because, as we carry on, we find it necessary to deal with more and more people, in more places, with a greater number and diversity of problems.
>
> (Gottmann 1989: 66)

The statement reveals one crucial ambiguity inherent in current processes of globalization. The processes which increasingly make the world a smaller place and integrate its population into a 'single society' (Albrow 1993a: 248ff.; Robertson 1992: 54) seem, at the same time, to imply an increasingly expanded, complex, shifting and accelerated everyday life for each individual in this world.

What has been called 'time–space compression' and 'collapse of spatial barriers' (Harvey 1993: 284, 293), means that individuals extend their scope of action and field of experience into a potentially global dimension, basically provided by access to global means of transport and communication. What has been described as 'contingent and accidental "otherness" in daily life' (ibid.: 301) implies for some an enjoyable ephemerality and variety of an increasingly internationalized environment. For others, however, it means the desperate search for local identity in a mobilized world, which they have to share with others who do not keep any longer to 'their' place in a fixed politico-geographical order.

Furthermore, Gottmann's statement recalls another important insight. In

THE DELINKING OF LOCALE AND MILIEU

the tradition of Spengler, Simmel and the Chicago School, the metropolis can be seen as *pars pro toto* of society, in its 'microcosm' displaying typical aspects of social life more clearly, and taking the consequences of changes in social life to an extreme (cf. Lindner 1990: 76ff.).

Not surprisingly, there has been an increasing interest in the role which global cities play within globalization processes (King 1990; Sassen 1991; Budd and Whimster 1992). However, attention has been largely paid to the economic dimension of microglobalization. None of these elaborate and detailed studies tackles the impact of globalization processes on a world city in the context of the lived experience of 'ordinary' people. As far as this aspect of London life is concerned we learn as much from reading Hanif Kureishi's novel *The Buddha of Suburbia* (1990) as from the academic literature.

Consequently, this chapter will not focus on the *global city*, defined as a key node of a global economy, competing in the global hierarchy of finance, banking and related services (e.g. Sassen 1991). Rather I will take as my starting point London as one of the few world cities which attracts people from all over the world, and thus brings together the most varied features of humankind in an environment of microglobalization. This intense microglobalization of the *world city* makes it a distinct epitomization of an increasingly globalized *life-world*.[1]

Therefore I shall assert here that the investigation of the microglobaliz-ation of the everyday life of a world city like London provides us with revealing insights into current processes of the globalization of people's everyday lives in general. To support my line of argument I shall draw on fieldwork, recently done in London, and bring together current thoughts on globalization with more established phenomenological perspectives in sociology.

From amongst the many features of microglobalization processes in people's everyday lives I shall concentrate upon the increased mobility and 'disembeddedness' of individuals' milieux. Milieux will be preliminarily defined as relatively stable and situated configurations of action and experience, in which individuals actively generate a distinctive degree of familiarity and practical competence (cf. Grathoff 1989: 344, 434). This configuration enables individuals to handle successfully the changing variety of microglobalization.

Microglobalization[2] will be defined here as the integration of global difference(s) and variety into a distinctive social environment. These differences refer both to humankind as such (ethnic groups, their habits, beliefs and practices) and the materializations of human activity (built environment, technologies) spatially scattered across the globe and distrib-uted in different historical epochs. Under conditions of microglobalization these are brought together in one place, making the environment attractive for people from all over the world.

Three different meanings are integrated in this notion of microglobaliz-ation of the world city, each of them making it a distinctive site of research: representation, intensification and symbolization.

First, the world city implies the notion of *metropolis* as the embodiment of the complexity, diversity and variety of the world as a whole, aptly described by Mumford through the metaphor of 'the most complete compendium of the world' (1991: 639).

Second, the world's complexity and variety are not only portrayed in a microglobalized environment, but rather are condensed in a bounded local and social setting. This *intensification* in metropolitan life encourages the emergence of new social forms, and allows us to study them in the making under 'extreme' conditions. Hence Park's metaphor of the city as a labora-tory in which 'human nature and social processes may be most conveniently and profitably studied' is especially appropriate for the world city (in Lindner 1990: 90).

Third, the world city is a *microcosm* in a two-fold way. In the first place, the variety and complexity of the microglobalized environment of a world city is an everyday experience for the people who live in it, and who conse-quently have to make sense of it as 'their' world of everyday life. Their daily routines draw upon, generate and (re)shape the reality of the world city. The attempt by individuals to mark the internal structure of 'their' reality through different kinds of symbolization and categorization illuminates the meaning of the world city for world city dwellers,[3] thus creating a 'cosmion' (cf. Schütz 1967: 336). Moreover, as the everyday lives of people in the world city are related in many ways to distant people and places all over the world, the 'cosmion' of the world city reflects these external global links in its symbolic expressions and their internal structure, making it a *symbolic microcosm of the globe*.

THE IMPACT OF MICROGLOBALIZATION ON LOCAL MILIEUX[4]

A world city like London attracts people from all over the world who, in times of global communication and mobility, are well able to keep up ties with their former places of residence and to sustain previous social contacts across distance. Hence, as already indicated, London materializes features of globalization in a revealing way.

The presence of many of the world's ethnic groups in contemporary London (cf. Merriman 1993), despite the geographical and political com-plexity of the globe, symbolizes the aforementioned 'collapse of spatial barriers' and 'intense time–space compression'. It also shows the increased mobility of people, who do not keep any longer to their assigned places in a traditional politico-geographical order.

The materialization of the aforementioned processes in London's everyday life is expressed in the following ways. Since people are attracted to the global city for different reasons, their motives for coming to London and life plans there are also different, by no means always implying a final settlement in London. Therefore London possesses a substantial *transient population*. Approximately three-fifths of London's population is born there, the rest are 'Londoners by adoption' (Hall 1990: 7). Although figures by themselves do not tell us too much, the annual turnover of 350,000 people is quite revealing, when we consider that this figure matches the population of the German town Bielefeld, host of the World Congress for Sociology in 1994.[5] It is also important to note that one-third of this number came from outside the UK (ibid.: 13).

Yet even living or/and working in London still means that most people are on the move fairly continuously, whether commuting between residence and work place, leaving London at the weekend, or using London's huge network of public and private transport in order to get the most out of the opportunities that London offers in terms of culture and entertainment. We should also notice that most 'Londoners by adoption' move house several times in order to find an appropriate environment in which to live (Hall 1990: 7f.). Therefore we can safely say that London has a fairly *mobile population*.

The mobile aspect of London life, of course, also reflects the ties kept up between 'Londoners by adoption' and their previous places of residence and work. One-sixth of London's population is born overseas (cf. Merriman 1993: 212; King 1990: 141), leaving aside the fact that many of the London-born people identify with an ethnic background. In particular the migration from overseas after World War II meant that 'all of Greater London's thirty-two boroughs became more cosmopolitan between 1971 and 1981' (King 1990: 141). Hence it is no exaggeration to speak of an *internationalized population* in London.

The assumption, therefore, can be made that people in London occupy a complex and constantly changing, and often disrupted environment rather than a homogeneous and stable one. Following Harvey, we could call this an *ephemeral environment* (1993: 21, 216, 292). People in London are well aware of this 'ephemerality' in their immediate surroundings. Especially the older generation, which enjoyed the close-knit street village communities before World War II and experiences this changing environment as the disruption of local communities and the decline of community spirit.

Herbert, now in his late 60s, was born and bred in the Elephant and Castle area, south London, and he recalls from that time that:

> In these working-class areas, every street or every two streets were like a village. Everybody knew each other within that street, and perhaps one or two of the neighbouring streets. . . . And I think one of the things that has happened to London now, and I'm jumping a bit here, is

59

that it's no longer like that. Because when I was young, people lived in these streets for generations, one generation was succeeded by another generation. But now the population in London is so transient that they move in and they move out again, you know. There is not the same association with a particular area and the same road.

Consequently Herbert left the metropolis and retired to a village near one of the 'new towns' outside London's green belt, in order to regain the feeling of a supposedly intact local community:

Coming to this village I regained a bit of what it was like in London in those days of my life, when London was a marvellous place to live, you know.

It is quite revealing to see the same problem approached by a 'Londoner by adoption', who is part of the 'ephemerality' Herbert complained about. Sarah, in her early 30s, is a professional, working in the City of London. Depending on the requirements of her job, she has moved in and out of London several times. She has chosen her current place of residence in south London because of 'easy access to the city', 'fresh air' and 'lots of open space'. She has a fairly distanced and rational view of the problem mentioned by Herbert:

I think the point about London is, very few people are in during the day, an awful lot of people are out working, so you don't get people sort of sitting at their windows and watching what's going on. You find the only people who really do know what's going on are the retired elderly people who do sit at their windows and look and see what's happening in the street.

Yet Sarah doesn't really mind, since her friends are scattered 'all over London' and, therefore, her social life takes place on 'neutral territory'. Her work and hobby (singing) require a lot of travel, and she likes travelling anyway. Hence London is more a place to explore the world from than to settle into a local community:

If you live in London, it's very easy to think about going somewhere else, whether it's outside London in the UK, or it's outside the UK altogether. I mean this year I've got an awful lot of travel organized already. And I've got weekends in Barcelona, and weekends sailing around the coast of France, possibly trips of course to Boston, and all sorts of things, which are easy for me to do because I'm based here. And I can just sort of buy a reasonably cheap ticket from London and get there easily after work and just go away for a long weekend.

These two quotations indicate a key dynamic of globalization, referred to by Giddens as 'disembedding', which basically implies the 'lifting out' of the individual's field of action from pre-given locales on the one hand, and the shaping of locales by distant social influences, on the other hand (1990: 19, 21, 79f.). Thus, while Sarah uses her residence as a resting place and convenient base for frequent and extended travel, Herbert 'helplessly' experiences the same process as unwanted mobility of his neighbours and disruption of the local community.

The point I want to make here appears to be very simple but it has deep analytical consequences. As long as people in their actions are confined to the limits of a specific, hardly changing locale, there is no awareness of people's active effort to come to terms with his or her surroundings – the gaining of practical competence in distinctive zones of everyday life. To speak in conceptual terms, locale and milieu converge into a local milieu. It needed the disruption of local communities and their completely 'localized relations' and the extension of people's field of action and experience beyond a specific locale in order to make us fully realize that the individual generates a milieu in an always changing environment, instead of just inhabiting a pre-given locale (cf. Giddens 1990: 101f.). The uprooting of people's field of action from a specific locale as ultimate reference point is a precondition for the extension of the individual's personal milieu beyond the immediate physical, geographical and social surroundings. This came about with the increase of individual mobility as a result of intense time–space compression. Therefore, the *delinking* of locale and milieu can be seen as one major consequence of globalization processes.

THE SITUATEDNESS OF EXTENDED MILIEUX IN THE BIOGRAPHICAL SITUATION AND ITS RELEVANCES

It is not surprising that concepts which focus on the individual's active effort to generate and maintain his/her own environment are having a resurgence in a period of history when: 'presumed certainties of cultural identity, firmly located in particular places which housed stable cohesive communities of shared tradition and perspective, though never a reality for some, were increasingly disrupted and displaced for all' (Carter *et al.* 1993: vii).

At the same time it is probably this emphasis on the willed activity of the individual which has made a phenomenological concept like milieu resistant to incorporation within the sociological paradigm which gave community and culture such prominence (cf. Chapter 2 of this book).

From the outset, the concept of milieu, as it was introduced by Scheler into German *Kultursoziologie*, was focused on the people's active part in the dynamic interplay between human beings and their related environment. Related to the person's 'value order', which stirs the practical approach towards the world, milieu thus can be defined as an environment, structured according to rules of preference, which consequently displays the

61

person's environment in its practically relevant aspects (cf. Scheler 1966: 148–72). Territoriality, therefore, is a function of the person's 'disposition', rather than of pre-given physical or geographical conditions.

Schütz elaborated this approach in a more mundane way. He sees individuals, living in a 'natural attitude', permanently structuring their situation in the world according to a 'system of relevances'. These 'relevances' are partly 'imposed relevances', deriving from the time–space structure of an ontologically pre-arranged world. But more importantly these 'relevances' derive from the individual's 'actual biographical state', which includes 'life plans', 'stock of knowledge' and (body-related) 'habitualities'. Since the 'biographical situation' determines the individual's access towards the world, it implies a selective structuring of the surrounding world according to zones, which are distinguished by the individual's practical interest in them, resulting in different degrees of familiarity. Those zones, however, are by no means ordered as concentric circles, but have fuzzy borders and open horizons (Schütz 1966: 116ff.; 1970: 167ff.).

There are at least two aspects of the milieu concept which make it capable of grasping changes in everyday life under conditions of globalization. First, it emphasizes the individual's active approach in relation to his/ her surroundings. Second, and relatedly, its notion of *situatedness* is based on the individual's *disposition* as focus of his/her 'configuration of action', instead of a specific locale. In consequence we see the emergence of a new view on the territorial and spatial structuring of mobilized everyday lives.

I now want to illustrate a few implications for the situatedness of milieux under the impact of globalized conditions. Locales, in which milieux might be focused to a certain degree, cannot be regarded simply as places, geographically located and referring to a physical setting. From the outset different people will have different views of the same physical setting, for the person's milieu as 'disposition' towards the surrounding world carries a *perspective* or direction. This personal perspective is certainly imposed on London as a whole, but also on very distinct places, as I will illustrate with the following example.

Streatham, an 'inner London suburb', recently saw the loss of its big department store, which used to attract shoppers from beyond the locality and, therefore, contributed to the reputation of the locality in London. However, what for many people, especially the older generation, is still known as Pratt's Department Store, is for others just a big ruin with boarded-up shop windows. Thus their different milieux provide people with a different perspective on the same site in physical terms. Conversely, different people can inhabit the same local environment and yet live in different milieux.

Furthermore, this example helps to reveal two more aspects referring to the importance of people's milieux in a changing environment. The milieu *transcends* the immediate physical setting of a place, not only in space, but in time. It goes beyond the actually visible, the perceivable, when people refer to the site of the former department store by saying: 'You see, this is where "Pratt's" used to be'. 'Pratt's', although (or because!) it is physically no longer there, is still something which practically affects many people's everyday lives in Streatham and, consequently, is still part of their milieux (cf. Scheler's notion of 'tradition' as extension of milieu in time: 1966: 161 fn.; cf. de Certeau 1988: 108).

Streatham's department store also makes clear that a single place can take on a symbolic role for a local milieu, symbolizing the identity of a former locale, after the locale undergoes irreversible changes, as Streatham did when it turned from the 'West End of South London' into 'just another part and parcel of that somewhat anonymous area known as "South London"' (Gower 1990: intro.).[6] A competent local voice might indicate how the loss of an intact locale confines locally based milieux to certain sites, which symbolize 'those days', and therefore help people to live in a *milieu of local tradition*.

> That's pride, that's deep-rooted pride. The people of Streatham still feel that they want to hang on to that rather nice way of life that they have known . . . from about 1949/50 into the 1960s, even up to about 1974/75, where they felt as though they were a cut above of the other parts of the Borough of Lambeth. After all they had a very big department store which was very well known, and the High Road contained a lot of major retailers. It was a good place to live, good place to work, good place to do shopping, and . . . a sought-after area in which to live.
>
> Now the situation has changed. But still, in the minds of a lot of people, they still live in those good old days . . . good old days . . . perhaps twenty years ago. They still haven't changed the way they think about Streatham. I'm pleased that they don't. Because I don't think it would be right to allow Streatham to go down. It needs to be kept at a certain level.
>
> (C. Barnett,[7] Committee member of the Streatham Association)

This view, not surprisingly, represents the perspective of those who, for one or other reason, deliberately or involuntarily, feel attached or are tied to this particular local milieu.

'SIGNIFICANT PLACES' AS THE FOCUS OF EXTENDED MILIEUX

The claim that personal milieux have become increasingly mobile and extended under the conditions of globalization does not imply a complete transcendence, an entire delinking of milieux from locales, but it does mean

THE DELINKING OF LOCALE AND MILIEU

the uprooting of milieux from particular locales. People's extended 'fields of action' are still woven around *significant places,*[8] where their daily routines are focused, providing a localized kind of situatedness. But again, this does not refer to the locale as such, but to the relevance of a certain locale to the person's milieu. *Home* is certainly such a significant place in a person's milieu. Yet, in terms of extension and mobility of milieux, what is considered to be 'home' largely derives from the person's ability to generate a special relationship to a place, less from the physical setting of the place.

Ira, in her late 20s, has lived all her life in London. She has moved house at least six times, always finding something unique about the areas she lived in. As she liked previous places of residence because of the variety of people she met there and not because of the local history of places, so she is attracted to Brixton because of its unique atmosphere, the uniqueness of which she tries to describe in the context of Brixton tube station:

> I've never come out of a tube station actually at any other place, where I thought to myself: 'My God, I can't believe these people, you know, I can't believe it' . . . I've come back from somewhere, tired as hell on a Saturday afternoon, and as soon as I'm at the bottom of the escalator I can hear Brixton, I can feel Brixton. Then you are going up the stairs, and there are loads of people on the stairs. And you're putting your ticket through, and suddenly there are four or five people, and they're either asking you for money, or are telling you something about the world or about religion, or they're trying to chat you up, or they're trying to sell you something. . . . There are just so many. And then you get to the top, and it's even more of that, you know. I think that's amazing. That's why I essentially like Brixton really.

Although she has lived in several areas in London and has developed the ability to get the most out of any place, Ira does not believe that there is no significant difference between these places. There are places of *biographical significance* for Ira, places of 'becoming a bit of an individual' – in her case, Islington:

> I think some places, you know, they have a significance for you if they kind of represent a changing period in your life, you know, or a discovering period in your life.

Furthermore, 'home' can develop a very *personal index*, related to personal belongings. Sarah, whom we have met already as a quite mobile and well-travelled Londoner, describes her 'feeling at home' in the following terms:

> But isn't it [home] related to this house I suppose largely as well? I would have the same feelings whether or not it is London I'm coming back to. I mean, for example, when I was travelling a lot and I lived out

in Oxfordshire, then that was coming home to me, but it was not London. So for me it's a more personal thing, it's more centred on my house. And I feel my belongings are here and, you know, my independence, if you like, is here. It's not sort of geographically.

'Home' in this sense no longer contradicts mobility, for it derives from people's ability to make themselves feel at home at different places. This point can be illustrated by taking an exceptional example. Barbara is an American expatriate in her early 60s, who had lived temporarily in London for two years. Accordingly, she only rented a single room in a shared house. Amongst the things she brought with her and which in a sense make her room, her 'home', are pictures and letters from her children, newspaper clippings and books – 'things that are meaningful for me and for other people . . . it's like my room and my things, that's my little world right now'.

However, as milieux are no longer confined to a particular locale, their extension and mobility allows them also to find situatedness in *associating with the like-minded*, instead of being confined to localized interaction. To illustrate this aspect we can stay with Barbara. Her milieu is not focused on the neighbourhood in Streatham, where she happened to come to live. Barbara's milieu centres on the social network of other expatriates, based at St Anne's and St Agnes' Lutheran Church in London, where she meets fellow-expatriates from all over the world, who share a similar milieu, or biographical situation (internationalized families, cosmopolitan life experience, temporary employment contracts). These like-minded people are also the 'resource people', as Barbara calls them, for the appropriate practical knowledge which is needed for developing an expatriate milieu in London:

> I found people in that setting that I like to associate with. Going to St Anne's and St Agnes' you meet people from all over. . . . And they are very friendly, because they're all trying to find their way in a big city. . . .
>
> So I think, the resource people you find, from going to the Lutheran Church, know how to take care of things or know how to get around to places you want to see in London. I found that quite helpful.

We can clearly see that the *uprooting* of milieux from given locales does not necessarily imply 'rootlessness' or 'homelessness'. Rather the opposite applies since the uprooting of milieux reveals the individual's ability to identify 'home' in an ongoing 'construction and organization of interlaced categories of space and time' (cf. Robertson 1994: 43). In this regard I completely agree when Robertson argues that 'in the present situation of global complexity, the idea of home has to be divorced analytically from the idea of locality' (1995: 39).

POLY-CENTREDNESS AND DECENTREDNESS OF EXTENDED MILIEUX

So far my argument has focused on the delinking of milieu and locale, that is the uprooting and transcendence of milieux from the conditions of specific locales. However, given that once milieux are uprooted and not rerooted, it follows as a consequence that there are *extended milieux*, potentially stretching across infinite time–space distances.

In times of global mobility, people tend to have more than one 'life-centre'. We can notice the multiplicity of 'significant places', both in biographical succession (birthplace, different living-places according to status passages: education, work, retirement), and/or the simultaneous co-ordination of life-plans, and even daily routines, around more than one locale as focal points.

The simultaneous integration of several 'significant places' in one milieu reveals further consequences. Milieu-bound familiarity, which is generated from 'being settled' into a certain environment, does not only derive from inhabiting places, but from repeatedly using certain 'paths' between places. Most London commuters seem to appreciate the relaxed feeling which derives from using the same route every day. They are able to carry on doing things almost 'blindfolded', like at home where things are ordered 'ready at hand'. Having a nap, reading a newspaper, putting on make-up, eating a snack while being on the move (an everyday experience on London's Network Southeast trains) are certainly activities which indicate the familiarity and relaxation of an 'extended home' and again imply a certain *decentredness* of milieux.

So we can see that milieux inhabit space rather than just places. Moving between 'significant places' is more than just technically bridging them. People's milieux have a direction, deriving from their general 'disposition' and actual 'desires'. From this point of view, places are no longer isolated, but interwoven in a 'biographical situation', connecting them according to 'biographical relevances'.

This connection becomes even more obvious when we talk about the integration of 'significant places' scattered across substantial distances. They are not linked by the permanent physical movement of people across them but are, nevertheless, important for the 'biographical situation' as the following illustrations demonstrate.

Ulla, in her early 80s, is a 'Londoner by birth' with 'Swedish background'. There are strong ties to Sweden (Stockholm, Uppsala), where all the relatives from her mother's side live. In the family she was the only one of three children who stayed in London, while her sister moved to New-foundland and her brother made a career on New York's Broadway. She made lengthy visits every year, alternating between Sweden and North America. Especially during the time when Ulla had to nurse her ageing parents, the trips to Newfoundland and New York were something which kept her going in London.

> My brother always sent me money to get out to him, to have a holiday. And I say, without those holidays I wouldn't have survived at all. So we had a great time. . . . He either sent me a round-trip ticket or money. I would go to Newfoundland, stay with my sister perhaps for a week, a week or two weeks, and visit all her friends, and then fly down [to New York] to my brother, and then we went on tour with him.

Far from the contacts ebbing away after the death of her brother and her sister, ties were still maintained especially between London and Newfoundland, encouraging regular travel in both directions. Ulla has made her own friends there during all the years she has spent visiting her sister. She knows about their biographies and is kept informed through letters, telephone and 'pigeon post':

> I've got to know all her friends, and I, you know, have heard all their stories and everything else. . . . And of course when you have all these friends, that's why I want to go this summer, because I've made so many friends there. My sister being three years older, I always made younger friends; not her's necessarily.

A special relationship developed between her and a woman who looked after her in Newfoundland when her sister was dying. This friendship, kept up by 'pigeon post', has even got features of a 'transatlantic support-service' in crucial situations of life.

> There was the daughter of the couple, Anne, who looked after me when my sister was dying. She put me in her guest-room and was very kind to me. So one year I flew over and looked after their home while they were having a holiday in Ireland. You see, that kind of thing. We were friends and we kept in touch, which is the important thing.
> Anne sends wonderful letters to me. She says it's another pigeon post, because with anyone coming to England, she gets some post over here. So she keeps me in touch all the time. And so I always know the latest things about her husband. . . . She is looking forward to seeing me. I rang her up at Easter.

Consequently, Ulla is as familiar with this part of Newfoundland and its people as she is with pockets of London and the people in her street in Streatham.

Barbara, the American expatriate, whom we have already introduced, pursues a life in London which, in diverse ways, is connected with her 'home' in the US. Her salary from the Methodist Church, some income from her ex-husband, health insurance, and many things more, are still held and run from the US. She feels that the administrative part of the connection is sometimes particularly difficult to handle, and can have a sharp impact on her life in London, i.e. 'when the money stopped coming from California'.

Sometimes she feels a little helpless and powerless when it comes to managing those things efficiently between 'here' and 'there', especially since she has been unable to make extensive use of the telephone for transatlantic phone calls due to her shortage of money. Referring to her health insurance she recalls:

> I asked them to tell me if the insurance would cover anything that happened to me in London, and they have never answered that. So it's very frustrating, and you can't just call up and say: 'Would you please answer my question!' I feel I can't afford that, so I have to just let some of that go.

Barbara's case at the same time indicates that *poly-centredness* of milieux does not mean that all 'significant places' are of equal importance, or conversely, that there is an absolute indifference. Again recalling the 'biographical situation' of the individual, the 'relevance' of the one or the other place might shift according to life plans, tasks and preferences.

Asked whether due to all those aforementioned technical ties, she would consider Nashville, where she still owns a house, as her 'home', she answers:

> No, I'm thinking of London as home now more . . . I still say home sometimes there, but more and more I'm saying this is my home. But I think of home as being more . . . London than Streatham. . . . But there are more things about here now than there used to be, obviously, because there are more people I'm with. But then again, I get mail from [Nashville], and I get information from friends and family and so on – that fairly makes me think about them. And there are some things that I miss here, and there are some things that make me feel good to know that they are there and I'm here, and that's OK. It's not as if I have to be there. . . . More and more I'm happy to be here.

These illustrations indicate two more implications of extended milieux and their decentredness. The milieu is not confined to the individual's field of action, and its perceptual field. Milieu as value-related environment extends beyond immediate practical interests into the realm of hope, desire, fear, expectations. Thus the 'biographical situation' also generates a shifting *affectual field* (cf. Waldenfels 1985: 183ff., 195f.). Consequently, milieu as related to the individual's 'affectual field' extends well beyond the place of the person's immediate bodily presence. I might be going along Streatham High Road but my thoughts are moving away to Bielefeld University where the scholarship board is just about to make a decision, which I hope will be in my favour.

Furthermore, the place of bodily situatedness is not always the focus of the milieu in terms of its emotional situatedness. Barbara, who just told us that her 'home'-feeling has shifted from Nashville towards London, but in fact 'goes all around, everywhere', is fairly determined to go back, not to the USA but the Philippines after her period in London. She spent a considerable period of her life in the Philippines before she came to London. This emotional bond to the Philippines has an immediate impact on her milieu in London. She made close friends with a Filipino family and attends the Filipino community festivities, either with this family or other Filipinos she has got to know.

> With the Filipinos I must say, I also feel at home with them, because, having lived in the Philippines for so long. So for instance with the Ferreiras, I was with them the whole day yesterday. We were looking for some familiar places, so we went to Chinatown yesterday. And when I was going to the British Museum, the girls of the Ferreiras were accompanying me there. I feel a little bit more familiar with them than with other nationalities.

So we see in Barbara's case not only the future life plans centring on a place other than London, but also the immediate impact of her emotional bonds to a distant place on her London milieu.

While Barbara's emotional bonds to the Philippines cheer her up and keep her going in London, Nicos, another Streatham resident, provides us with another insight into the influence of distant places on a London-based milieu. In his case, however, the connectedness with 'back home' has a rather unsettling impact on his London milieu. His case is of additional interest, since it reveals the impact of media on the linking of distant places in personal milieux.

Now in his early 30s, Nicos has lived in London for twenty years, since he came over in 1974 due to the war in Cyprus. Two years ago he set up his own catering business, but it failed after one year of hard work. Ever since then he has wanted to leave London, for he can't find 'real value in life' here. On the other hand he cannot go 'back home', before he has lived up to the Cypriot media-generated image of London, imposed on him from 'back home'. Nicos feels pressurized by this image all the time in London:

> The ideology is that you are in London, you should have made a lot of money, you should be somebody, you know. They expect you to go back home on holiday with lots of money in your pocket, because they have this illusion about, you know, the 'golden streets of London', you know, this is rich pickings. And, you know, if you spent ten years in London, or twenty years in London [people will ask:] 'Why haven't you got a lot of money? Are you an idiot?' The fact is that you are not an idiot, the fact is that life is hard.

These examples of the impact of distant places on the situatedness of London-based milieux, whether it is by the immediate presence of previous biographical sequences (Barbara), or by the intermediate and diffuse pressure of expectations (Nicos), bring us back to where we started this discussion.

CONCLUSION

The shifting and extended situatedness of milieux according to changing biographical relevances

All the aforementioned aspects of the situatedness of milieux under conditions of globalization: 'uprooting', 'transcendence', 'decentredness', 'poly-centredness', which can be summed up in the phrase 'extension of milieux', lead to one final consequence. What has been described in terms of society as a general 'compression of time–space' has its equivalent in the *potential convergence of 'here' and 'there'* in individuals' milieux. This means that extended milieux not only transcend the surroundings of specific locales, but that they inhabit space by meaningfully integrating (geographically) distant places into a biographical situation. This implies the structuring of people's lives around more than one focus, as well as the immediate impact of distant places on the place of bodily presence.

In extended milieux 'here' and 'there' do not equal 'near' and 'far', that is 'familiar' and 'unfamiliar'. Familiarity thus is no longer solely related to the person's immediate physical environment in 'readiness at hand'. It extends to distant familiar places and their interwovenness in a uniquely personal way. Consequently, the situatedness of 'personal milieux' derives from the person's determination to hold together the different significant fragments of an extended field of action and experience, rather than from long-term settlement in a specific locale.

Hence the competence of a person to handle an extended milieu is a crucial individual attempt to create and maintain spatial and social order in an ephemeral world of time–space compression. In a time of 'geographical mobility' (Harvey 1993: 294), 'collapse of spatial barriers' (ibid.: 293), 'imploding spatialities' (ibid.: 304), when 'time and space have disappeared as meaningful dimensions to human thought and action' (ibid.: 299ff.), it is the individual in his/her milieu who actively generates a unique spatial order and situatedness. The collapse of geographical distances does not imply the absence of any spatiality, but physical distance is embedded or even replaced by spatiality, set by shifting 'biographical relevances'. The collapse of a pre-given geographical order of places does not imply their dispersal in pleasurable indifference, but their meaningful integration into a biographical story or sequence. Distance is measured by biographical 'relevance'.

70

This applies for both extremes of time–space compression, where the world's differences have imploded into one locale (the world city), as well as the potential extension of people's field of action into a global dimension. Two illustrations highlight this point. Sarah enjoys the cosmopolitan variety of places and people, integrated in London. Yet, in order to be able to enjoy it, she refuses to be exposed randomly to this variety. Consequently she attempts to structure her daily life in London according to her preferences. This implies for Sarah setting differences where there are no obvious physical or geographical differences.

> So for me there is an enormous psychological difference where I have my entertainment. I don't stay in the centre of London, because, if I finish work I want to go and switch off and relax totally. The way I do that is to come home and change my clothes, and go out to somewhere that has nothing to do with work. I hate going out straight from work, which a lot of people tend to do. I hate meeting up with people for drinks straight after work and then going on to the cinema or something in the West End, because I just don't feel that I have changed gear at all, and that's very important for me. So I feel in a way that, you know, although we are geographically quite near the City here, I feel it is a world apart.

Ulla, despite her age, still flies every year to friends and relatives in Newfoundland or Sweden, and stays there for a substantial period. But the local commitments to friends in the street remain and sometimes it is difficult to plan the nearest future between local and transatlantic relevances.

> I'm still waiting to book [the flight]. I want to make my dates with Susy, because Rob [her husband] has got his special anniversary . . . when he retires. I want to know the dates before I say: 'I'm going off to Newfoundland'.

Finally we can state that the meaningful integration of distant places into the shifting biographical 'relevances' of 'here' and 'there' in a person's milieu provides an 'original spatial structure' (cf. de Certeau 1988: 109), deriving from creative manipulation of 'seemingly contingent geographical circumstances' (Harvey 1993: 294). Consequently, the person's competence to focus successfully the intermingling local, regional and global relevances of his/her milieu, not only provides a mobile and extended kind of situatedness, but at the same time constitutes a concrete structuration in which the expanding world of the individual becomes (re)united.

In this sense, then, extended milieux could be considered as one concrete realization of 'sociospheres' (cf. Albrow, Chapter 3 in this volume), in which individuals inhabit a shrinking world, co-existing, overlapping, and intermingling with other people's milieux, and thus negotiating the relevant spaces of 'their' worlds. The situatedness of this particular conception of

71

extended milieu, therefore, refuses the nostalgia that some phenomenological approaches are rightly accused of (cf. Robertson 1992: 157). In this version it rather stresses – even if it does not identify itself with – the generation and transformation of forms of 'the concrete structuration of the world as a whole' (ibid.: 53).

ACKNOWLEDGEMENTS

I would like to thank Martin Albrow, John Eade, Neil Washbourne, Darren O'Byrne and Laura Buffoni for comments made on earlier drafts of this chapter.

NOTES

1 This obviously brings up the problematic issue of differentiating between a 'global city' and a 'world city', something which is discussed by John Eade in Chapter 1 of this book. It might seem that my use of the term 'world city' contradicts Eade's attempt to detach this volume on the lived experience of a 'global city' from previous attempts in the paradigm of world systems theory to define a 'world city' simply through its role in the 'capitalist world-economy'. However, my decision to opt for the term 'world city' derives from the attempt to approach the lived experience of the global city form a phenomenological perspective, usually focused in the term 'life-world'. A '*world* city' in this sense than can be considered as an affirmative territory of the life-*world*. The use of the term 'world city' is also consistent with my use of the term 'microglobalization', the prefix 'micro-' does not imply a (systems related) 'macroglobalization' as counterpart, but refers to the intense globalization of the 'microcosm' of the life-world of a world city.

2 The term should not be confused with Robertson's notion of 'miniglobalization', which refers to the fact that 'historic empire formation involved the unification of previously sequestered territories and social entities' (1992: 54).

3 This includes to different degrees commuters, tourists and many others who actually come to the global city.

4 Since this chapter is concerned with the mobility of extending personal milieux, its concern with locale refers to 'significant places' in relation to the 'situatedness' of these milieux, not to a particular London locality defined by administrative or community boundaries.

5 Having lived in both cities for substantial periods of time over the last three years, it is the difference between London and Bielefeld which, in the 'lived experience' of my own milieu, time and again brings home to me the distinction between a city and a world city.

6 See John Eade's study on the redevelopment of London's Docklands in Chapter 8 of this volume for a detailed analysis of how the (re)construction of one locale in different 'symbolic unities' attempted to serve different social milieux.

7 Name has been changed.

8 This category, and a few of the following categories are inspired by two essays in Waldenfels (1985: 179ff. and 194ff.).

5

WORKING-CLASS CULTURE
Local community and global conditions
Darren O'Byrne

In this chapter[1] I will, after outlining my general perspective, investigate the following assertions:

(i) that the processes of 'globalization', and their 'local' impacts, result not simply from economic factors or from global social interaction, but from an orientation to compete within the global arena, and that such an orientation operates as a form of cultural capital;

(ii) that such an orientation is often seen to be in conflict with the localist perspective, which is among the cultural values of 'traditional' working-class communities;

(iii) that these cultural practices combine with material factors to produce certain exclusionary mechanisms; and

(iv) that the 'global' is itself constructed through these local practices, and that the construction of 'locality' is a fluent social process built around essentially political struggles over the 'ownership' of space, place and identity.

Throughout the discussion, I will use, by way of illustration, responses given by residents of a predominantly white, working-class housing estate in Roehampton, south London, to a series of questions asked as part of a research programme investigating the possible impact of globalization at the local level.[2]

I

My aim, then, is to consider the relationship between, on the one hand, these global processes which result in such displacement and fragmentation of communities, and, on the other, the continued existence of a strong sense of localism. Such a localism is found in a particular normative structure, that of a working-class culture. Arguing against certain hasty assumptions which may be made of such a relationship, I shall argue that, despite this emphasis on locality and territoriality, working-class communities have always been political constructs based on issues of conflict; sites of political struggles between 'insiders' and 'outsiders'. Changes in the relationship between such 'insiders' and 'outsiders' have always occurred due to the interplay between local and non-local cultures and world-views.

Thus, localities can be seen as constructions of a tentative social order in a world of flows. Indeed, it is my contention that identity – such as that of 'being working-class' – is constructed only with reference to: (a) the objective structure of material conditions, physical location, and flows of people; (b) the normative structure of values and traditions; and (c) the interaction of people and of cultures in a given physical locality, which produces a constant negotiation and renegotiation of 'the local'.

Some points of clarification need to be made regarding my perspective. First, attention is paid to the importance of the political dimension, by which I mean the relations of power within the locality *as a site of power and conflict*, and not, on this occasion, the artificial and arbitrary distinctions between certain wards, boroughs, constituencies, or the like. I do mention this latter usage once, briefly, on page 85 below. From this emphasis on conflict, I see space and place (whether local or global) as social processes, based on shifting definitions. Thus, I am concerned with the conflict-creating interplay between the fixity of places and the constant flows of people.

Examples from the interviews will show a fierce loyalty towards locality and community in Roehampton. In the sample, only one respondent admitted to an intense dislike for life on the estate, and all of the interviewees admitted a strong reliance upon the local facilities. Harvey (1993: 3) seeks to understand why 'place-bound identities' are becoming 'more rather than less important in a world of diminishing spatial barriers to exchange, movement and communication'. Indeed, territoriality, for Harvey emerges as a renewed psychological concept of place, materialized through the 'threat of time–space compression' (ibid.: 4). Following Heidegger, he reminds us that the shrinking of time and space creates existential fears for local inhabitants of displacement and homelessness (Harvey 1993: 10) – such is our reliance upon our spatial security. This is reflected in references to the local as somehow 'good' when counterpoised with the 'global', which is 'bad', and in the need to 'defend' one's 'territory' (itself an assumed point of stability upon which to base a fragile need for 'belonging') against the 'threat' of 'outsiders'.

But how does this emphasis on locality come about? It may be, I will argue, that this localism is the result of (class) cultural practices which, in many cases, produce a conscious resistance to external forces and a mistrust and rejection of globalist values in favour of a defence of local activity. However, another possible explanation needs to be addressed – one which derives from an organicist tradition in sociology. Here, such localism may be viewed as an adaptation to these wider processes. This would be based on a (hasty) assumption that global processes constitute totalizing social change. It might thus be argued that culture and identity are being reconstructed in accordance with this change and, therefore, that this localism is a form of reaction or adaptation.

Such a perspective would be problematic because it might assume that globalization is in fact a totalizing concept, forcing involvement (positive or negative) and reaction from other processes and phenomena, such as class culture. It would come close to depoliticizing class and reducing human action to merely reaction. In other words, by reducing class identity to a reactive adaptation to global processes, it becomes depoliticized and relative.

In trying to avoid such a reductionism, I hope to show how an alternative perspective may stress the relative autonomy of both globalization and class culture; acknowledging the growing impact of globalization upon localities, while asserting the importance of those localities as sites of struggle and conflict, as well as of 'commonality'. Such a perspective, however, would necessarily involve a hermeneutic understanding of the world-view[3] expressed within the cultural arena (in this case, the locality) itself, and view such changes as active processes. But first, I should briefly discuss what is meant by 'globalization'.

II

Globalization can, loosely, be defined as the dialectical social process based around the emergence, by virtue of a material phenomenon, 'time–space compression' (Harvey 1989), and a cultural one, 'globality' (Robertson 1992), a specific world-view built on an image of the globe itself as an arena for social action. This 'world-view' will be the focus of my attention in this chapter. For Robertson, the key component is globality, which he defines as 'consciousness of the world as a whole' (1992: 8). He views this as a purely cultural phenomenon, but the nature of the dialectical relationship is such that it cannot be divorced from political and economic processes, and Lash and Urry (1994) have gone some way to exploring globalization and related processes in terms of the relationship between social, economic and cultural flows.

There is a growing body of literature focused on the impact of globalization upon localities, but most of this has essentially been economic in its focus (e.g. Sassen 1991). The corresponding shift towards 'localization' has been charted by writers as a parallel process: the decline of 'national' primacy creates an awareness not only of the globe but of the more immediate local sphere (Lash and Urry 1994). The effects of these changes need to be understood at the local level, and with regard to more than simply economic processes. Awareness of 'the world' as a place, interaction, and orientation towards it, constitute levels of analysis which require an understanding of the locality as lived by its residents. Indeed such an interpretation of the 'local' is so crucial to Robertson's neo-Durkheimian understanding of globalization that he has suggested that the term 'glocalization' would be more appropriate (Robertson 1995).

Recent research has made the claim that even the most 'isolated' or 'traditionalist' community relations are subject to increasing global influences (Albrow *et al.* 1994). Factors such as increased mobility, migration and the arrival of 'new residents' have altered the appearances of communities traditionally viewed as homogeneous. These factors, coupled with 'wider' political processes, which seem to have radically transformed the spatial boundaries of the world as a whole, constitute elements of a process of global change which requires us to challenge essentialist, generalizing statements about what local community 'is' or 'should be' in favour of an appreciation of the changing meanings, requirements and desires attributed to 'locality' and local 'community' by residents. Thus: 'The presumed certainties of cultural identity, firmly located in particular places which housed stable cohesive communities of shared tradition and perspective, though never a reality for some, were increasingly disrupted and displaced for all' (Carter *et al.* 1993: vii)

My argument here is that this awareness of the globe as a perceivable whole is the product of cultural capital, and that structural material restrictions limit access to this cultural capital to some members of society and exclude them from full participation in these processes. I am drawing here specifically on studies of working-class culture. I will return to this later.

III

Like globalization, social class can be understood as the defining term for the dialectical relationship between cultural and material forces. In its cultural sense, it is an idea, associated with a set of codes and values; an abstract source of shared identity and social belonging. Thus, in the construction of a world-view, locality and self-identity, the individual draws upon collectivist concepts – in this case, the concept of 'working class' which carries with it a set of associated values; a milieu.[4]

Localism has not always been viewed as a core ingredient in working-class culture. E.P. Thompson (1963) focused on the growth of class culture beyond immediate localities. However Hoggart's classic account of working-class community stressed the significance of locality: 'The core of working-class attitudes . . . is . . . the local . . . first the family and second the neighbourhood' (Hoggart 1957: 32). Hoggart, of course, deals with a specific group, and does not attempt a reification of class culture. In dealing more generally with the tradition, Bourke summarizes thus: 'the "community" was the neighbourhood, which was in turn the class' (1994: 138).

John Clarke sees a similar relationship between the working-class and localism, stating that working-class culture is 'identified with specifically local experiences, relationships and practices . . . articulated around specifically local points of reference, contact and conflict' (Clarke 1979: 240). He adds that this localism was affected by changes in the economic, political and industrial structures. However:

> localism continues to have cultural importance in a number of forms. Locality continues to act as a focus for some working-class cultural identifications, often among those who are in some senses marginal to production and to the collective solidarities generated there. Locality continues to act as a basis for collective activity among working-class adolescents, both in the sense of providing cultural identities . . . and of constituting their 'social space'.
>
> (ibid.: 251)

There is clearly no 'real' definition of what actually constitutes such a 'working-class community'. It is generally understood that significant 'ingredients' include solidarity, close-by family and social networks, shared lifestyles, and limited spatial mobility (although this last point is particularly contentious). Territoriality – and the use of 'communal spaces' such as pubs, corner shops, etc. – is considered significant, possibly as a constructive attempt at the 'rediscovery' of lost community (Cohen 1980: 85). Bourke (1994) shows how such examples involve a nostalgic romanticism, written through oral histories, in which conflict gives way to commonality (ibid.: 137).

Bourke goes on to say that an alternative definition of 'working-class community' can be found in progressive socialism, in which the 'community' is the shared experiential world of the working-class itself. Such a 'community' represents the 'innate socialism of the workers' (ibid.: 137), which was manifested in sociability and solidarity at the local level, so that 'community' becomes 'a weapon against the power of other classes and a defence against . . . authorities' (ibid.).[5] Clarke adds that this significance of locality exists among older and younger members of the 'community' alike. It serves to defend nostalgic or imaginary conceptions of community against change and, we might add, the encroaching global forces. As Pahl has said: 'conflict from without creates solidarity within' (1970: 102).

All these 'qualities' are brought together in the stereotypical portrayal of the local community; it is regarded as an extension of the family. In media presentations, particularly television soap operas such as *EastEnders* and *Coronation Street*, not only is the significance of local space emphasized, but also the apparent 'normality', 'human-ness', or 'down-to-Earthness' of the localized characters. Even newer characters, characterized as being more 'mobile', soon become engulfed within the activities of the locality, as if they do not have, and never have had, a life elsewhere. Characters are winning through their apparent normality: they are 'flawed but decent', whatever that may mean. For example, characters may flirt with racist intolerance or express male chauvinistic opinions, but, 'deep down', they are just 'ordinary, decent, working-class folk looking after their own'. Thus the most defining factor expressed in these shows is the support each character shows for her or his neighbour in times of crisis, even when such support seems to go against 'type' (Geraghty 1991: ch. 5).

In these soap operas or in the oral histories of life in working-class communities, what tends to be presented is a portrait of consensus. Clearly, this is an over-simplification. There are always times when an individual member of any community – however 'close-knit' that community is – feels alienated from it. And as the passage from Bourke quoted above suggests, this emphasis on consensus leads to a 'glossing-over' of the conflictual elements in a given community, which Suttles (1973) argues are more important components of such a culture than the consensual ones. Suttles suggests that consensus primarily occurs when the community as a whole is attacked from the outside, and as such, consensus is a defensive measure, uniting otherwise conflicting forces against a common 'enemy' (quoted in Bourke 1994: 150). Otherwise, there are always 'outsiders' – those who 'do not belong'. People from different classes, ethnic backgrounds, or with different lifestyles are particularly susceptible to such exclusion. As such, the significance of locality in working-class culture is a political one. The immediate locality is the site of these political struggles between 'insiders' and 'outsiders'. Indeed, this exercising of power within the locality, it could be argued, has always been a reflection of the lack of power at national level. One can see this in the classic studies of working-class communities, such as Dennis *et al.* (1956) and Tunstall (1962), which reflected a stage of *national* capitalism so accurately analysed by Marx.

If this has served as an introduction to the relationship between localism and working-class culture, it is now necessary to turn attention to the views of those who live in such a 'community' – those inhabitants of the estate in Roehampton, as mentioned in the introduction.

When asked to express their feelings towards the locality, most respondents were positive in their appraisal, and it seemed particularly important to the residents that, on the estate, people remained 'loyal'. As one would expect, this is particularly true of older residents. Thus Beryl, who is 61 and retired, said:

Of the original settlers to this part of (the estate), we've lost only a quarter, and many of those families who have moved on have tried to get back. We're very community minded.

Jean, a 51-year-old housewife, agreed:

78

Lots of residents here are second generation Alton Estaters. Lots of people who have to move away want to come back. Lots of people who were born here want to live here for the rest of their lives.

And Gladys, a 63-year-old community worker, commented that:

[There are] second-generation families bringing up their children here. . . . [My son] went to school here. Now, he can knock on the door of four or five friends who are living here with their wives and kids, or girlfriends. . . . So nothing has changed.

But perhaps this 'loyalty' is best represented by the words of a younger woman, Carol, a 36-year-old housewife:

I've lived here all my life. I don't know much other than Roehampton. I really like it here and I wouldn't want to move. My parents lived here, and still do. I met my husband at school, and we never wanted to live anywhere but here, close to our families. My family is very important to me.

If this localism is to be expected among many respondents, then perhaps so is the distrust of 'outsiders' and 'strangers' that has been associated with working-class communities. Again, the clearest examples come from the older residents, such as Beryl:

We are frightened of losing our community. Newcomers rarely integrate into the community. Lots of youngsters have no respect for people living around here, including the youngsters living at the [nearby college halls of residence]. [Our] kids . . . are far better than any of them.

She added:

Problems arise from newcomers, such as DSS scroungers, ex-convicts, single-parent families, and other younger people who are having everything paid for them, and people who don't want to work, plus the druggies.

It is easy, then, for Beryl to identify the 'outsiders'. They come clearly packaged, and labelled: 'druggies'; 'scroungers'; ex-convicts; even students. These groups are all in some way antithetical to a Puritanism, a work-ethic and a distinct anti-intellectualism associated, according to 'classic' studies, with working-class culture. But the Alton Estate is, traditionally, a predominantly white estate, so clearly the presence of other ethnic groups poses other questions. Maggie, who is also retired and is 57, mentioned these 'newcomers':

I think one of the biggest changes is the number of ethnic minorities that have moved into the area, and on the whole most of them have

integrated well – the West Indians especially. . . . It's more difficult with
. . . the Asians, because they tend to stay within themselves, and
although they will talk to you, they don't want to get involved in local
things. . . . It's very difficult with people like that to bring them into the
community, because they don't actually want to be part of it.

Clearly, this revolves around the issue of conflict and diversity. I have stated
how such a community exercises a distrust of outsiders, particularly non-
white outsiders and middle-class outsiders. Although space prevents me
from discussing issues of ethnicity and racism here, it is worth mentioning
that most respondents seemed generally far from hostile towards black or
Asian families on the estate (despite the acknowledgement of distinction
and 'otherness' expressed in the language of the respondents), and one
respondent suggested that, with young people of all ethnic cultures and
diversities growing up together and playing together, there is hope for the
future. If this is the case, it would suggest that the 'difference' between
insiders and outsiders is less one of class or ethnicity, but instead of
territorialism. Those 'known' on the estate are 'in', be they black or
white, manual or non-manual. Locality and local solidarity and loyalty
become the central concepts in inclusion and exclusion.

However, this tolerance may only stretch so far, and not as far as a
commitment to cultural pluralism. Inclusion may rest upon involvement in
the local community, and an acceptance of the values associated with that
host community; an 'assimilationist' frame. If 'those Asians' tend to 'stick
together', then they are frowned upon by their neighbours, and excluded.
Similarly, these 'new' residents, neither insiders or outsiders, may be
defended by the 'community' against external challenges, but this may
not amount to an acceptance of them, and in fact this solidarity becomes
exclusion and conflict once within the 'confines' of the 'community'.

So this assumption of 'working-classness' on the estate needs to be further
explored. Despite its history as a predominantly white, working-class estate,
hostile to outsiders from different cultures and classes, it is clear that the
estate cannot be reduced to such a homogeneous position. Roehampton is
now a mix of cultures. Indeed, it is noticeable from our respondents that
class is not mentioned in the discourse of locality, and as such it may be
misleading to assume a direct link between class and localism *per se*. 'Newcomers' are welcomed regardless of class, ethnicity, etc., as long as they
integrate into the 'host' community. (Although even this white, working-
class 'host' community is largely a migrant one.) In other words, we may be
faced with new insider/outsider relations, which appears to suggest that this
localism is a 'pure localism', drawing an analogy with Giddens' (1991)
concept of 'pure relationship': the significant relationship being between
shared orientations of the individuals to the locality, developed through an
individual's familiarity with that place regardless of its qualities.

I make this point because it is possible to make a (somewhat hasty, in my view) assumption that global change involves a necessary change in the economic structure which reduces the significance of social class, and from this that it might be argued that maybe this localism is in fact not related at all to a particular class culture. Alternatively, global flows and social processes may have radically altered the very foundations of a 'traditional' working-class. Thus Lash (1994: 127) describes the existence of a new, 'reflexive' working-class, based on information structures which allow for international competition, and which rely upon training and access to these information flows.

Nevertheless, I understand 'working-class identity' to be an unwritten (and unspoken) code underlying the nostalgic or imagined perceptions of solidarity in this community. These people are identifiable as working-class people because they share the values of working-class culture.[6] Thus, even if we accept that there has been a shift in insider/outsider definitions, we can still see that the estate is dominated by an ethos traditionally associated with working-class culture.

Let us move beyond the immediate community towards wider events. When asked about such events, the consensus within the Roehampton sample suggested that world events played little part in the everyday lives of Altoners. Carol stressed that:

> Whatever happens [elsewhere in the world] . . . it doesn't affect me. I've got my life and my family to look after. They come first. Nothing that happens out there is going to change that, or help me. I don't really care. It's all talk. At the end of the day, it means nothing.

Beryl agreed:

> I don't think it's a smaller world. I live in my own little world, and my set patterns mean an awful lot to me. When people move out, I think it means just the opposite: the world gets bigger. I'm content with what I do. It's no good looking for things you can't get. I'm proud to be English, but people are happy to knock England these days. People have no respect. I think it's all down to the upbringing.

Beryl is happy to mention both locality and nationality in the same breath. For her, they are almost indistinguishable, because a loyalty to both represents a nostalgic defence of tradition in the face of modernity. Gladys makes a clearer distinction, when she states that 'community is more important than country'. There were, of course, exceptions. Dave, a 35-year-old electrician, said:

> I don't think it's healthy to stay in one place for too long. It's good to get out. Otherwise you have a really closed view of the world. . . . I'm not totally 'local' but then again I'm not really 'global'. I don't see things

81

the way someone who spends most of his life in one area might see things, even though I probably do rely on my area quite a lot. But I don't think I have a great desire to see all of the world. I think it's important to know who or what you are, and I think I'm British. That's how I see myself: British first.

My point is that this localism, and essentially this anti-globalism, is produced by the cultural and material components of working-class culture, and, because of its fluent nature, this emphasis on the local feeds into, rather than detracts from, the emergence of the global.

IV

So, this emphasis on local community solidarity may result from specific aspects of working-class culture, constantly being reconstructed and re-negotiated in the light of globalization. Willis (1977) showed how working-class children so very often end up in unskilled working-class jobs, turning their backs on education. He found that certain values existed in the family structure and the school structure which worked continuously to keep the working-class youths in their 'place' in society. This took the form of a transmission of culture. A similar argument can be raised about the production or transmission of a localist perspective. Lack of encourage-ment from family or peers, lack of facilities, etc. may all play their part in transmitting this view. In a sense, to play on Willis' terminology, they may be 'learning to be local'.

One head teacher in Roehampton was concerned that the children in the area are not encouraged by their parents to learn. Thus locality breeds in them a limited world-view. He described the educational facilities as limited, but also as reflecting a general lack of interest. Again he puts this down to their parochial outlooks. He also told me that, according to enquiries made in class with his pupils, less than one-third of them were planning on going off the estate during the coming week. This may be due to restrictions on access to funds, but it is also a product on restrictions on outlook. The Roehampton ethos is one of 'looking after one's own', and no world-view is encouraged. In many cases it is positively rejected as it seems to go against the entire ethos which is central to life on the estate. This view was shared by a youth worker, who added:

Kids don't leave the estate. They don't want to. Kids in Brixton go all over London. Here in Roehampton, they don't want to know.

Do they want to leave the estate when they are older?

No, they couldn't bear it. All they want is the estate. All their friends are here; all they know. On a trip to London, we saw Big Ben, and they asked me what it is!

Is this because the estate is so isolated?

> It must be, but Putney's not that far away. There are buses. They can go into town. They don't want to. I think it's because they're left alone to make their own fun. Their parents don't spend a lot of time with them.

One young person, when asked how often he leaves the estate, replied: 'Saturdays, and some Sundays. I go swimming. I go to Kingston.'

Here we once again come across the estate's 'localism'. I would go on to suspect that the number of people born and still living there with partners (childhood sweethearts?) is unusually high. Roehampton's isolation, unemployment, and poor travel facilities have hit it hard. All these factors are significant. We cannot reduce this construction of locality to simple matters of economics. Although important, economics must complement cultural factors in our analysis: neither is truly reducible to the other. Cultural factors are transmitted which 'restrict' the individual to a certain outlook. Economic restraints exist which limit the individual's opportunity to break free of these cultural 'trappings', or which serve to justify them further. Class position is significant in terms of the family from which those values were transmitted originally to the individual. Neither created the other, but they have merged over time to create a continuous cycle of constraint.

So how do these young people 'learn to be local'? What codes are being used by which local people can be identified? For example, if a young person talks about going to 'the chippy' or 'the park', is it automatically assumed that local people will know what is meant, thus distinguishing them from non-locals who would be less aware of these terms? And how is one expected to act, to dress, to speak, etc. when one is 'hanging out' on the street? These are all unwritten codes of belonging in a specific social group which is linked to a specific locality.

'Hanging out' is itself seen as 'an essential part of growing up' on the estate, according to the head teacher, so to some extent these codes require a visible presence and face-to-face interaction. More 'elaborate' codes may utilize non-personal forms of communication, but this physical proximity seems important among young people on the estate. If a young person bases his or her rules of inclusion and belonging upon membership of the estate, then too much time away from the estate may cast a doubt even over that person's status as belonging in the locality. By spending too much time away from the centre of activities, that person may be cast into a non-space between inclusion and exclusion: not an outsider, but no longer truly 'one of us' because the estate no longer dominates that person's social activities.

So, a specific type of cultural capital relates to knowledge of the estate itself: a resource of knowledge regarding the codes pertaining to that physical space. Nevertheless, this assumption that the youth sub-culture on the estate relies upon both its locality and the values of its parent culture needs qualification, particularly since, as Cohen and others have shown, the emergence of youth sub-cultures has historically been detrimental to the role of the family as a force of solidarity in working-class communities, through conflicting allegiance to both the 'traditions' of class culture, and the 'new hedonism of consumption' (Cohen 1980: 83).

The consensual portrait of working-class communities assumes a form of static loyalty to an area, and in doing so treats the concept of a working-class community very much in isolation from other cultures, other sets of values, and other influences and aspirations. This is misleading, as the presence of a working-class culture is itself inseparable from the socio-economic, and more importantly ideological, conditions in which it evolves. Richard Johnson, working within a Gramscian tradition, has said that working-class culture cannot be totally 'brought into line' by the dominant culture, but that ideological hegemony serves to keep it 'in its place'. This is transmitted through the ideology of not only the mainstream culture but of the working-class culture, itself an instrument of oppression, in its inability to acquire a sufficiently 'complete' or 'oppositional' world-view (Johnson 1980: 60).

I have sketched how the combined effects of economic position and cultural capital may encourage a localist perspective, even – perhaps especially – under globalized conditions. Thus, regardless of the increasingly significant developments that promote the process of globalization, full access to the key aspects of the process is still restricted.

Lash's new, 'reflexive' working-class relies upon access to the information and communication structures (Lash 1994: 127–32). Those who are excluded constitute a new 'underclass', who are, according to Lash, the sons of those 'traditional' working-class fathers studied in the mid-1970s by Willis (ibid.: 131). The decline in factory-based manufacture, together with the breakdown of neighbourhood communities, has produced an anomie which results in: 'a gang-bonding of young males and racial violence. This of course applies not only to the urban minority ghettos but to the white ghettos of Britain's council estates' (ibid.). In other words, this generation brought up 'learning to labour . . . only to find there are no working-class jobs' (ibid.) turns instead to a specifically male (violent) type of habitus.

Under such altered and challenging conditions, locality becomes a central source of loyalty and belonging. It becomes an essential part of one's 'identity'. This is even more relevant with regard to the decline in national identity, and to the alleged breakdown of the concept of class as an economic phenomenon. For many this localization is based on a nostalgic view of local community.

Despite the considerable technological advances, access to the 'means of compression' is still clearly restricted by economic constraints. Travel and communication may be faster, easier and cheaper, but not everyone is in a position to take advantage of that. Similarly, access to the 'means of globality' is still culturally restricted through education, socialization and the transmission of cultural capital. Accordingly, globalization is far from a universal process.

V

It is necessary to stress that 'locality' has always meant a variety of things. In a sense, localities exist on a series of dimensions, each of which is in constant interaction with the others. We can, for example, identify the *historical* dimension, in which a particular village or hamlet is still identifiable and definable even though it is now part of a larger city. Then there is the *political* dimension, often based on an 'imaginary line' which defines which constituency, borough or ward an area comes under, and thus determines the political profile of the area. There is a *social* dimension, which was the focus of attention of traditional community studies concerned with the local interactions of residents. A *cultural* dimension is identifiable, in which individuals are attracted to areas because of the cultural make-up of that locality, such as Tooting with its high Asian population, or Brixton, the hub of London's African-Caribbean activity, or Camden with its prominent 'counter-culture' influence. Such areas may become magnets for people wishing to be 'amongst their own'.

A *subjective* dimension – how individuals define their own locality – clearly borrows from each of those mentioned above, and draws on external influences upon the individual's world-views. In the case of working-class localities, then, such a subjective dimension relies heavily upon the recognizable cultural dimension of the area, and, in most cases, its political, historical, and social dimensions as well.

None of these dimensions of localities can be seen to be 'fixed' or permanent. They require constant maintenance and reconstruction. Be they the social relations of residents, the political boundaries, or the Chicago School's ecological models, they are subject to all manner of external and internal 'interference'. For example, the construction of place is an active process negotiated through the competition between places in the capitalist logic (Harvey 1993: 6).

In *The Condition of Postmodernity* Harvey called for:

> a recognition that the dimensions of space and time matter and that there are real geographies of social action, real as well as metaphorical territories and spaces of power, that are sites of innumerable differences that have to be understood both in their own right and within the logic of capitalist development.
>
> (1989: 355)

It is in these sites that the daily realities, and conflicts, of local cultures and global flows are encountered and fought out. These struggles are political struggles as much as they are struggles of identity. The politics is class

85

politics. I would now like to discuss the way local residents, as social actors, present a form of social power to their 'place', that is, what has been called, in a thorough and useful materialist analysis of the social construction of 'place' within the capitalist logic, 'the power of places' (Harvey 1993: 21). I agree with much of Harvey's analysis, and my task here is to extend this notion into the realm of predominantly *cultural* capital.

Localities should be seen as socially defined spaces, building on socially constructed historical dimensions, but reified through historical processes. So the locale – be it 'the estate' or 'the village' – is a reification; a universal which is lifted above the properties of its constituent components, and which, as an autonomous (or relatively autonomous) 'reality', becomes a central stage for human action *on its own terms*. Thus, this reification is seen to exercise power over the daily lives of individuals living within it, be it through material factors such as spatiality, or symbolic ones, such as the establishment of a set of norms which require, for example, the resident's loyalty to his or her locality. Power can be exercised through the people but 'on behalf of the community' (whatever that is), via sanctions. As Appadurai (1993) states, localities are 'fragile social achievements' built around a 'local' knowledge . . . of how to produce and reproduce locality' and about 'producing reliably local subjects as well as about producing reliably local environments within which such subjects can be recognized and organized' (1993: 1, 3).

This ability for a reified 'locality' or 'community' to exert power over residents, and to reproduce both itself and its 'subjects', has been achieved as an ongoing historical process. Localities have never been absolute, fixed entities: they have instead existed as sites of political struggles, constantly caught in the flux and flow of 'external' power relations (such as the economy) and 'internal' social constructions. Changing social, economic and technological structures have required the localities to renegotiate and reconstruct themselves accordingly. The 'myth' of community could hardly be sustained with the arrival of the first motor-car, or more widespread mobility, unless its internal workings and meanings were flexible enough to be adapted to new challenges.

I have stated that the existence of localized working-class cultures cannot be read as merely resistance or adaptation to global processes, nor can it be used as evidence in denial of a process of globalization, as such a process is, I have suggested, not a universal one. In fact, even the most local of cultures has always been forged by the interplay between local and global forces. The culturally constituted, fluent nature of class-based communities is entirely consistent with the extension of wider, global social relations. This, it might be argued, has always been the case. (In such processes of change as urbanization, modernization and industrialization, the respective forces of change have emerged in no small part due to developments

86

relating to the relations of change, that is, to cultures, orientations and world-views.)

From such a perspective, we are able to place more emphasis on the constructive, creative abilities of actors. What we have received from Roehampton, then, have not been inseparable responses. Each has its own peculiarity, its own subjective construction of locality, based on each respondent's own life experiences. On the surface, we have a 'traditional' community based on solidarity and locality. But this community itself cannot be reduced to the transmission of a common culture. The estate, and the area in general, has clearly been affected by the 'world outside'. Newer residents, many of whom are middle class, now dwell on the fringes of the estate. We would argue that these different 'groups' exist at different 'spheres', different 'scapes', living out their lives and giving meanings to their locality, but at different 'horizons' which remain both spatially proximate and culturally distinct. This might suggest that these communities exist in a state of consensual harmony brought about by this 'civil inattention'. However, such a reading would be hasty. Conflict is present in all such communities and is the result of structural forces as much as of group dynamics.

Let me clarify this point. The responses above, individualistic for sure, are inseparable from collectivist concepts and problems. This is significant in at least two ways. First, even in the individualistic process of identity-construction, the individual must draw from collectivist concepts such as 'white', 'black', 'working class', etc. Second, in developing or constructing concepts such as identity or locality, and in being able to participate in local and global processes, individuals are often constrained by structural factors such as the economy, or the transmission of cultural capital. Such factors limit access to some members of society and exclude them from full participation in these processes.

Working-class communities have always abounded with conflicts between 'insiders' and 'outsiders', and the words of our respondents themselves suggest the presence of an 'insider' who is, at the same time, an 'outsider', an Other. These struggles are political struggles, be they between black and white, rich and poor, local and global. In such struggles, the locality, divorced from any practical significance for its residents or the state, retains its ideological significance as the site for these struggles. Politics, essentially, is local.

The emergence of the globe as a meaningful social arena creates further tensions for the cultural capacities of individuals in the social construction of locality. I have stated that community and locality exist at a number of interactive, relative and objective dimensions built around such factors as history, politics, economics and culture. Furthermore, individual actors operate within a general framework influenced by these existing dimensions, and it is possible to shift, meaningfully, creatively, between them and select from them, in order to construct objective definitions. Under globalized conditions, the actor is faced with a more diverse, fragmented and often displaced variety of dimensions, and thus is theoretically able to construct a view based upon the globe as a meaningful point of reference, and to alter his/her perception, or construction, of locality and community in accordance with this global perspective. Similarly, individuals are no longer restricted to essentialized self-definitions (e.g. black, British, Londoner, etc.), but may find themselves shifting between such definitions in accordance with different situations (Centre for Bangladeshi Studies 1994; Eade and Albrow 1994). This is a radical shift away from simplistic, stereotypical images of identity: new conditions suggest that no identity is fixed or absolute.

However, this process is constrained by limitations made upon the individual actor's ability to select from the range of dimensions by structural processes. Education and life-experience are significant in developing a 'world-view', but limitations on these may produce a more localist view, closing off certain avenues from which to construct one's perspective, and/ or opening up other ones. Some families are always 'on the move'. Their children are more likely to develop a non-local perspective. In most cases, the dividing line between localism and globalism is less clear-cut: the avenues lead to a series of points on a continuum between the two.

Adopting a viewpoint that class culture is not static, but is socially constructed by individuals drawing from the (often limited) options and values available to them, which then act back on the individual through external processes, it is possible to see both globalization and class culture as originating as relatively autonomous social constructions which depend on the individual's own life experience, and the climate of the world in which s/he lives. Changing social processes allow for changing cultural perspectives, but these are still socially constructed. Under global conditions, networks become dispersed, and cultural influences become more diverse. Yet the attraction of the 'local', particularly when it affirms a set of cultural codes and 'values', remains as strong as ever.

In this chapter, I have attempted to defend a hermeneutically informed analysis of working-class culture as a way of life, and locate its emphasis on locality within the general debate over the processes of globalization. I have not sought to analyse these concepts in any macro-political way, but, in conclusion, I would call for such an analysis to explore the relationships between the dynamics of local cultures and the concentration of power and profit from the representation and extension of these local cultures in the global economy. Questions emerge as to who actually benefits – culturally, politically *and economically* – from the transmission of this cultural capital. Perhaps Bourdieu might be as useful a guide as Wallerstein in understanding the mechanics of the global capitalist system.

NOTES

1 This chapter is a revised version of a paper given to the 1995 conference of the British Sociological Association. I am grateful to Martin Albrow, John Eade, Steven Groarke, Neil Washbourne and Jörg Dürrschmidt for comments on earlier drafts.

2 See Albrow, Eade, Fennell and O'Byrne (1994). The research involved a series of interviews with residents of various locales within the London Borough of Wandsworth. My illustrations all come from the Roehampton sample.

3 Described for the purposes of this paper as a 'set of experiential contextures which makes up the common footing upon which a multiplicity of individuals together learn from life and enter into it' (Mannheim 1982: 91). The author goes on: 'What is presupposed here throughout is that fundamental experiences and attitudes do not emerge in the substratum of individuals' lives in isolation, but that individuals who are classed together in the same group share a basic stock of experiential contents . . . [which] are not . . . found in isolation . . . but . . . possess an internal coherence and thereby constitute what may be called a "life-system"'(ibid).

4 It needs stating that by 'traditional' working class I refer to a 'stereotype' which is primarily white. The relationship between this white working-class culture and 'Otherness' will be discussed below. To avoid misunderstanding, I am not in any way suggesting that this stereotype represents a 'real' working-class culture. In fact, far from it, particularly as my very definition of the term requires a self-defined identity of 'being' working class. See, for example, Centre for Bangladeshi Studies (1994), in which a number of 'educationally successful' young Bangladeshis had identified themselves as being working class, although this self-image was being challenged due to their educational achievements.

5 In this sense, working-class culture has always been a 'global' phenomenon. A shared identification with a particular set of values suggests that it is not spatially restricted, and the importance of nostalgia in the construction of community and commonality shows how it is not temporally restricted. As such, 'local' culture (in this case, working-class) could be said to revolve less around a locality than around a milieu. See the chapter in this volume by Dürrschmidt.

6 It is worth briefly contrasting the responses from the Roehampton sample with those from another sample, in the 'middle-class' locale of Northcote, south Battersea. Here, a transient middle-class population expressed a delight in the strong sense of community in the area, but this 'community feel' seemed to revolve very much around interactions between like-minded people, with less clear reference to the actual locality itself. In fact, a working-class respondent stood alone in denying the presence of this community spirit. She said: 'Community spirit is dead. Few people, especially not the newer tenants, seem to care about the community anymore.' In this locale, then, the 'community' has been appropriated by the newer arrivals, the 'yuppies', while the older residents, having failed to co-exist with their newer neighbours, have been reduced to the role of '"outsiders", tolerated "others"' (Albrow et al. 1994: 11–14).

6

LOCAL LIVES – DISTANT TIES

Researching community under globalized conditions

Graham Fennell

INTRODUCTION: THE BIAS TO THE SOCIAL

Sheldon (1948), in a classic study of elderly people in Wolverhampton after the Second World War, defined a close relative as someone who lived within five minutes' walking distance, being a measure of the distance a hot meal could be carried from one dwelling to another without reheating. Successive studies of close families and the way they operate have followed this steer in taking 'close' to mean 'near' or 'interacting frequently face-to-face'; and, by extension, significant, important, meaningful. This privileges *nearness* (one meaning of closeness) against relationships which unavoidably involve distance and separation; and *close* relationships and people who have them (as for instance in the accolades routinely conferred on the '*close-knit* community') as against those people who do not have them or those areas not apparently 'close-knit'.

We are aware, however, that there is no necessary association between nearness and significance. We can live and interact with and be near people to whom we feel distant or from whom we feel estranged (warring neighbours are a case in point). We can have close relationships (in the sense of intimate relationships, relationships with people we love, relationships which are important to us) even if we are separated by oceans and continents and see one another only infrequently. People throughout history have been forced into diasporic relationships – the nineteenth century, for instance, saw massive population movements in and from Europe; the Irish potato famine caused a massive exodus, as did rural poverty in many other countries. Whole peoples have been and are driven out and excluded from territories by armed force and have had to reconstruct their lives as diasporic and dispossessed. England in the twentieth century has not been invaded, occupied by armed forces, riven by civil strife or blighted by plague or famine and it may be a particularly English privilege to hold in esteem the 'close-knit' local community: many people in the world have not had the privilege or, because trapped by poverty, might regard it anyway as an overrated idea.

Two polar archetypes stand out from English community studies: we are likely to remember Mum from Bethnal Green, standing arms akimbo on her doorstep, her grandchildren playing at her feet, her married daughters living next door or a few doors away, and two hundred named relatives within a square mile (Young and Willmott 1957; Townsend 1957; Marris 1978). We may also remember 'the most isolated individual we ever met' (Rex and Moore 1967), an elderly Estonian refugee encountered in Spark-brook, Birmingham, a man who had lived in England for many years but apparently had no English, no friends, no family, no known relatives. Many people doubtless occupy positions between these extremes, but if we regard their situations as outcomes, they are as much a matter of luck and historical context – being in the right or wrong place at particular conjunctures – as indicative of moral worth. What we have tried to do in our study is collect data on some aspects of relationships without imposing too many *a priori* assumptions about better or worse. We have not sought a special place to conduct our study, or selected special types of people to study; and we have not sought to privilege any type of relationship over another, though we have admittedly prompted and prodded for infor-mation about global or international connections which have too commonly been left out of earlier work. Findings from our own recent survey are introduced immediately, to contextualize the critique.

While we do not necessarily advance any *special* claims about the area, timing or methodology of our admittedly limited local survey, it is neces-sary briefly to explain that it was conducted in the London Borough of Wandsworth in the early summer of 1994. Interviewing of a sample of 221 adults was undertaken by a small group of graduating social science students from the Roehampton Institute, London, trained and supervised for this purpose by two external consultants with extensive field research experience, working under the direction of Graham Fennell. The focus of the research and schedule of topics were set by the principal investigators, Graham Fennell, Martin Albrow and John Eade; initial funding was pro-vided by the Roehampton Institute, London. It was informed by pilot interviews conducted by Darren O'Byrne, reported in the previous chapter.

Wandsworth was chosen because it is the local borough in which our academic department is situated: social science departments commonly try to develop a symbiotic relationship with their local area – supplying the area with educational services and information about itself, using it also as a resource for students and as a local laboratory in which to gather data and formulate ideas. Wandsworth is a large London borough, containing a considerable mix of classes, types of residential area and ethnic groups: we sampled randomly in all twenty wards in the three main divisions of Battersea, Putney and Tooting. Adults aged 18 and over were approached and screened by doorstep interviews at home, located by means of a 'tightly controlled' quota sampling and random walk procedure. Technical details of the survey are available from the author.

We might note that there is relatively little industry or employment in Wandsworth and we have characterized it elsewhere (Albrow *et al.* 1994) as an 'inner London suburb' – a place where people are more likely to live or travel through en route to work, than to work itself. As to the timing, one relevant detail is that the survey was conducted before most respondents had taken their 1994 summer holiday (if they had one); and this renders even more noteworthy the numbers who had already travelled abroad that year – before our interview – in the first seven months of 1994 (the figure was seventy-two or one-third of the sample).

Social scientists cannot escape the prejudices and cultural assumptions within which they and everyone else at the time are embedded and the possible distortions or biases in their work may not become apparent until we can look back at some decades removed when new emphases and preoccupations have become important to us and we feel frustrated by the lack of attention to or information about certain topics in earlier studies. It occurred to us, in the 1990s, that there were at least five ways in which the relationship between locality, living, connectedness, belonging, family and community could be confused – and perhaps in a sense overstated – by methodological biases in previous work; to say nothing of possible changes in 'modern' times (that is to say, the period in which investigators always regard themselves as living) – as for instance the mobile phone – which may begin to affect the way things are and the way people operate.

FIRST BIAS: LOOKING IN BUT NOT OUT

A first bias may be introduced by deciding on the *physical boundaries* within which the research will be located (the village, the town, the borough, the

Table 6.1 Purpose of last visit abroad

Purpose	No.	%
Holiday	130	59
Visiting family/friends	42	19
Business/work	15	7
Other	12	5
Working holiday	4	2
Education	3	1
In armed forces	3	1
Never been abroad, etc.	12	6
Total	221	100

Table 6.2 'Did you meet anyone abroad whom you already knew?'

Answer	No	%
Yes	113	51
No	97	44
No ans.	11	5
Total	221	100

city, the region, the nation-state); and then focusing the questions on what occurs *within* these boundaries. This imposes a frame of reference that *this* defined area has some special significance and makes it more important, the people who live within its boundaries more important, than other places and peoples. For instance, when we asked our respondents if they had been *abroad* recently, the majority agreed that they had been abroad primarily by way of a holiday, and many also for reasons related to work or education. But included among the 'miscellaneous other reasons' was someone who had recently been abroad 'to get married', clearly a significant, in this case non-local, activity.

We asked if, when our respondents were last abroad, they met anyone abroad whom they already knew; and further, if they had formed any new relationships with people with whom they planned, or were continuing, to keep in touch. Table 6.2 shows that over half our sample had indeed met up with someone abroad whom they already knew.

A quarter of the sample had formed new relationships while abroad, making contact with new people with whom they continued to keep in touch, or had plans to maintain contact (Table 6.3). We would maintain that these contacts are *prima facie* potentially as important as local ones.

SECOND BIAS: FINDING THE SAMPLE

A second bias may be introduced by the way we go about *sampling* people to study within the geographical areas previously defined. The sampling method may introduce a bias in favour of the *local*, the *resident*, the person who *belongs* to an area, compared with those who, while not meeting these conditions, are in some sense 'in' or 'use' the area. Moving from the notion

Table 6.3 Plans to keep in touch with new people met abroad

Intention	No.	%
Yes	54	24
No	154	70
NA	13	6
Total	221	100

Table 6.4 'Have you ever lived in any other country?'

Answer	No.	%
Yes	69	31
No	152	69
Total	221	100

that some people 'belong' (for instance, because they were born there, spent their childhood there, 'have their roots' there or have lived there for a considerable time), it is easy to reverse the equation and think that, as well as people belonging to an area, an area 'belongs to them', that they somehow have greater rights over it, including a greater right for their voices to be heard in social research than others. We are then easily led into the classic demarcation disputes between 'locals' and 'outsiders', 'traditionals' and 'newcomers', 'insiders' and 'cosmopolites', or 'transients'.

The questions we used in our survey to shed light on these matters included asking where people had been born and where they grew up, whether they were still living in the area they spent their childhood (assuming – itself a questionable assumption – that people predominantly spend their childhood in one place which they think of as their place of origin, or think of as 'home'), whether they had ever lived outside the United Kingdom and whether they expected still to be living in the same area in five years' time. The results were very interesting and are displayed in Tables 6.4 to 6.12.

Table 6.4, for instance, shows that nearly one-third of the sample had lived in another country. (By 'lived' we meant something beyond a holiday, some established period of residence in which people would describe themselves as 'living abroad', having a postal address overseas, being established in that place for a period of time. This would include those who had been posted overseas with the armed services.)

Table 6.5 Age at which respondents left childhood area

Age	No.	%
Never left	58	26
0–9	19	9
10–17	35	16
18–21	67	30
22–29	33	15
30–39	5	2
40	1	0.5
72	1	0.5
NK	2	1
Total	221	100

Table 6.6 Age at which respondents left childhood area (quartiles)

Age left/if left	No.	%
Originals	58	26
Childhood	54	24
18–20	59	27
21 or over	48	22
Missing	2	1
Total	221	100

When we asked at what age people had left their childhood area, the question interestingly revealed fifty-eight 'original inhabitants' (about a quarter of the sample), people who had *never left* the area in which we found them. Inspection of Table 6.5 shows that the majority – about one-third of the sample – 'leave home' around the age of attaining their majority, in the age-band 18–21, with relatively few leaving their 'child-hood area' when they are middle aged or older.

This is confirmed if we try to divide the sample into quartiles – four equal parts. Just over a quarter are 'original inhabitants', just under a quarter have left their childhood area during childhood. The modal group (27 per cent) leave in the narrow age range of 18–21. Those leaving after that age are less than a full quarter of the sample – only 22 per cent.

This naturally prompts speculation as to whether times have changed or are changing: did people *used* to live longer in one place, spend more of their lives in the area in which they grew up? We cannot answer this question in general, but we could examine in our own sample the relationship between the respondents' current age and the age at which they had left (or not) the area in which they spent their childhood. Table 6.7 shows that at most only twenty people (9 per cent of the sample) could be described as 'elderly original inhabitants' of the area; and they in turn accounted for approximately one-third of the 57–85-year-old age group in our sample. This rather arbitrary age-band was again arrived at by dividing the age spectrum into approximately equal quartiles.

Comparing the percentages along the rows of the table gives some indication of change over time – the older respondents are *more* likely to be 'original inhabitants' than the other age groups; and older people were more likely to leave their childhood area *later* than younger age groups. Conversely, it is the youngest age group (the 18–28-year-olds) who are most likely to have left their childhood area at the age of majority.

This second bias, giving unnecessary primacy to the *local*, may be exaggerated by the way in which samples are designed and drawn. In designing our 'community sample' we might implicitly make use of a residence *test*, as we do if we make use of a sampling frame involving a

Table 6.7 Age respondents left childhood area, by age now

Age left	Age now				All ages (quartiles)
	18–28	*29–36*	*37–56*	*57–85*	
Originals	15	12	10	20	57
[row %]	29	22	19	36	26
Childhood	13	13	14	13	53
[row %]	24	24	26	24	24
18–20	20	16	19	5	59
[row %]	37	29	34	9	27
21 or over	6	14	11	17	48
[row %]	11	25	21	31	22
Totals	54	55	53	55	217
[row %]	25	25	24	25	100

residence qualification – like the electoral register. We might also work from lists of patients registered with local doctors, or approach people through residents' associations. Without consciously doing so, we exclude the people in the area who do not qualify for inclusion. In opening our interviews, we might screen out, through the opening questions, people who do not live there, who do not 'belong' in the sample.

THIRD BIAS: THE LENGTH OF RESIDENCE TEST

Additionally, and this is the third main possible (unconscious) source of bias, we may impose a *length of residence* test on our informants, feel that we will get the most useful information from long-term residents, people who really know the area (because they have lived and worked there for a substantial time), perhaps people who have local standing, are known in the area – which is likely to be achieved, generally (though not exclusively) by long-term residence.

To counteract these possibilities in our own work we decided against using any form of population *listing* – since these almost invariably imply some 'length of residence' qualification. We used instead a 'cold-calling', 'random-walk' technique, designed to yield interviews with whomever we found behind the door – whether on the electoral register or not, whether registered with a local doctor or not, whether a person lacking legal rights of immigration or not; and we accepted interviews regardless of how long people had been living in the area, avoiding any bias towards the 'long-established' resident. One residence test we did impose, however: our respondents had to define themselves as 'living' in the area (that is, having

96

some form of 'home' or base in the area) and we excluded anyone who was simply visiting, or in the area for work but living elsewhere.

This data, also, we found very interesting. We completed interviews with 221 adults in Wandsworth, 94 per cent of them at the address where they lived and 6 per cent who happened to be at someone else's address when we called there; and we asked them, 'How long have you lived in this area?' The answers ranged from a maximum of seventy-eight years (four members of the sample had lived in Wandsworth for more than seventy years) to 'less than a year' for nineteen people (9 per cent of the sample). It is helpful to see the full *range* of the distribution, to remind ourselves how variable and different people's lives and situations are. This is done in Table 6.8.

The *median* length of residence (the mid-point which divides the sample equally in half), in our random sample of adults was ten years in Wandsworth. If we split the sample into quartiles, about one-quarter (fifty-five people) had lived in the borough for three years or less; another quarter from four to ten years; another quarter from eleven to twenty-five years and the remaining quarter twenty-six years or more. Among the most enduring residents there was naturally a slight, but not significant, bias towards elderly women: women, as we know, have considerably greater chances than men of living longer, anywhere, *ceteris paribus*.

The range of length of residence is thus between the newly moved in (less than one year) through to a maximum of seventy-eight years, with a median length of residence of ten years. There is no significant variation by sex of the respondent, as can be seen if length of residence is grouped into quartiles. Predictably, however, there is a larger number of older women who have lived in the area longest. Table 6.9 gives the length of residence by sex, grouped into quartiles by length of residence.

Table 6.8 Length of residence in the area

Years	No.	%
One or less	19	8
1–4	46	21
5–9	29	13
10–14	26	12
15–19	18	8
20–24	29	13
25–29	14	6
30–39	16	7
40–49	10	4
50–59	7	3
60–69	4	2
70–79	4	2
NK	3	1
Total	221	100

Table 6.9 Length of residence, by sex

Years	Men	Women	Both
3 or less	27	28	55
[row %]	26	24	25
4–10	27	29	56
[row %]	26	25	26
11–25	28	27	55
[row %]	27	24	25
26 or more	21	31	52
[row %]	20	27	24
Totals	103	115	218
[row %]	47	53	100

Table 6.10 'Would you expect to be living in this area in five years' time?'

Answer	No.	%
Yes	134	60
No	55	25
Can't say	32	15
Total	221	100

Table 6.11 Expectation of continuing to live in area, by current age

Answer	18–28	29–36	37–56	57–85	All Ages
Yes	21	36	33	43	133
[row %]	39	66	60	78	61
No	26	14	10	5	55
[row %]	48	56	18	9	25
Can't say	7	5	12	7	31
[row %]	13	9	22	13	14
Totals	54	55	55	55	219
[row %]	25	25	25	25	100

We asked people if they supposed they would still be living in the same area in five years' time. A quarter of the sample definitely do not expect to stay in the area; over 60 per cent do, the remainder being unsure: Table 6.10 shows the distribution.

The distribution of responses by sex is virtually identical, however there is a strong variation both by *age* of the respondent (Table 6.11) and by the *length of residence in Wandsworth* (Table 6.12): older respondents and those who have lived longest in the borough and more likely to have a continuing expectation of living there than the youngest age group, or the most recent arrivals (these are not identical categories).

Table 6.12 Expectation of continuing to live in area, by length of residence there

	Years of residence in area				
	3 or less	*4–10*	*11–25*	*26+*	*All years*
Yes	24	29	37	42	132
[row %]	44	52	67	81	61
No	24	18	8	4	54
[row %]	44	32	15	8	25
Can't say	7	9	10	6	32
[row %]	13	16	18	12	15
Totals	55	56	55	52	218
[row %]	25	26	25	24	100

What this demonstrates is that approximately 60 per cent of the sample reckon still to be living in the area in five years' time but that the long-established residents have a greater propensity to have this expectation (over 80 per cent of them). Conversely, about a quarter of the sample expect to move on, but the most recently arrived (three years' residence or less) have a higher expectation of moving again (44 per cent expect to move). There is very little age or length-of-residence variation among those who are uncertain.

FOURTH BIAS: QUESTIONS OF INCLUSION AND EXCLUSION

Having secured our sample of informants, a fourth source of bias may enter in the questions we ask them. There is a limit to how much information an interview can carry: just working to map an informant's kinship connections systematically can take hours, so we tend to be selective, focusing on the *most immediate*, the most significant. If we ask people how often they see their children we will ask about the nearest, or closest, or those seen most often (sometimes we ask about the 'first-named', the first ones to come to mind, and this *might* arguably be better from our perspective, but is less common); and similarly for other relatives and friends. Mapping most people's social connections will otherwise exhaust the patience of the subject and the concentration of the inter-viewer, and the real questions, the questions we want to get to, have hardly begun. But this does mean we *systematically* tend to ignore relatives and friends who live in other parts of the world, the people we left behind when we moved here from Bangladesh, a son who lives in Australia and comes to visit every five years or so, a daughter who moved with her husband and family to South Africa some years ago?

A possible change, in our more modern times, is time–space compression

Table 6.13 'Have you ever travelled abroad from the UK?'

Answer	No.	%
Yes	210	95
No	11	5
Total	221	100

through technological advances. We can, wherever we are, perhaps pick up a telephone and speak to our friends and relatives (after no longer a delay than in phoning the house next door) by satellite connection anywhere in the world. With a little organization and substantial expenditure, we can travel to the other side of the world within twenty-four hours or so. And these technological and financial advances are more widely disseminated in populations (less the privilege of the elites) than the best equivalent forms of communication might have been in earlier times.

We do not know what difference these changes in technology and living standards have made (because we lack baseline data) and we must be cautious of linear assumptions – that everything gets better progressively; that things in the past were more rudimentary, less efficient and less satisfactory; that our times represent the pinnacle of evolution. Postal services, extensively used in the nineteenth century, may be less efficient and reliable today, the telegram and the telegraph of sharply declining significance. But it can be salutary to remember that Virginia Woolf, with three or four postal deliveries a day, would be used to inviting people to tea by post the same day; and post by sail packet to and from the West Indies was as fast in Nelson's day as by airmail today. So we must be on our guard against modernist fallacies, that everything today is new, better, faster, the dilemmas and challenges never before encountered. Some things

Table 6.14 'When did you last travel abroad?'

Answer	No.	%
In current year (1994)	72	32
Last year (1993)	59	27
Year before last (1992)	17	8
Three years ago (1991)	5	2
Four years ago (1990)	11	5
Five years ago (1989)	7	3
6–10 years ago	15	7
11–20 years ago	11	5
21–30 years ago	6	3
40 + years ago	6	3
Never been abroad	12	5
Total	221	100

young adults want to live close to where they work in the city and have no ties which require them to journey back and forth (young childless professionals, for instance); there are others (night workers in the broadest sense) who need to live close to where they work because of the hours they have to keep and the lack of transport at those hours; there are tourists and other transients through the city, business visitors, people who are not staying long and want to be central. There are those whom Gans called the trapped – poorer, elderly perhaps, working-class people who might like to move away but are unable to do so.

For those other than the trapped, however, Gans argued that residential choice is largely governed by life-stage. Although a cosmopolitan city will always contain a variety of alternative lifestyles, perhaps at least 90 per cent of the British have, since the eighteenth century, gone through a cycle of leaving home, forming a heterosexual union, getting married and having children and establishing separate nuclear households. It is the pressure of forming a long-term union, a long-term household, a new family which in Gans' view prompts the quest for larger accommodation, more space, more fresh air, safer streets, quieter environments, better schools which has been the suburbanizing pressure.

Hence a convection current develops, leading to an earlier, misguided, belief that cities kill people – for death rates in cities exceed birth rates. But this is not because the city has a rapacious maw, sucking people in to kill them, or that people go to cities to die. Rather, it is that parents and prospective parents move to the suburbs for babies to be *born* and children to be raised. After the children have been raised, they are likely to want to leave home and, likely as not, a good proportion of them will head for the city to work, sample the social life, mate-select and pair-bond, the reverse rotation of this slow convection current. Their parents *may* stay where they are, or think of limiting their outgoings by moving to down-sized accommodation, or contemplate (assuming they have been working) retirement migration – perhaps to the seaside or the 'real' countryside.

Clearly the ease with which people make these transitions is affected by the resources at their disposal – and some have more than others – but given this association which Gans conjectured between life stage and locality, should we attach any special importance, any primacy to *long-term* residence, is it a signifier of any greater virtue? Some people have lived longer in a place simply because they have lived longer, they have had more life to live. In any random sample, therefore, we must control for that opportunity, otherwise some of the 'short-term' residents are simply younger people, artefactually. And some people may stay longer, because their lives have *not* followed the typical modalities of new household formation and child-rearing; or because, lacking resources, their opportunities to move are restricted.

OTHER GLOBALIZATION INDICATORS

In a modern global city we might now expect to find people of various nationalities and ethnic groups but, since there is a tendency for a degree of residential clustering to occur, a random sample will tend to hop over those clusters and will mainly select white British residents (as we have noted, 87 per cent of our respondents gave their nationality as British). Table 6.19 shows that it was also a predominantly white sample, with 16 per cent indicating a different ethnic group.

We included in our survey various indicators of people's exposure to, receptivity to and interest in countries *other than England*. For instance, we asked if people spoke any language other than English; we asked if they had cast a vote in the recent European elections; whether they were interested in what goes on in other countries and whether they felt their lives were affected by things in other countries. Nearly half the sample claim to speak at least one language other than English (Table 6.20).

There is no variation by sex but there are some quite sharp variations by age, with the middle aged being most likely to claim a language other than English and the oldest age group least likely to be conversant with another one (Table 6.21). The pattern is virtually identical for both sexes: the *highest* number claiming another language is to be found among women aged 37–56, 63 per cent of whom say they are proficient.

The final cluster of questions dealt with the respondents' engagement or sense of engagement with the world beyond Britain's national boundaries. Table 6.22 shows that almost half the sample claimed to have voted in the most recent European election (a figure somewhat above the actual turn-out, so on a simple 'yes/no' question like this, they may have exaggerated their civic virtue somewhat, for the benefit of the interviewers – we did not probe any further).

As many as 68 per cent of the sample *felt* that their lives were affected by people, events and organizations in other countries, as Table 6.23 shows.

Table 6.19 'How would you describe your ethnic group?'

Answer	No.	%
White	186	84
Black Caribbean	14	6
Black African	1	1
Black other	2	1
Indian	4	2
Pakistani	4	2
Chinese	3	1
Other Asian	5	2
Other responses	2	1
Total	221	100

Table 6.20 'Do you speak any languages other than English?'

Answer	No.	%
Yes	99	45
No	122	55
Total	221	100

Table 6.21 Proficiency in language other than English, by current age of respondent

	18–28	29–36	37–56	56–85	All ages
Proficient	27	26	34	12	99
[row %]	50	47	62	22	45
Not proficient	27	29	21	43	120
[row %]	50	53	38	78	55
Totals	54	55	55	55	219
[row %]	25	25	25	25	100

Table 6.22 Voted in last Euro-poll

	No.	%
Voters	104	47
Non-voters	117	53
Total	221	100

Table 6.23 'Is your life affected by people, events and organizations in other countries?'

Answer	No.	%
Yes	150	68
No	69	31
Unsure	2	1
Total	221	100

Adding together responses to another question, as many as 84 per cent claimed to be interested in what goes on in other countries – 38 per cent claiming to be very interested, 46 per cent 'quite' interested and only 16 per cent professing no interest in other countries (Table 6.24).

CONCLUDING REMARKS

Times change, societies evolve, people both adapt to conditions they cannot influence and exploit opportunities which they begin to perceive. In studying anything, these things can be exaggerated or down-played by the way in which we characterize our research into people's lives, the way we design our studies, select our samples, frame our questions, interpret and report the results.

In any local area we might be able to home in on the archetypal indigenous inhabitant, or spot the typical 'cosmopolite'. We may be tempted to suggest there is at least a latent conflict between them, as if the 'originals' stand for tradition, immobility, continuity, community, moral worth and truth, the 'cosmopolites' represent newness, mobility, discontinuity, superficiality and all that is beguiling but false in the modern world: there is powerful nostalgia in the ahistorical perspective. But our argument is that to play with such dichotomies is to misrepresent both: the forces at work affect all our lives – traditional locals take holidays in Spain or see their children married in exotic locations; quintessential cosmopolites seek out the local delicatessen and involve themselves in local organizations such as parent–teacher associations. Both may belong to national institutions with local branches (such as political parties), or supra-national organizations like Greenpeace or the Roman Catholic Church: we argue for a greater interpenetration of the global and local than has hitherto been acknowledged, and have tried to show how a different approach to issues of inclusiveness and exclusivity in key areas of sample design, question design and reportage can begin to illuminate these matters. However slow or rapid the pace of secular change, we must also be aware of the limitations of cross-sectional sample design, and allow for the slow convection current of

Table 6.24 'Are you very interested, quite interested or not interested in what goes on in other countries?'

Answer	No.	%
Very interested	84	38
Quite interested	102	46
Not interested	35	16
Total	221	100

Table 6.25 Target and achieved sample quotas

	Target	Achieved	
Age 18–29	75	75	
Men employed	25	24	1
Men non-employed	11	13	+2
Female employed	27	24	−3
Female non-employed	12	14	+2
Age 30–59	101	97	−4
Men employed	38	35	−3
Men non-employed	11	10	−1
Female employed	34	35	+1
Female non-employed	18	17	−1
Age 60 and over	45	49	+4
Men employed	4	6	+2
Men non-employed	13	15	+2
Female employed	3	2	−1
Female non-employed	25	26	+1
All males	102	103	+1
All females	119	118	−1
All employed	131	126	−5
All non-employed	90	95	+5
All categories	221	221	

new household formation, consolidation and dissolution, associated as it typically is with residential changes through the life course.

7

RETHINKING POVERTY IN GLOBALIZED CONDITIONS

Laura Buffoni

THE MACRO AND THE MICRO LEVEL

Poverty, with its local manifestations and interplay of global, regional (national) and local causes, can be considered as one of the phenomena in which the 'global' meets the 'local'.[1] In this chapter it will be argued that:

1 polarization occurring at global (macro) level has dramatically increased in the last decades confirming the image of a 'North/South' divide, although the 'poles' might be scattered all over the globe;
2 because of the influence of globalization processes on individuals' everyday lives (defined as 'microglobalization'), poverty in 'affluent' societies has involved various ways of adaptation and forms of social coping, producing more complex patterns in the way poverty is perceived and experienced.

The focus of this chapter will be upon the latter aspect. By looking at people's life histories and at their subjective perception of poverty we can collect insights into the processes shaping the lives of individuals. I define poverty as the lack of material and cultural resources which restrict one's ability to socialize and, in a dynamic sense, as a 'trajectory' of progressive decline and of reduced availability of options in everyday life. How do these features change under globalized conditions? By collecting individuals' reflections and evaluations on poverty, I have attempted to gain information on the way and the extent to which external events and phenomena of social change, in this case microglobalization, have affected in one way or another (positively or negatively), the well-being of people and their access to material and cultural resources.

The discourse on 'consumption' and access to various lifestyles has a clear part to play in research on poverty. As globalization processes influence people's everyday lives in various ways, I think it is necessary to look beyond stereotypical images of the poor and not take for granted seemingly widespread patterns of consumption. Globalization has contributed to the increase of social polarization, but at the same time it has transformed class structures. Globalization has fractured consumption groups, on the one hand creating new needs, on the other, cutting across traditional barriers of non-access. If globalization has an impact on stratification systems, it might well distort the manifestations of poverty and, in general, of access to resources: poverty in a global city or under 'globalized conditions' might be experienced by people who are in fact not marginalized or excluded and are still able to profit from and participate in various activities, thus alleviating the burden of poverty. On the other hand new forms of exclusion and marginalization could arise for those who do not seem to belong to the social category of the poor. The concepts of capability and functioning, as discussed by A. Sen, will be central to my analysis of poverty under globalized conditions, since they incorporate the notions of rights, quality of life and fulfilment, and the notion of freedom (Sen 1990: 23).

Global economic trends have consequences on national economies and on people's well-being at local level. The actual regime of 'flexible accumulation', characterized by liberalization and privatization at global level, influences local economies and national welfare institutions. Furthermore the practice of 'global sourcing' pursued by transnational companies and the accelerated technological changes in production have an impact on the localization of production and on the international division of labour, thus creating areas of extreme labour fragility in many traditionally industrialized areas. But my intention here is to consider the issue from a different perspective.

I want to look at the way globalization has an impact on everyday life through its local manifestations. Globalization processes

1 inform people's values (globalism);
2 transform and/or increase access to images, information and commodities (globality);
3 influence people's mobility and their ability to maintain social relations across the globe (time/space compression); and
4 transform the interplay between local and global forces, thus changing the patterns of local communities.

It is from this perspective, that I will consider qualitative changes in the experience and perception of poverty in a specific locality of the world: London.

THE GLOBAL CITY:
GOING BEYOND THE DUAL CITY

Cities represent an ideal site for observing processes occurring within the wider society, especially changes in the relationship between people and their environment and among people themselves.

Like a magic box, the city can offer its 'presents' both in terms of opportunities and social participation as well as in terms of exclusion and anonymity. Poverty is not a distinctive feature of urban areas (quite the contrary), but it can develop specific characteristics in cities, where the contrasts become more visible, failures and success more showy, and where exclusion is ignored or hidden in the city's crowded labyrinths.

The idea of 'dual city' or 'divided city' – discussing the contrasts between opulence and poverty in urban areas – is a classic theme of urban sociology (see Castells 1989; Logan *et al.* 1992, for example).

> Poverty is manifest, affluence is ostentatious. Gentrification sits besides the devalorisation of old properties.
>
> (Cross 1993: 1)

Globalization processes, in the sense we described above (globalism, globality, time/space compression, transformed local communities), might well have an impact on the experience of poverty and social exclusion in a global city, but they do not necessarily support the idea and image of a divided and dual city. Three aspects of poverty may change in globalized conditions, giving way to more complex patterns of stratification:

1 A polarization of life chances may take place since a 'global' standard of living – made of financial expertise, technical knowledge and access to global means of communication – is reached by the higher echelons of society whereas the 'old poor' are left further behind because they are unable to display the necessary capabilities in terms of economic resources, cultural resources and knowledge. Furthermore, local communities, inhabited by various 'dislocated cultural identities' (Hall 1992b: ch. 6), might lose their importance as settings for social relations, leaving the poor locals deprived 'even of the sense of deprivation . . .' (Albrow, in this volume, p. 54).

2 On the other hand, the proximity of 'global facilities' and specialized services may spread access and may offer opportunities – independently from one's social class and economic position – to those able to develop new and alternative forms of social coping.

3 The idea and perception of poverty, or better, of relative poverty, might assume different characteristics. Globalization in terms of physical mobility, means that people cross national and cultural boundaries looking for better opportunities in life. Global communications and media make us aware of the living conditions of people across the globe. Global cities are multi-cultural environments. Because of these factors we should rethink the idea of relative poverty. Poverty is and remains relative, but the question is, relative to whom do people perceive their poverty?

112

GLOBALIZATION AND POVERTY: PROCESSES AND DEFINITIONS

A series of questions arises when we attempt to link globalization and poverty. Poverty has traditionally been studied with regard to the structural (economic, social, political) characteristics of spatially delimited societies (in which society is mainly defined in terms of the nation-state) or through comparing individual countries or groups of countries of similar socio-economic status. But what happens in 'globalized conditions' when national boundaries do not limit social phenomena and instead 'global events' profoundly influence everyday lives? In other words, how should we look at the well-being of increasingly multi-ethnic/multi-cultural societies under the influence of globalization processes? How should we revise and adapt the concept of 'relative poverty', since it is increasingly difficult to circum-scribe social phenomena and perceptions, and consequently, to tell relative to whom people are less poor or poorer? How does globalization affect the sociologist's analysis of poverty?

I will consider two major contributors to the debate on poverty, in order to look at the way concepts have been used in 'traditional' research on poverty and in the current debates on the conceptualization of poverty. The first, Peter Townsend, leading figure in the study of poverty in Britain, is one of the main theorists of the idea of relative poverty.

In his latest work Peter Townsend analyses 'relative deprivation' in an international context. The way he defines and conceptually organizes the idea of 'relative deprivation' is nevertheless not fundamentally different from his previous analysis:

> People are relatively deprived if they cannot obtain, at all or sufficiently, the conditions of life – that is, the diets, amenities, standards and services – which allow them to play the roles, participate in the relationships, and follow the customary behaviour which is expected of them by virtue of their membership of society. If they lack or are denied resources to obtain access to these conditions of life and so fulfil membership in society they may be said to be in poverty.
>
> (Townsend 1993: 36)

Townsend proceeds to argue that:

> People may be deprived in any or all of the major spheres of life – at work, where the means largely determining positions in other spheres are earned; at home, in neighbourhood and family; in travel; in a range of social and individual activities outside work and home or neighbourhood in performing a variety of roles in fulfilment of social obligations.
>
> (ibid.)

113

In order to identify those living in poverty in a given area, a poverty line can be drawn, either looking directly at those whose needs are unsatisfied, or looking for a level of income below which people are unable to meet minimum needs. Under the 'relative deprivation' approach a threshold of: 'income is conceived according to size and type of family, below which withdrawal or exclusion from active membership of society becomes disproportionately accentuated' (Townsend 1993: 36). The idea of 'relative deprivation' has been disputed from different directions, basically on the premise that inequality (on which the concept of relative deprivation draws) is not the same as poverty. Amartya Sen, who has worked in the field of economics and moral philosophy, has argued for the maintenance of an 'absolute nucleus' in the concept of poverty.

According to Sen, absoluteness of needs does not mean their 'fixity over time'. Using Adam Smith's example of the necessity of an Englishman in the eighteenth century to have leather shoes in order to avoid shame, Sen argues that there is no question of being less ashamed than others but not being ashamed at all – an absolute achievement (Townsend 1993: 125). Of course each society varies enormously in the commodities and resources needed to participate in community activities: so, in poor communities these can be very little indeed, whereas richer communities would have much higher demands.

Sen's absolute nucleus consists of 'functionings' and 'capabilities', because they are common to any society: 'Functionings represent the part of the state of a person, in particular the various things that he or she manages to be in leading a life' (Sen 1993: 31). Some functionings are elementary, such as being adequately nourished, being in good health and may be strongly valued by all. Others may be more complex, such as achieving self-respect or being socially integrated, but are no less important.

In order to perform subjectively valuable functionings we need 'capabilities'. Each person's capability set (which is not to be confused with any functionalist approach to poverty referring to personal abilities, values or knowledge) depends on a variety of factors, personal and more importantly social ones, and determines the person's freedom to choose between different types of life, access to opportunities and well-being (Sen 1993).

RETHINKING THE CONCEPT OF POVERTY IN GLOBALIZED CONDITIONS

Some of the concepts discussed by the above-mentioned authors are particularly useful in looking at the qualitative changes of poverty in a globalized setting. Others have to undergo substantial revision, since globalization strains older concepts formed for nation–state sociologies (see chapter 2, pp. 34–5). In this sense the following issues represent a digression, from 'traditional' approaches to poverty, though maintaining the importance of some of the concepts, and in particular Sen's capability-approach.

Rethinking the notion of poverty should involve the use of the concept of 'capability'

The concept of 'capability' may prove particularly useful for two reasons. On the one hand, it can be argued that under 'globalized conditions' new sets of capabilities are needed in order to have access to life chances or a global lifestyle characterized by the use of technological innovations, financial expertise, mobility, flexibility and access to global means of communication. Those unable to display these capabilities – in terms of economic, social and cultural resources – risk being left further behind and being excluded even by basic functionings, like being socially integrated and able to participate in social activities.

Technological innovation and growing informatization have transformed the nature of knowledge (Lyotard 1984). Individuals need to enact flexible strategies and a wider range of knowledge and capabilities in order to have access to technologies used in everyday life. On the other hand, access to information technology and to global means of communication might reduce the sense of social isolation experienced at local level through worldwide networking (for example, the use of the Internet and e-mail or simply by using communications and by travelling). Various technologies and 'global facilities' might represent a viable way of organizing an alternative form of social coping, though lacking relevant economic resources.

Credit cards are a typical example of a global service: they are imagined for a global market, they are based on the integration of different technological families (electronics, media and materials), they are managed by globalized organizations (Petrella 1989: 5). But are they of any use to the worse off?

In the last few years the Child Poverty Action Group, has pursued research on the way information, technological innovation and financial services – relevant commodities offered by a globalized social setting – are truly accessible and helpful to all strata of society. The global financial market with its rapid diffusion of 'plastic money' and sophisticated services is a good example of how technological innovation is extremely useful in serving the 'better off' and in helping to increase the profits of financial firms, but excludes from its advantages the unbanked, those who do not have a regular job and are therefore unable to demonstrate their credit-worthiness as well as the computer illiterate (Golding 1986). Looking at the development and widespread use of the credit card, Ritzer considers it as an example of today's quantity-oriented society: 'Plastic money is more efficient than cash: it is a better means to the end of spending money' (Ritzer 1993: 82).

Through the media, the message becomes pervasive: credit cards, mobile phones, use of computer technology and leisure activities (in particular travelling) are given an image of familiarity, affordability and prestige, and at the same time they are presented almost as indispensable. But if it is true that many of these services become increasingly less expensive, the lack of capabilities may become more and more stigmatizing, even if they are based on built-up needs and not on necessities.

Globalization and the transition to an 'extended relativity'

Given the complex and heterogeneous nature of globalization processes, a definition of poverty under such circumstances has necessarily to be relative, although the 'boundaries' of this relativity are difficult to trace because they are rapidly shifting and not necessarily linked to a spatial dimension. A notion of poverty based on nationally consumed commodities or on a nationally defined poverty line does not represent a standard definition of who is poor any more. An increasing number of individuals know about and relate to poverty in different parts of the world, either through the media or personal experience. 'Global awareness' contributes to relating oneself to a wider social space.

Awareness about processes going on in the world (globalism) and knowledge about poverty worldwide might change individuals' perceptions of their own and others' poverty. An 'extended relativity' can be induced by the media, by travelling, by migrating, by relating to people coming from or living in various parts of the world. Furthermore, the co-existence of ethnic and cultural minorities within a dominant culture makes the notion of relative poverty more complex. Originally from 'poor' countries where they might have been relatively well-off, 'newcomers' may feel particularly marginalized and dispossessed in the 'new', host community. But the sense of loss and deprivation might be mitigated if a community of people with the same cultural origins and lifestyle is (re)created in the host country, and a stratification system (re)produced within the community itself.

On the other hand, time–space compression, enabling social relationships to be maintained at a distance, may reduce felt exclusion and the perception of social deprivation. Individuals may embark on new coping strategies and display enhanced capabilities through worldwide networking.

Poverty should be considered in terms of conditions of risk

The notion of risk is related to a condition of isolation and social exclusion. People who experience social isolation lack a 'safety net' in terms of adequate social and economic support networks, and they are therefore requested to display more flexible capabilities. When living in such a condition individuals find themselves just 'at risk of poverty' since any

116

single negative event could result into a 'slipping' into a condition of poverty (Daniele 1995: 53). In other words, an additional loss of resources could result in reduced possibilities of converting capabilities into useful functionings.

The interviews reported below represent examples of people who have a direct experience of poverty in the present or had it in the past, or people who, more than others, are at risk of poverty. For them, one single negative event or a minimal reduction of capabilities may result in a sudden, significant reduction of the quality of life and/or exclusion from social relations.

Sharing the world city: the use of space and the transcendence of boundaries

The variety of opportunities, both in terms of magnitude and range of activities, offered by the global city can be used in different ways by different actors, but still in some cases represents a viable resource for those who are worse-off. Free exhibitions can become a warm place for rough sleepers. Matinées or films on particular days of the week are accessible cultural/free-time resources for those living on income support or other forms of social assistance. International events like the Notting Hill Carnival can represent one important option of the global city, which gives the opportunity to participate in community life and express one's creativity, even if lacking material resources. So the global city, with its 'concessionary' opportunities and commodified leisure activities, contributes to the construction of a complex web of social activities, or 'socio-spheres', which, though spatially very close, do not come in direct confrontation and therefore mask profound conditions of inequality (see p. 54).

The idea of the 'transcendence of boundaries' as manifested in the global city, with poverty and wealth co-existing side by side,[2] can help us to relate the barriers of access and non-access to a spatial dimension. As we mentioned before, the 'transcendence' of boundaries implies the encounter of both poverty and wealth in the same locale, the global city. The same opportunities and areas are used at different times and/or with different aims, creating a system of 'shifting' purposes throughout the day or the week, but it is this difference in purpose and timing which reflects the uneven access to resources. Inhabiting the same locale makes it necessary for the poor and the better-off to negotiate the use of space. Space is negotiated in terms of its territorial organization (using the same locality for different purposes) and sequential order (inhabiting the same place at different times).[3]

Spheres of access and non-access are redefined and eventually less intelligible, but not eliminated, and can be associated with the idea of 'time–space stratification': 'Time–space social stratification is the frame within which inequalities of access to resources and life chances are contained today which are more acute than any which prevailed during the period of class-based industrial society' (see p. 54)

Sociospheres of 'poverty' or 'wealth' can be (re)produced wherever people find themselves (re)located. In this sense the analysis of poverty in a global city is less dependent on the actual local settings, since spaces (and times) of the city are constantly negotiated and 'discovered' in terms of opportunities and resources.

SPEAKING POVERTY: MEANINGS AND PERCEPTIONS OF POVERTY IN THE WORLD CITY

The interviews, carried out across London, present a variety of situations and conditions of people living 'at risk of poverty' (as previously discussed), or of people who, directly or indirectly, have and/or have had an experience of poverty. They present different types of social coping and various ways of experiencing unemployment, underemployment and homelessness. The social space of non-work is lived in ways that go beyond stereotypical images of impoverished worklessness. I selected these interviews to show active modes by which individuals make use of the resources available in their social worlds, and how they display a variety of capabilities which are converted in important functionings (participating in one's ethnic community activities, doing volunteer work, maintaining social relationships). They also show how perceptions of individuals' relative poverty might be constructed.

Apart from John, an old-age pensioner, and Bill, who is in daily interaction with other members of his family living in the area, the interviewees do not express a particular attachment to the specific locality they inhabit. Their indifference may also be described as 'disaffiliation': poverty and the every day struggle for existence lead to a relative autonomy from a specific locale and to a detachment from the external world, if the locality itself cannot be converted into useful resources because of lack of money or other capabilities (a stable job, a fixed address). The local dimension can become relevant only if it offers opportunities of participation, for example a community activity involving members of the same ethnic group or other services (free meals, charity shops, cheap supermarkets). Toni, for example, has a particular relationship to Notting Hill, but he lives in a different area which he uses as a place from which to base his activities (Albrow *et al.* 1994). For those who are worse-off and have been homeless or at risk of homelessness, a place to live, whether a bedsit, a hostel or a council house, is not a free choice. To the extent that choices on housing are taken by the 'administration of poverty' (social services or local council) poor people,

118

sometimes only because they are unemployed, lose the ability to 'make territoriality' (Pieretti 1995), since decisions about their accommodation and spatial mobility in the city are taken outside of their sphere of control and without any possibility for negotiation.

Trained as a fishmonger in Hastings, Matthew, who is 30, came to London because he could not find a job on the coast, but lonely and unemployed he rapidly found himself on the street. The vicious circle of homelessness–unemployment–homelessness has been interrupted by Matthew since he started working for the *Big Issue*. He is now living in a council house in south-west London with no telephone and no TV, looking forward to a brighter future and considering himself among the lucky ones, since he feels he is relatively better off, both compared to people around him and relatively to people living in other parts of the world. In describing his own condition of poverty Matthew uses the 'traditional' relativity concept, and also refers to the contribution participation in social relationships can make to one's well-being:

> I wouldn't class myself as rich. Well, I wouldn't say I am poor, poor. It is not like when you haven't got a pound in your pocket or poor when you are hungry and you haven't got nothing to buy food with. That is poverty. . . . But I have good food, I have a social life, I am not *that* poor, but I *am* poor. Compared to the normal, to the average, I am in the lower half, the lowest part. But if you have got friends and you have got no money you can always lend a fiver here and there. . . . Compared to the Third World, we are well-off countries, like America, England.

The image of the 'dual city' is recalled in Matthew's words, since the city is on the one hand a site of desolation and loneliness:

> In these big cities everyone is for themselves, like America or here, you will always find people on the streets. I think if you go to the countryside, you won't find anything like that over there. Totally different people, kind to each other. Whereas in London it is such a big city and everyone is for themselves. They don't care about anybody else.

On the other hand, the city is a place for opportunities, where ideas from all over the world are collected, and where there is room for hope in a better future:

> I can see the world definitely getting better. . . . You know, the *Big Issue* to me is a sensational idea. I mean, three years ago a homeless person never had the opportunity to get involved with a company like this . . . but for me . . . I was around on the streets and in hostels for nearly one year before I knew about the *Big Issue*. And the moment I found out about it I said: 'Yeah! it's a good idea'. I think that homelessness is

getting better from this. I think a lot more people are paying attention. In America it's really good. We got the idea from America. It is sold in twelve different states over there. It is called *Streetwise, Streettalk* . . .

The idea of the *Big Issue* – and of street magazines in general – comes from the United States and is now to be found in various countries, adapted to local realities. It permits the creation of new forms of social coping for homeless and ex-homeless people, who use the magazine as a (temporary) way of access to material resources, whilst possibly planning other strategies and building up capabilities.[4]

In some vendors' opinion the *Big Issue* must necessarily be a temporary experience, since they feel their image and condition of homelessness has been exploited, without any reward in terms of participating actively in the magazine itself. Denouncing a situation in which homeless people do all the distributive work and 'the staff' only are in charge of the production of the magazine, Joseph is very disillusioned and feels exploited by people who 'in reality do not care about the homeless', 'do their own business' and 'only for money'. None the less he uses the magazine as an easy way for making good money in his 'position' in Soho and relates to distant conditions of poverty, displaying a deep global (class?) consciousness. The slogan 'think globally, act locally', formulated some decades ago and still capturing the imagination of people across the globe (Esteva and Prakash 1994), pervades Joseph's words, suggesting the possible creation of a 'world poverty movement' and the need for making people aware of conditions of poverty at the global level through acting locally:

> I see a problem in our country: we must help ourselves before we help others. It's easier for me to see the people who are in front of me who are suffering, rather than people who are in another country suffering. I know they are there, I know they are suffering, but I can't reach out to them, if I can't reach out towards who is in front of me first. . . . Our commune at the moment acts locally. It is very smallsighted, because we must build up ourselves first. When we have become older, stronger, wiser and bigger, when we are ready, then we will reach out to other sites of the world. Hopefully, maybe, we can take children off the streets in Brazil where they are killed by despots and give them a holiday over in this country. . . . If we can help the homeless from other sites of the world to gather with the homeless of this country, then, maybe, those children together will have a better way of learning about each other than I have had in learning about others.

Toni, who came to London as a child, remembers his days in Trinidad and his direct experience of living in poverty and in 'hardship'. Now in his 40s, Toni is a freelance photographer, but most of his time and energy are spent working for the Notting Hill Carnival. Toni now has his own band and his council house in Acton has become more a workshop for the preparation of costumes than a home. The Carnival, as an opportunity for interaction between various cultures offered by the global city, gives Toni the opportunity to participate in the activities of the Trinidadian community and to fulfil his creativity. He distances himself from the hectic and unbearable rhythms of the city and from a commodified lifestyle:

> People might see that as being laid-back. I remember my father jumping around and I mean . . . he got a stroke when he was in his 50s, because of the stress and all that. . . . You know, when I see people around me running and killing themselves on material things and unnecessary things, I just look at them . . . and prefer the way I am.

The concern about contemporary patterns of consumption is also mentioned by John, a 74-year-old pensioner who was in the building trade for most of his fifty-year-long working life. He is now retired but still works 'for friends'. John receives help from the council in order to pay the rent, but as he says 'that is the only thing I claimed in my life. I was never unemployed':

> I've got the feeling that [despite] the commodities that people have in these days such as vacuum cleaners, fridges, washing machines – these 'luxuries of life' as I call them – living was better [in the old days] and people were more friendly.

John feels that he lives in an area where the sense of community has disappeared, although he has contacts with a few neighbours. His most important social relations are with his son and his son's family and with the friends in the local stamp club. The future of the stamp club has become a source of concern since 'the rents of the rooms are so high, and we had to close up'.

Living on a basic pension John finds various essential goods expensive, and considers himself a victim of the cuts in welfare spending. According to John, housing is the biggest problem. Food and clothing are also expensive but 'you look around' and 'find something cheaply'. The combination of age and low income limits John's access to relevant functionings (see Sen 1993: 31) in terms of social activities since it would be 'a bit too expensive if you went out for a meal'.

> The older ones, they need a lot of heating. . . . They need more heat and clothes and things like that. . . . They cut out all this help one used to have with spectacles, dentures, things like that. You have to be on social security before you get just a little bit off. . . . Health is a problem with all these hospitals shutting down, kicking old people out. I think they want us to die so that they don't have to pay the pensions any more.

121

John knows about the outer world through the media which contribute to the building up of his own awareness and knowledge about the wider world: 'poverty is all over the place . . . also in wonderful America, but worse-off places are Haiti, China and India'. He seldom uses his bank account and has never had a credit card:

> I won't touch a credit card. You get into debt too quickly. They keep sending them through and I keep cutting them up and throwing them away. I have heard of too many people who have gone into trouble. There are a few things I pay by cheque, like rent, but all the others I pay cash.

Elderly people seem really to be in the worst-off category, according to the perceptions of most interviewees. Julie, who is in her 70s and now living on her nurse's pension, talks of 'elderly people living on basic pensions':

> I don't know how they can exist. Although social services gives free medicines, if you are just over you have to pay for a lot of things. Many people are too proud to ask for help and sometimes filling the forms and all the paraphernalia can be difficult and people feel they lose their dignity.

Even when dealing with the bureaucracy of social assistance, individuals need specific capabilities. In this sense elderly people are more disadvantaged, since capabilities belonging to the past – filling in forms, reading and writing a certain (bureaucratic) language, going to various offices – have to be recycled, and a possible failure in doing this may result in a sense of loss of dignity and self-confidence.

Julie's definition of (other's) poverty is absolute: 'poverty is not having enough to eat', but this poverty is not a far away one, it is near and experienced. Subsistence poverty, defined in terms of physical well-being, has not disappeared in affluent societies for those who live on a basic pension. But the problem is not only of maintaining one's well-being and efficiency, but a question of pride and dignity:

> Everybody should have at least a little bit of good nourishment, but everything is so expensive. You can do without meat and eat other proteins, but fish is important. Eggs and butter are expensive. Basic things like clothes, bedlinen are so expensive. Maybe to spend £40 for clothes is not so much for some who has a salary, but it is too much for someone living on a pension. Poverty is also about pride. Poverty is degrading.

As a major manifestation of global processes of social change, international migrations have generated a massive movement of people around the world, and have created new ways of assessing personal and others' well-being. Denzel, a former environmental officer who came from Mali nine years ago, has worked as a cleaner, petrol station attendant and mini-cab driver since his arrival in London. Now doing a PhD, Denzel describes the process of globalization in terms of the diffusion of Western culture across Third World countries through the media and particularly education. The creation of new needs transforms the perception of well-being, and consequently of relative poverty.

The middle class in poor countries whose aspirations are blocked feels cheated. Poverty has to be considered relatively to the economic standards of the society you live in. But through education and communication the middle class has been exposed to different standards. So, although relatively to their own society they are not poor, their aspirations are blocked, since they cannot achieve the higher living standards they well know.

On the other hand, the lack of information and comparative data, making people relate only to their own reality, can have – according to Denzel – its advantages: 'the rural poor do not aspire to a different way of life; they do not feel cheated'. However, global forces inevitably expose people all over the world to cultural, economic and social processes which influence their lives, thus in some cases putting at risk their physical and cultural well-being, as Denzel says:

> Communications and easy financial flows provoke the impoverishment of people because resources are calculated in terms of Western resources, US dollars. But, if I am a . . . tribesman why can't my richness be valued in terms of my resources, cattle and crops, rather than in US dollars?

Denzel supports quite a few people at home in Mali by regularly sending money to members of his family. He keeps contact by writing and sometimes by telephone if it is an urgent matter. For the time being he has not been back to Mali but his sister has come over to London.

Bill's 'living the world city' contrasts with the world of Joseph (see above) who lives in a commune for ex-homeless people, temporarily without telephone and electricity. Bill is a 40-year-old long-term unemployed person living in Elephant and Castle. He used to work in a quango but lost his job 'for political reasons', and got blacklisted from the Civil Service. He managed to get another job, but after a few months he injured his back badly and has not worked since. After nine years of invalidity pension, he was recently judged fit to work by a doctor, and is now back on income support (£45 a week). He lives in a Church Commission flat with his girlfriend who will soon have a baby. In the last nine years Bill has been engaged in volunteer jobs in the social welfare sector in the council estate next to his house. He also edits the journal of a sports association from a Macintosh computer which he has at home. With a lot of free time he 'reads all the time', goes to the library, free exhibitions and to the cinema sometimes on Monday when the price is £2, thus enjoying as much as he can the opportunities offered by the global city.

Bill has developed an expertise in managing his very scarce resources:

> What I tend to do is . . . to juggle with money. It's like, I pay one bill and there's another one holding in a limbo and then there's another one. . . . And the same with money. So what I do is, like tomorrow, I get £90 of two weeks' unemployment benefit. . . . I take £30 of that and buy £10 of electric, gas and telephone stamps and with the other sixty quid I'll buy £30 of shopping and then keep £30 for myself. . . . And then, that lasts for a little while. And then the following week, the second week, I just have to see what I can do, you know . . . I can borrow some money off someone or whatever . . . and that's how it works basically . . .

Sue, waitress and mother of four, came to London from Mauritius when she was 5 years old. Her life as a teenager in Britain was very hard since her father was an alcoholic and violent towards her mother: 'We were poor . . . I mean they are still poor.' She started working very early, at 16, and at 20 had her first child. Her husband is an electrician and was born in St Kitts. He became redundant some time ago because the company collapsed and Sue has now to cope with the mortgage. According to Sue life in London is so fast and expensive that it represents a continuous struggle:

> London is very fast . . . everything is more expensive than outside. You have got to have more money to go out and go around. You need money for everything. Only to go down the road can be 60p by bus. Everything is a struggle. Everything has been a struggle in my life. Even now. . . . Now I have got a car and my husband has got a car. I don't drink and I don't smoke. But still at the end of the week we have to struggle for the bills. My mother-in-law helps us buying the clothes for the kids, if not, I couldn't have a car. I feel my life has been just struggling.

Sue does not have any contacts outside the UK. She is waiting for a British passport and she is looking forward to it in order to go on holiday 'where everybody else is going, like Tenerife or Spain'.

CONCLUSION: SHIFTING BOUNDARIES OF POVERTY IN THE GLOBAL CITY

Social phenomena and individuals' everyday lives undergo major change in globalized conditions. In this paper, I have looked at poverty experienced across a city, in order to provide illustrations of the way global processes can have an impact on individuals' lives at local level, and in particular at the way people respond to globalization itself, by changing their perceptions of their own and others' well-being.

Going back to my initial working definition – poverty as lack of material and cultural resources which restricts the ability to socialize – we can observe some transformations currently at work. For some respondents the possibility of maintaining social relations across the world and of knowing about poverty in the world transforms the perception of their own relative poverty. Denzel's insights are due to personal experience. John has constructed his 'awareness' through the media. And Joseph works actively for changing conditions of relative poverty in the world, both in his local environment and in the international setting.

The respondents' worlds imply that living in a global city can result in a variety of forms of social coping, in which individual strategies are played on an extended horizon. The opportunities offered by the global city, in terms of technology, communications cultural and social opportunities, can be transformed into relevant social resources (a 'recreation of the community of origin' in the case of Toni or maintaining cultural interests in the case of Bill), if one has the necessary capabilities despite lacking material resources.

On the other hand, the dislocation of local communities brought about by globalization may be an element of additional disadvantage for those who are worse off and do not have access to 'global networking'. They experience further isolation and see their social resources decrease. A reduced set of capabilities due to age, material resources and technological illiteracy makes life in globalized conditions even more difficult. For elderly people who are confined to a limited area of society, since they are out of the working environment and have a reduced amount of friendships and marital relationships (Taucer 1995:156), technologies and access to communications are of little use, if they lack the necessary capabilities to make use of them. Additional capabilities in terms of socialization and ability of making new friends have to be recycled from the past in order to maintain and/or create relationships which are no longer available within the local community.

The image of the global city is one of complexity but not of duality: a place where isolation and destitution is a lived everyday phenomenon, but at the same time it is a place where opportunities are available even to the 'worse off'. A variety of forms of social coping and capabilities is built up, in a puzzled socioscape constituted by sociospheres of uneven access to resources. The various social worlds are not closed but draw resources, meanings and knowledge from the outer, global social setting, thus dissociating the boundaries of access and non-access. Poverty in a globalized setting results in a shifting reality, which in turn means that 'poverty' as a concept has to undergo constant rethinking.

NOTES

1 The problem of the complex relationship between the 'local' and the 'global' has been discussed by Robertson who argues that the local is itself *'an aspect* of globalization'. To avoid any confusion it is necessary, according to Robertson, to introduce the concept of 'glocalization' because 'what is called local is in large degree constructed on a global, or at least pan- or super-local basis'. In other words 'the promotion of locality is, in fact, done "from above"' (Robertson 1994: 35). While acknowledging the existence of complex relationships between the local and the global I will in this chapter use them as parallel and intermingled but not opposite notions.

2 Looking at the relation of environmental risk to globalization and referring to Beck's 'boomerang curve' (the hazardous consequences of risk return to their sources and adversely affect those who produce them; so pesticides and toxins will return on imported foodstuffs, sulphur emissions will turn rain to acid, carbon dioxide emissions will alter the climate of the planet, etc.), Waters points to the fact that the 'boomerang effect puts the poor and the wealthy in the same neighbourhood', suggesting another aspect of the way space is shared in globalized conditions (1995: 62). In this sense the one who consumes more also contributes more to the creation of environmental risk but the consequences are (almost equally) shared by the whole population.

3 A good example of this phenomenon is London's Strand (Davies 1995).

4 Working for the BI allows registration for a council house and the organization itself helps vendors in finding a home. Having a fixed address means in turn enhancing one's chances of finding a job and/or being entitled to social assistance.

8

RECONSTRUCTING PLACES

Changing images of locality in
Docklands and Spitalfields[1]

John Eade

INTRODUCTION

In this chapter we turn to a different area of the 'global city' – Docklands
and Spitalfields in the east London borough of Tower Hamlets. We also
view more closely themes which have only been touched on during the
previous chapters, viz. the issues of race and ethnicity associated with the
global flows of migrant workers. At the same time we meet again the
divisions of class as the flow of global capital transforms the socio-
economic character of 'localities' in far more drastic ways than are evident
within other areas of the city.

Docklands and Spitalfields have attracted the attention of numerous
social scientific commentators (cf. Eade 1989; Colenutt 1991; Mellor
1991; Schwartz 1991; Jacobs 1992; Rhodes and Nabi 1992; Bird 1993;
Dunn and Leeson 1993; Cohen *et al.* 1994; Fainstein 1994; Cohen 1995).
These studies have revealed the sharp conflicts of interest and re-imagings
of place as local working-class residents engage in active political resistance
to the transformation of the localities within which they live. While
Harvey's discussion of space and place and the politics of difference in
the context of global capitalism has clearly inspired a number of these
interpretations other issues raised by the globalization literature have
remained untouched.

In my account, therefore, I want to focus on the implications which the
disjunctures between the different scapes described by Appadurai and
Albrow have for the discussion of the politics of difference and resistance. As we have already seen Appadurai contends that the global cultural
economy is relatively autonomous because of 'certain fundamental disjunctures between economy, culture and politics' (1990: 296). Individuals
navigate a variety of scapes which are defined as 'imagined worlds' which
are 'constituted by the historically situated imaginations of persons and
groups around the globe'. These scapes are not just individual constructs,
therefore, nor are they detached from processes of power and inequality

since through these 'imagined worlds' people can 'contest and even sub-vert' those constructed by officials (state bureaucrats, for instance) and entrepreneurs.

Appadurai's (1990) model of asymmetric flows and disjunctured scapes retains a belief in the stability of communities and networks through which people move. However, we have argued in Chapter 2 that an adequate understanding of globalization requires us to move beyond conventional assumptions about the stability of place which are conveyed through such terms as 'community'. In Chapter 3 Albrow has claimed that socioscape can be used to portray the degree to which places have become delocalized amid a 'growing indeterminacy' in the everyday application of such terms as family, community, friendship, partnership, enclave or lifestyle group.

Albrow's application of socioscape to analyse delocalization and indeter-minacy challenges those who wish to retain 'old structural terms' like class, neighbourhood and community. We have already seen O'Byrne in Chapter 4 arguing for the reconstruction of the concept 'working-class culture' in the global city, and in many respects Spitalfields and Docklands present a similar picture of strong working-class solidarity combined with a fierce sense of localism. Discursive traditions in Spitalfields and Docklands are shaped partly by a political rhetoric which has long sought to forge a close link between class and community which can, in certain instances, accom-modate the divisions of religion and 'race' (cf. Eade 1989, 1991). These rhetorical conventions are reinforced by political and social practices which incorporate local community activists into the political arena where the conventional procedures of nation-state decision-making prevail.

What Appadurai and Albrow among others are emphasizing, however, is the emergence of new rhetorics and practices which problematize social, cultural and political conventions shaped by nation-state struc-tures. Attempts may well be made by white residents to incorporate 'outsiders' like 'black and Asian' settlers into a local working-class culture and community. Nevertheless, the emerging literature on hybridity, dias-poric communities and new ethnicities indicates the manifold ways in which global migrants and their descendants are defying assimilation into con-ventional political discourses and practices. Indeed, their supra-national links enable them to challenge these conventional modes of interpreting the world within specific territories.

There is much to recommend Harvey's call for a new politics of place which Bird, in his analysis of Docklands, describes as 'capable of recogniz-ing and exploring the instabilities of and contradictions present in all areas of social life and political formations' (Bird 1993: 134). Yet the need which Bird discerns for 'practices that symbolize the bridging of individual experience, cultural difference and collective representations' (ibid.) requires us to look beyond reformulations of indigenous political, cultural and social discourses and practices based on the nation-state and class formation. In our academic quest for these new understandings we can especially rely upon the interpretations of global migrants as they engage in the dialectical tension between traditional and translated identity formations (Hall 1992b: 310). They navigate the disjunctures between different political and cultural formations and attempt to make sense of these differences in ways which do not necessarily conform to a specific tradition. Their journey is largely an imaginative, reflexive movement where they can draw on traditions in other parts of the world and in the process construct their own translation. (I am not implying that the nostalgic vision of an heroic working class should be replaced here by a romantic construction of migrant communities since people's engagement in the dialectic of tradition and translation can lead them to assertions of the most virulent forms of traditional, exclusivist identities.)

The ideological construction of place by global migrants and their descendants can be compared with attempts by those who see themselves as 'insiders' to understand the changes taking place within the global city. These people may be playing a key role in the transformation which they seek to interpret to themselves and to others. They may also engage in the dialectic of tradition and translation but may have at their disposal different political, social and cultural resources as they move between the diverse scapes of the global cultural economy. Before we see how these general formulations apply to Spitalfields and Docklands the historical context within which these changes are taking place needs to be briefly outlined.

SOCIAL AND ECONOMIC CHANGES WITHIN TOWER HAMLETS

Those living and working within the east London borough of Tower Hamlets have experienced in the most acute form the economic and social impact of international and global forces. The building of docks during the eighteenth and nineteenth centuries ensured that the lives of its residents were vitally affected by the flow of international trade as Britain's 'industrial revolution' and overseas trade became closely intertwined. The areas which now constitute Tower Hamlets developed a predominantly working-class character, although religious and regional loyalties also served to differentiate its inhabitants. A sharp social boundary overlapped with the territorial frontier between Tower Hamlets and the City of London, the centre of Britain's national and international finance and banking houses. Railways and roads cut through the poor localities within the old boroughs of Stepney, Poplar and Bethnal Green to enable the armies of white-collar commuters to travel swiftly to their places of work in the City and the West End. Goods imported and exported through the docks were also transported with little concern for the interests and needs of local inhabitants.

Between 1880 and 1980 a fairly stable pattern of social and economic division was maintained, although there were obviously significant developments within that pattern. Residents developed a clear sense of working-class culture which was bound up with local struggles at the workplace and within the expanding political arena. The Labour Party was the main beneficiary of local electoral support within the area from the mid-1920s and until its defeat in the borough election of 1986. Religious differences and conflicts involving racist exclusion of Jewish settlers in particular enabled political organizations on both the Left and the Far Right to gain some local successes at particular times, but the 'municipal socialism' of the Labour Party held overall electoral sway across the three boroughs which now constitute Tower Hamlets. Labour support was sustained through the trade unions which emerged within the docks, transport and garment industries and through the zealous recruitment of local community activists operating outside the political arena. The expansion of council housing and the 'redevelopment' of bomb-damaged localities after the Second World War also provided the Labour Party with an important constituency to satisfy – working-class residents with fierce attachments to local territory. At the same time, as the classic Young and Willmott study in post-war Bethnal Green revealed, these closely integrated communities were frequently breaking up through the very process of 'urban redevelopment' and the movement of skilled manual workers to the new towns outside the metropolis.

By the 1970s the historic role of the docks had been played out as one by one they closed. The social and political alliance between the Labour Party, the trade unions, community activists and substantial sections of the working class occupying council housing began to crumble as newcomers from Bangladesh in particular began to make an impact on local community and political organizations. The period between 1986 and today has highlighted the extensive social and economic changes which were already at work in the early 1980s and which have created a more complex, diverse society.

The creation of the London Docklands Development Corporation in 1980 and the rapid redevelopment of the redundant docks have been the two most important elements within this rapidly changing picture. A massive redistribution of resources has resulted in the influx of global elites and white middle-class 'immigrants', global and national corporations relocating from the City of London, a movement from industry to services and the re-imaging of 'Docklands'. Both white and Bangladeshi members of the local working class have been largely excluded from this redevelopment. White working-class resentment of 'immigrants' has largely focused on Bangladeshis whom they see as competing for scarce council housing and the British National Party gained a brief electoral success in 1993 on the back of this resentment. The Labour Party returned to power at the 1994 borough elections and has to confront a potent mix of diminished public resources and high expectations from working-class residents who are confronted in their daily lives with the social and economic polarization fostered by 'Docklands redevelopment' (see Crilley *et al.* 1991).

Spitalfields has also experienced, albeit less dramatically, the polarization between a highly paid, white middle class entrenched within the service sector and a working-class population dependent on local manual occupations and predominantly Bangladeshi in terms of country of origin. Georgian houses built by earlier 'immigrants' (Huguenots) have been gentrified and 'protected' through the establishment of a 'conservation area'. Prices for these houses reached the giddy heights of around £500,000 during the late 1980s housing boom, while political and community activists were calling for action to improve the standard of accommodation and amenities experienced by Bangladeshi and white tenants of council and privately rented housing. The recent closure of substantial local businesses, especially the Truman's Brewery and the Spitalfields Fruit and Vegetable Market, has highlighted the tension between demands for office space and services linked to the City, for conservation of urban heritage and the needs of working-class (white and Bangladeshi) residents.

IMAGES OF LOCALITY AND LOCAL TRANSFORMATIONS

After this highly condensed and inevitably sketchy portrait of various crucial developments in Tower Hamlets I will now focus on the images of place in the context of two localities – Docklands and Spitalfields – in order to contextualize the broad developments outlined above and to relate them to the opening discussion.

Docklands

The name 'Docklands' is largely a recent construction designed to replace or reinterpret older placenames associated with working-class communities (the Isle of Dogs, Wapping, Limehouse, Cubitt Town). The promotion of 'Docklands' was intimately bound up with the creation of the London Docklands Development Corporation (LDDC) and was intended to describe an area far beyond Tower Hamlets, i.e. into the Royal Docks of Newham and the Surrey Docks across the river in Greenwich. A certain symbolic unity had to be provided for a highly disparate range of localities as part of the strategy of attracting outside investment and presenting a rival magnet to the City of London.

The advertising hype which surrounded the physical reshaping of the area emphasized the 'unique' blend of a maritime heritage and a 'state-of-the-art' financial and commercial centre which was leading Britain into the twenty-first century. A harmonious relationship was also claimed between

131

this energetic newcomer and the City of London while references to the local 'community' ignored contemporary divisions of race and class (see Bird 1993). When social divisions were acknowledged they were located in accounts of the area's 'history' and frequently in the context of crime. Late 1980s advertising for a new development in a former docklands warehouse now renamed the 'Tobacco Dock' described, for example, a nineteenth-century past where the criminal population of the area stole the goods from Britain's international trading empire or preyed on the wealthy entrepreneurs who owned these warehouses, ships and other related businesses.

Far more detailed information about Docklands was provided by the LDDC at its visitors' centre on the Isle of Dogs and in the literature, pictures and videos a much more nuanced picture of local history and contemporary life emerged. However, this was consistent with the LDDC's strategy of constructing a new image which would attract middle-class settlers and visitors from across the world. Although the rhetoric changed during the late 1980s to acknowledge local communities the LDDC perspective consistently fails to give due weight to the alternative approaches proposed by local pressure groups, political activists and community organizations such as the Docklands Consultative Committee and the Docklands Forum (see Brownhill 1990; Colenutt 1991). The 'wild frontier' of the 'East End' where local working-class residents constituted a dangerous exotic 'Other' was being made safe for City of London corporations, global investors and members of the 'new service class' who followed the relocation of their firms into Docklands or sought a home in a rapidly changing area where the River Thames and the old docks were the focus for leisure and recreation rather than international trade.

Who these newcomers might be and what would attract them were questions raised during recorded interviews with three Docklands estate agents. According to one of these estate agents there were two main categories of investors in the new property built in Docklands:

You've got two different types. You've got the major city companies and international financial companies who are investing in properties for their employees to live in and to entertain their people visiting from overseas. For example, Texaco bought about twelve or fifteen apartments in one particular development in Greenwich and they put their visitors in there and also they are relocating their staff for a few weeks until they find their own place. Every major city company, as far as I can see, has bought something in Docklands and none have sold yet . . . because I think they think it's a good investment for the future.

The other people we have are companies from overseas wanting to invest here, again for relocation purposes or investments for the company. Individuals from everywhere – Hong Kong, America, Taiwan, Kuala Lumpur. . . . We've just sold to the Acting Governor of the

132

Falkland Islands. All day we're receiving faxes from all over the world. We sold to people in America and Spain. The High Trade Commission of Hong Kong have just moved here. So it's quite exciting really!

Given the lack of knowledge among these global investors about the different locales within the Isle of Dogs where most of the Docklands development had so far taken place this estate agent had to point them in the 'right' direction. The 'unattractive' council housing estates on the Isle of Dogs and white working-class hostility to 'newcomers' could deter these high-spending customers. The estate agent explains that clients are warned to avoid the council estates:

> There's one area where – I must admit . . . when I give people a map I say: 'These are the areas [to avoid]' and I 'X' off the council areas because they are not going to buy there anyway so they don't want to wander around these places.

Some long-established public houses were safe for the newcomers to visit and clients were encouraged to mix with 'East Enders' who were, in general, 'very friendly':

> we encourage people to go locally and we give people lists of places to go and the names of the publicans and where they can eat . . . I love the East Enders: they're absolutely great. They're very friendly. They're very like the North of England people . . . I lived in the North for several years. The typical Londoner, to me, is not friendly. Nobody speaks to you on the tube or bus . . . [The East Enders have] had a tough time with all this building going on [but] . . . I think now they've realized they're onto a good thing and the area's improved. . . .But they're lovely people.

This description of the locality and East Enders establishes a number of themes which are underpinned by stereotypical images. Clients should avoid the council estates where East Enders live – it is claimed that they do not want to buy them anyway – but once they come to live in the area they can mix with certain friendly 'locals' in safe meeting places (public houses). Despite the poor image which white working-class East Enders may have acquired, on account of a perceived hostility to newcomers, they are really friendly unlike the 'typical' Londoner. East Enders are even beginning to see how the changes around them can benefit them financially and environmentally as the area 'comes up in the world'. The fundamental harmony between different sections of the 'local community' was asserted at a later stage of the interview when the issue of racism was raised. White hostility to Bangladeshi settlement had helped a Far Right (British National Party) candidate win a local by-election, for example, but this recent political event was dismissed as 'a little bit of a hiccup'.

In another interview with a member of a very large company of surveyors the blend of British 'yuppie' and overseas customers is described as well as Docklands' relationship to the wider London market:

> We're viewing the definitive yuppies. . . . We've people buying from all sorts of cultures and creeds and they can be East Enders. But if we sell to East Enders they will be people who were born in the East End, made their money [or] whatever and have a house in Essex and now want a *pied-à-terre* in London for access to their business. So . . . [we] describe ourselves as the East End's West End.

Old images of the East End which, for example, conjure up a violent past are avoided in his company's bid to attract up-market overseas customers:

> If you try to [use these traditional images] you'd be banging your head against a brick wall because you [would] still have Jack the Ripper in mind for anything that's to do with the East End. The Orientals: the Far Easterners, Malaysians, Singaporians, Hong Kongese are most receptive to Docklands as an idea because they have seen it. Since the rejuvenation of their countries thay can relate to anything modern. Then you have some cultural reasons for wanting to be on water and being high up. But anything old is frowned upon.

British middle-class yuppies, overseas investors and the traditional East Enders may live close to each other but move within their own social worlds. However, the arrival of former East Enders who have 'made good' has brought about some of the social integration which all estate agents wished to emphasize:

> If you go down Westferry Road and on to Manchester Road . . . you've got all the new developments next to the [River] Thames. [When] you come across the road you've got all the yuppies living there or whatever you call them these days. Then you've got local people who have lived in council places for years and years on that side of the road. I think in the 1980s when the yuppies started moving in it was separated and *they* did not want to cross to *that* side and *they* did not want to cross to *that* side. Now . . . East End people [are] moving on to the island [Isle of Dogs] into the new developments which I think is helping integrate people because they know [local] people.

In both interviews the estate agents make scant references to Bangladeshi settlement in the locality despite invitations to do so. They do not deal with Bangladeshi clients and they take little or no interest in the issues facing Bangladeshis and other ethnic minority groups in the borough. They appear to know more about white working-class residents, regarding them as the 'real' East Enders and having more sympathy for their interests. Bangladeshis might be part of the global labour market but these estate agents

134

operated within a wealthy niche of this market at a local level where working-class Bangladeshi needs are not their concern.

Spitalfields

Spitalfields, for over two hundred years, had received new settlers from overseas. The Georgian houses built by Protestant Huguenot silk weavers were occupied by Irish and Jewish settlers in the nineteenth century and were now close to the heart of the Bangladeshi community. Brick Lane had acquired a reputation as an alternative tourism centre as the more 'adventurous' visitor who was drawn by its ethnic mix of leather and textile shops, cafés and restaurants. Spitalfields' role as a major industrial and commercial centre has been steadily eroded by the demand from the City of London for office and up-market business space and by the gentrification of the Huguenot houses in the conservation area of central Spitalfields. The closure of two large sites in the ward – the Truman's Brewery and the Spitalfields Fruit and Vegetable Market – increased local fears of massive redevelopment by City property corporations. The collapse of the property market in the late 1980s ended the more ambitious plans for the area but estate agents were still able to attract clients willing to gamble on the next upturn in the housing sector.

The area had long been associated with East End stereotypes of violence and strangers. The 'Jack the Ripper' murders of the 1880s constitute one of the most important elements in this mythology and contemporary walking tours capitalize on this aspect of the locality's 'heritage'. Violence could be presented in ways which did not deter the visitor, as a local estate agent explained:

> You've got to keep a bit of the original Jack the Ripper territory because, obviously, that's a great big pulling point for the tourists around here. It was around Spitalfields that a lot of the supposed murders took place . . . So you've got to keep that otherwise you'll lose what was the City, the East End of London and what people remember of it. If you talk to Americans all they think of is: 'Have you got the fog?' and 'Where's Jack the Ripper?' and 'Isn't this quaint?' and they're the sort of people that want to see these Georgian buildings.

Danger was to be made safe in a package which directed the visitor's gaze to the famous historic buildings redolent with urban 'tradition':

> When you are selling things residential I think people are actually harking back to what used to happen years ago. . . . Things like Christ Church, Spitalfields . . . the weavers' silk lots in the Huguenot houses and . . . down Brick Lane they've opened up an old music hall, a typical East End old music hall. So I think a lot of people like the old

traditional things . . . but they want it brought back to them in a clean, nice, packaged way.

The reference to 'a typical East End old music hall' is interesting because it was only recently established in the former Truman's Brewery and caused a certain amount of scandal among the leaders of the nearby Brick Lane mosque (housed in a former synagogue which was originally a Huguenot church). Publicity for the music hall conveyed an image of a rumbustious working-class East End:

An evening of rare rapport and sophisticated sauciness awaits discerning pleasure seekers . . .

Escape from reality into a world of abandoned frivolity, scrumptious suppers and bargain beverages.

Each week will bring named artists at prices only we can afford, complementing the musical director, our master of ceremonies, a bewitching bevvy of beauties – and the legendary Dockyard Doris.

Dine before the show. A scrumptious three-course dinner served each evening.

Latkas a speciality.

Popular media images of an Edwardian era when different classes rubbed shoulders in an atmosphere of raunchy fun (partly modelled, it seems, on the television music hall series, *The Good Old Days*) are combined with more local evocations of the docklands and Jewish heritage (*latkas* are potato cakes). Former East Enders and American Jewish tourists could enjoy a pleasurable nostalgia with Dockyard Doris, a drag act.

Understandably tensions were generated by conflicting local and more global interests concerning developments within Spitalfields. The estate agent emphasizes the lack of conflict between the wealthy newcomers and the working-class white and Bangladeshi residents but he acknowledges a sharp division based on class:

You're going to have two distinct situations – them and us – with the new people coming in . . . whether you're going to get them mixing I doubt it somehow, unfortunately. At the end of the day it's the same old class situation which we're never going to get rid of.

OLD AND NEW IMAGES IN A CONTEXT OF SOCIAL AND POLITICAL CHANGE

The previous section has described the imaging of urban space in two areas – Docklands and Spitalfields. In the first area a new identity has been constructed as part of a major redevelopment financed by national, public investment and private finance from national and global corporations. Businesses within the service sector and members of the new service class have received considerable financial inducements to settle in the area made safe partly by a process of image construction where dangerous stereotypes about an old, hostile, working-class East End are associated with a distant past. Stereotypes of friendly 'East Enders' evade the conflicts along the fissures of race and class. The heritage of buildings and community spirit are linked to images of a bright, new Docklands where natural resources (water) forge a link between the past, present and future. The changed environment can be used to establish a global identity for the area so that investors across the world can be encouraged to buy property here rather than in those cities which are London's global competitors.

Redevelopment in Spitalfields focused even more closely on heritage and conservation. Once again images of an old, dangerous locality were reworked to fit a portrait of a lively East End where wealthy settlers and tourists could be safe. At the same time there was an acknowledgement that in an area of considerable poverty and a large Bangladeshi population the divisions of class and race could not be erased by even the most careful marketing of an urban landscape.

The visions of locality by LDDC publicity agents and such gatekeepers to property as estate agents clearly do not conceal traditional cleavages, but neither do they present an illusory picture of the new social groupings which are emerging in Docklands and Spitalfields. The changes brought about by 'redevelopment' have had major implications for the social and political life of the borough and both publicity and estate agents provide particular insights into the interpretations by powerful groups of local people as to what is happening and how those interpretations might shape other people's perceptions of those changes. They reveal a highly mobile elite of global investors and senior managers of global and national corporations briefly visiting offices in the area as well as those 'yuppies' and others within the 'new service class' who are beginning to make a more permanent social investment in Tower Hamlets.

These newcomers may well be contributing to the growing indeterminacy of social allegiances described by Albrow but they do so in a context where traditional social and political relations have been disrupted and marginalized by central government intervention. A political disjuncture between the LDDC and the local authority has been paralleled by a social disjuncture which has reproduced – albeit in new, more variegated and globalized forms – the sharp inequalities of wealth which have long been displayed in this part of London (see Crilley *et al.* 1991). These disjunctures are created by developments which extend to the level of the nation-state as well as far beyond the boundaries of this particular country. At the same time we can also see the crucial part played by publicists and estate agents in maintaining those disjunctures through specific promotions of Docklands and Spitalfields and everyday transactions with those who want to invest, work and live in re-imagined localities.

LOCAL ASSERTIONS OF BELONGING

In the publicity discussed above very little space is created for the diverse voices of working-class residents. A general impression is created of an area which was socially and economically deprived before 'redevelopment'. What does not emerge within this picture are the counter-claims to urban space constructed by diverse sections of those relying largely on manual work jobs and small business. Alternative plans for the development of the area (see Brownhill 1990; Colenutt 1991) are ignored or demeaned. The direction of public resources into areas which promoted the interests of the new service class and global corporations are seen as an inevitable aspect of a national strategy to compete with other post-industrial countries across the world.

Several studies have recently analysed the reaction of the white working class to developments in 'Docklands' (Foster 1993; Cohen *et al.* 1994; Cohen 1995). A central theme in those analyses is the varied reaction to the gradual increase of Bangladeshi residents within the area. Conflict particularly revolved around scarce public resources, especially council housing. The local and national press gave extensive coverage to incidents of racial violence and to the ways in which local political activists, especially those within the British National Party, benefited electorally from white working-class disaffection.

A key theme in these events is the assertion – by some people at least – that the locality belonged to them and others like them rather than to 'immigrants'. However, since the late 1970s, if not earlier, Bangladeshis have publicly maintained their right to live in Tower Hamlets, to share in and contribute to its resources and to participate in its political life.

As part of a global labour migration process which included the oil-rich Gulf States, the first generation of Bangladeshis had settled in the borough during the 1960s and 1970s. According to the 1991 Census they constituted almost a quarter of the borough's population (36,926 of 161,042) – by far the largest concentration of Bangladeshis within Britain. In the wards adjoining the City of London their presence was far more commanding and they formed the majority of Spitalfields' residents (see Table 8.1). The first generation had worked in the borough's garment industry, cafés, restaurants, small shops and hospitals and was now joined by a second and a third generation. These younger inhabitants had made a significant impact on the local political structure, local administrative services and the educational system (see Adams 1987; Eade 1989, 1990, 1993; Forman 1989; Gardner and Shukur 1995). The youth clubs, cultural centres, prayer halls, traditional educational centres, mosques and political rallies were visible markers of to the contribution which these three generations were making to the localities within which they lived.

During the 1980s members of the second generation, in particular, entered the local political and community organizational arena to challenge

Table 8.1 Bangladeshi population in Tower Hamlets by ward, 1991

Ward	Bangladeshi total	Total pop.	Bangladeshi (% of total pop.)
Blackwell	875	4780	18
Bow	396	8203	5
Bromley	1572	9632	16
East India	541	6881	8
Grove	297	5182	6
Holy Trinity	2269	9410	24
Lansbury	753	8383	9
Limehouse	1683	8476	20
Millwall	1082	13771	8
Park	201	5302	4
Redcoat	1559	6571	24
St Dunstan's	3757	10015	38
St James	721	5940	12
St Katharine's	4824	13807	35
St Mary's	2351	5659	42
St Peter's	2383	10360	23
Shadwell	3565	10038	36
Spitalfields	5379	8861	61
Weavers	2718	9771	28
Total	36926	161042	23%

Source: OPCS (1993)

exclusivist versions of local belonging which defined themselves and other Bangladeshis as inherently 'Other'. In their constructions of locality they looked far beyond Tower Hamlets and Britain to their country of origin and to a variety of social groupings. While some employed the language of socialism and class struggle in their alliance with white left-wing activists, they could also engage with other Bangladeshis across Britain, in Bangladesh and areas of the globe where solidarities could be constructed around kinship, village, language, religion and race, for example. After the Labour Party's defeat in the 1986 borough elections and the demise of the GLC and ILEA there was greater room in the borough's political arena for the expression of highly localized links with the country of origin as well as global visions of an Islamic community (*umma*). Issues raised during *The Satanic Verses* controversy and the Gulf War could be related by Muslim activists to local Bangladeshi concerns about religious facilities and other resources where public authorities played a key role (see Eade 1992, 1993).

These developments can be interpreted as further evidence of 'disembedding' and delocalization. Political and social events were lifted out of their particular context and became the topic of debate and action in various parts of the globe (Gardner 1994). People could imagine themselves as members of communities which spanned the globe and transcended nation-state boundaries and nationalist formulations of belonging. The rootedness of place became more questionable as people became aware of the wider range of imaginary worlds available and the possibilities of moving across social and political boundaries.

The ways in which some second-generation Bangladeshis were engaging in these new worlds can be gleaned from a pilot study undertaken during 1993 among twenty second-generation Bangladeshis in higher education (Centre for Bangladeshi Studies 1994). For the purposes of this chapter I refer to accounts which focus on locality and the wider world and which were usually raised in the section on identity. The questions invite respondents to consider the meaning for them of such local categories as East Ender, Cockney and Londoner. Before these questions, however, they discussed more general identities – working class, British, Bengali, Bangladeshi and Muslim. Other categories which could be located within local or more global contexts were gender, class, black and Asian.

The explorations of locality reveal a variety of interpretations which problematize and look beyond conventional political and social boundaries. Let us look at the most localized set of identifications first. In response to the questions about his identification with the terms 'East Ender' and 'Cockney' Rahim replied:

> I am an East Ender. I used to have more of a Cockney accent before I came to this college. My Cockney accent was really strong like in *East-Enders* . . . [I wouldn't] describe myself as a Cockney any more. The Cockney is somebody who is fixed with that dialect and I am not an English person who has been living in this country so I can't really be a Cockney. . . . Yes, I am an East Ender. Although I am an East Ender I don't act like an East Ender. All my friends are not in the East End.

Here Rahim defines 'Cockney' in terms of accent and explains that he used to be Cockney because of the way he spoke before going to college. However, as he continues his explanation he introduces the concept of authenticity through his description of the true or 'original' Cockney who, unlike him, is 'an English person who has [always] been living in this country'. He is also prepared to describe himself as an 'East Ender' – presumably because he was brought up in Tower Hamlets – but he concludes that he is also no longer a true East Ender because he has moved on; his social relations have been made with people outside the area.

Rahim's belief that the terms 'Cockney' and 'East Ender' may have originally applied to him is interesting because many white working-class residents appropriated the terms to themselves. The racialization of the boundary between white East Enders and others may have been implicit in Rahim's references to 'original' Cockneys. The everyday experience of moving through a locality where white people resented the presence of a culturally different group and regarded themselves as the 'real' locals is powerfully described by Fatima:

> As a child I remember in the area I lived in there used to be more white people around; not in our particular street but streets adjacent to us. And they used to be quite abusive – swearing, taunting us because we always start our Islamic studies early on. . . . And we used to go to mosques and we wear the *hijab*[2] . . . they would pull our scarf off (the local kids) and they would jeer at us . . . most English families breed dogs and they did let the dog yelp at you . . . the bark is more frightening than the actual bite . . . But I think once past the age of 9, 10 I would be answering back so once you start answering back people are less keen to start on you . . . I have always been fortunate in the sense that I have lived in an area with so many Bengali people around me. The community was so strong that anybody else – like white or black people – they were the outsiders.

Fatima reveals here an intimate identification with a locality which is dominated by her own 'community' and as she grows up in the area she becomes ready to challenge those who do not consider her to belong.

The way in which a sense of being part of a local 'working class' was expressed in status differentials based on education, wealth, occupation, accent and dress was reflected in several of the young Bangladeshis' discussions:

> At the moment I would describe myself as working class – right at the bottom of the ladder. Well if you take the advertising classifications – A1, A2, C2 and all this – I've got no money so I must be at the bottom. The class issue has been talked about since the year dot in this country. It is still here. . . . It is because of where I live, because of how rich I am. . . . If I manage to get a good degree, get a job, I think I will always think of myself as working class but maybe I won't be so impoverished.

Here Kadir explains the way in which class is popularly associated with money, education and jobs, but also how educational achievement does not necessarily change an individual's self-definition as being 'working class'. This issue of social mobility and personal identity is taken further by Rupna:

> I would say I was between classes . . . I come from a not very educated background and in my life I have tried to educate myself so I can become something my parents aren't. So I would say I am in a mobile state. If I got a job as a teacher it would mean that I would be in a very different class from my parents . . . I would say that class is more associated to employment now although for a lot of people it is very much part of their cultural identity. . . . People living in the East End

would consider themselves a certain class . . . it is [a] working-class environment.

Rupna stakes a claim to being 'working class' but Azad warns that white people may not accept Bangladeshis as 'real' members of a British class society:

I don't believe in class but this society would class me as working class. . . . If you talk about class then in a sense I am moving up the stage from working class to middle class. But I will never . . . be middle class in this society. . . . On the streets you are still mainly Asian or Pakki. Class has got no say in it.

This response showed the importance of the Bengali/Bangladeshi background of informants and the ways in which they looked beyond national boundaries in order to make sense of their place within Britain. Being socially and culturally different from white British who frequently racialized differences between them encouraged some to identify with others who were 'black' as Naima explains:

I am a British citizen. It is to do with having certain rights in this country and I have lived here for so long. I don't think I could live in Bangladesh although I keep on going on about my loyalties and affiliations . . . I don't really identify with white British people but I identify with people who are black and British. There are a lot of us now. About three million . . . I don't feel nationalistic about being British . . . it is just another aspect of my identity.

While most respondents attached considerable importance to the relationship between their social identity and place some wished to minimize the significance of location. Noor explained that:

'British' just means location. Where I am. And 'Londoner' basically is also a place. The 'East End' is a place. It is just sort of describing where you are from, what part of the world. I don't think it would be any different if I was somewhere else in the world. It is not that I think these questions are difficult – it is just that I don't really think about me as a Bangladeshi or where I am from because I sort of go anywhere and I suppose if I went to . . . [the] States and lived there I think I would be a New Yorker or whatever. It doesn't really mean anything to me.

Mujib asserted his lack of interest in nostalgic or patriotic attachments to a particular place:

I don't have any romantic ideas about place. I wouldn't say I was a patriotic person. Even though I identify very strongly with being Bengali I don't think it has anything to do with countries. It is to do with culture and the people at the time, not a place. So it is about where I am at the moment and who I am living with.

The reflections of these highly educated individuals are not presented here as 'representative' of a community or even a particular generation. Their educational attainments and career prospects awareness were exceptional compared with the attainments of the political activists from the same generation, for instance. Nevertheless, their reflections on various social allegiances are illuminating both in their conformity to well-established narratives and their exploration of movement and possibilities. They are keenly aware of linguistic, racial, class and national boundaries and how these can combine to form a highly localized set of allegiances which exclude them. Yet some are also eager to stake their claims to locality where an identification with Islam and Bengali community plays a central role. Locality is here reinterpreted through discourses and practices which refer to imaginary communities far beyond Tower Hamlets and nation-state frontiers. The exploration of new combinations and possibilities also leads to the breaking of the conventional association between Britishness and nationalism as well as the rejection of romantic attachments to particular places and an openness to future movement around the globe, i.e. migration to the United States.

GLOBALIZATION AND THE RECONSTRUCTION OF LOCALITIES

I have focused in this chapter on the ideological reconstruction of certain localities within London where the economic impact of global capitalism is strikingly evident. How do the issues raised here relate to the interpretations of globalization offered in other chapters in this volume and elsewhere?

In some respects Docklands and Spitalfields resemble Roehampton where Darren O'Byrne locates his discussion. All three localities are occupied by residents who express a fierce attachment to a long-established working-class culture and exclude newcomers who do not accommodate their constructions of local social and political history. Bangladeshi settlers have 'learned to be local' and their community activists have played a crucial role in competing for resources in the local political arena. Yet beyond these superficial similarities a more complex picture emerges in East London. The Bangladeshi political representatives operate across more than one political arena drawing on links which transcend British national boundaries. Bangladeshis outside politics are also highly aware of the manifold possibilities provided by the diverse links which require new understandings of the localities within which they have grown up.

143

The perceptions of the highly educated Bangladeshis provide us with 'empirical possibilities' which indicate ways in which localities are being globalized across London. Their reflections draw on a history of migration and associations with others which problematize any notion of a local, homogeneous working-class culture. Attempts to forge an unbending link between local and national cultural formations are also contested as associations between nationalism and citizenship are challenged and identifications with places demystified.

These understandings of locality appear to complement those discussed by Martin Albrow in Tooting – an impression strengthened by the contrast between these interpretations and the images developed by LDDC publicists and local estate agents for other settlers, i.e. City of London corporations, global investors and the new service class. Different scapes have been created as these localities have become increasingly economically, socially and culturally both heterogeneous and highly fragmented. Despite the sharp disparities in wealth which have emerged in London's East End this heterogeneity has so far produced a situation where unequal social actors have looked past each other and kept their (social) distance. Conflict has usually occurred around a racialized boundary between working-class whites and their Bangladeshi neighbours. The globalization of locality in Docklands and Spitalfields has not produced a new politics of place where social and cultural differences can be accommodated within a strategy of local working-class resistance.

The racialization of local and national political discourses has played a major part in preventing a new politics of place emerging. However, I want to suggest that the diverse constructions described in this chapter indicate the presence of perspectival disjunctures which have not been adequately understood by those operating within the local and national political arenas. The disjunctures between scapes have been reinforced by (consciously created and sustained) economic, social and political disjunctures which transcend national frontiers. Those wanting to sell the 'locality' to global newcomers both operate within and sustain those disjunctures as they conjure up a bright new world where the traditional working class is relegated to a shadowy, sometimes dangerous, sometimes bucolic role. Bangladeshis also show signs of operating within different social, cultural and political worlds, but they also engage in the process of translating between different discourses. As they move across ideological boundaries they reinterpret their localities through global connections and problematize conventional understandings of place. In their awareness of possibility and movement they indicate the kind of detachment from a nostalgic, essentialized notion of locality which is required for the development of a politics of resistance which can actually confront the forces beyond the existing local political arena.

ACKNOWLEDGEMENTS

I would like to thank Darren O'Byrne, Neil Washbourne and other colleagues in the Globalization Research Cluster at the Roehampton Institute as well as Chris Mele (University of North Carolina at Wilmington) for their help in preparing this Chapter.

Permission has also been given by B. Blackwell for the extract from D. Harvey (1989), *The Condition of Postmodernity*.

NOTES

1 This chapter is a revised version of a paper given at the British Sociological Association conference, University of Leicester, 10–13 April 1995.
2 *Hijab*: loose fitting outer garment which almost totally covers the body.

9

IDENTITY, NATION AND RELIGION

Educated young Bangladeshi Muslims in London's East End[1]

John Eade

INTRODUCTION

In the previous chapter I introduced a number of young educated Bangladeshis who live in an area of London which dramatically reveals the disjunctures of the global cultural economy. Here I want to examine further their responses to other questions in the survey which invited them to explore different social and cultural identities and the ways in which these identities might be connected. Through a description of their varied responses we can both deepen our understanding of how people's perceptions relate to the general discussion of globalization developed within this volume and challenge the lingering influence of traditional sociological assumptions concerning the relationship between individual perceptions and group solidarities.

During the last decade social scientists have become increasingly interested in issues of social identity. Their interest can be partly explained in the context of Western political developments where national solidarities established after the Second World War have been challenged. The emergence of ethnic revival movements in many West European countries, the dramatic resurgence of ethnic assertions in Eastern Europe, the former USSR and Yugoslavia and the elaboration of ethnic and racial solidarities within the USA are some of the areas where the issues of social identity and group boundaries have become heavily politicized in the arenas of both rhetoric and policy making.

In the United Kingdom considerable attention has been paid to the development of a populist national rhetoric by the New Right during the 1980s and the heyday of 'Thatcherism' (see Barker 1981; Gilroy 1987, 1990). Furthermore, several commentators have analysed the way in which such rhetoric marginalized 'immigrants' and their descendants through the racialization of ethnic differences between the white majority and black and

Asian citizens (see Reeves 1983; Miles 1988; Solomos 1989; Hall 1992a; Anthias 1990).

These racialized constructions of national belonging have been challenged by young black British artists who have contributed to a politics of cultural representation which celebrates difference through the construction of new ethnic identities (see Hall 1992a: 257). New ethnicities point to a liminal third space – the boundary between the opposites of insider/ outsider – where counter–narratives of belonging can be formulated (see Bhabha 1990: 300–15; Feuchtwang 1992: 1–13). Through these new ethnicities hybrid identities can be constructed as 'black British' citizens in Britain, for example, establish imaginative ties with a diasporic culture linking black people to the Caribbean, Africa and Asia (Hall 1992b: 258; see also Gilroy 1987; Bhabha 1990; Cambridge 1992).

The politics of cultural difference and the process of identity construction are not confined to Britain's ethnic minorities, however. As national belongings in the West are challenged by local and more global imaginings of community the assertions of a 'British', 'English', 'French' or 'Belgian' cultural hegemony become more tenuous – the rhetoric of national unity notwithstanding. Nationalist discourses construct 'imagined communities' (see Anderson 1983) but these discourses are riven by the ambivalences of referring to a mythic past while recognizing the modernity of the nation-state and civil society (see Bhabha 1990: 1). Moreover, the changing social and cultural character of those communities belies the tendency towards constructing an essential unity rooted in the past (see Eade 1992).

In these constructions of belonging the various and sometimes competing claims of nationalism and religion have been highlighted. Contributors to public debates during *The Satanic Verses* affair and the Gulf War, for example, have discussed the loyalties of Britain's Muslim settlers to Britain, to their countries of origin and to their fellow Muslims across the world. Since the majority of British Muslims hail from South Asia any consideration of these loyalties must examine the influence of political struggles, economic developments and cultural dynamics in the Indian sub-continent (see Modood 1988; Eade 1990; Werbner 1991; Gardner 1992). British Muslim constructions of identity challenge, therefore, narrow definitions of the 'black experience' (see Modood 1988). They also contribute to the recent rethinking of cultural processes which confronts essentialist and reductionist interpretations of community evident in many popular and academic discussions of the British, the Muslim community and black people.

The development of new ethnicities, hybridity and diasporic communities can be understood within the context of the disjunctive order of a global cultural economy (Appadurai 1990: 296) where individuals are engaged in the construction of multiple 'imagined worlds' around the globe which can challenge the definitions and practices of political and

147

economic elites (ibid.: 297). Of the various 'imagined worlds' suggested by Appadurai the most relevant for an analysis of hybridity and new ethnicities is the 'ethnoscape': 'a landscape of persons who constitute the shifting world in which we live: tourists, immigrants, refugees, exiles, guestworkers and other moving groups' (ibid.).

While the general discussions of the global cultural economy cast fresh light on traditional sociological debates concerning social solidarity they still operate within an assumption that individual perceptions are intimately associated with those individuals' membership of social groups. Appadurai, for example, still remains convinced that individual perspectives can be analysed in the context of stable social networks and communities. Appadurai still operates within a model of inter-group relations which has dominated the analysis of ethnic minorities in Britain (cf. Watson 1977; Werbner and Anwar 1991; Ballard 1994; Lewis 1994) and which usually assumes a socio-cultural foundation created by family, kinship and religious ties (see Eade 1996). We have already challenged this approach towards individual perceptions in previous chapters and I want here to substantiate our critique by exploring further the views of the young Bangladeshis who were introduced in the previous chapter.

Furthermore, while the analyses of different scapes, hybridity and new ethnicities have encouraged recent rethinking of essentialist formulations they have not produced much detailed substantive information about how the different 'imagined worlds' are constructed by individuals in local situations. In the following case study we also have an opportunity to enter the imaginations and discourse of 'ordinary' people who inhabit and construct 'ethnoscapes' – the sons and daughters of 'immigrants' within Britain – and, in the process, see more clearly how they interpret group identities.

As yet there are very few detailed accounts of how 'ordinary' young black and Asian Britons engage in identity construction (see Eade 1990; Samad 1992; Back 1993; Alexander 1994). The pilot survey which we undertook in Tower Hamlets during 1992 was limited in the amount of people contacted but was rich in the qualitative information provided. In this chapter we will explore the variety and complexity of the young Bangladeshis' views concerning national, local and religious identities. In the process we are led far beyond the construction of local and national boundaries to consider supra-national loyalties which constitute part of the contemporary global cultural economy and the emergence of new social configurations.

BANGLADESHI SETTLERS IN LONDON'S EAST END

As we have already seen in Chapter 8, Bangladeshis constituted a substantial proportion of Tower Hamlets' residents (22.9 per cent). The vast majority of these settlers hail from the district of Sylhet in north-east

Bangladesh. The first generation settled in the UK during the 1960s and the early 1970s. These predominantly male elders were joined by their wives and dependants during the 1980s, although strict controls on immigration have played a large part in slowing the process of community formation (see Carey and Shukur 1985–6; Gardner 1992).

The second generation of Bangladeshis is still heavily reliant on the employment sectors which their elders had entered, i.e. the local garment industry, ethnic retail and wholesale shops, cafés and restaurants. They are confined to predominantly working-class neighbourhoods in a borough whose southern wards have been dramatically transformed by the 'regeneration' of London Docklands. Their relations with white working-class residents are frequently soured by racist incidents as both groups compete for scarce public resources which have been systematically cut back during the last decade.

Since the vast majority are Sunni Muslims of the Hanafi school these community facilities include mosques and other Islamic centres which are financially supported by Muslim countries, viz. Saudi Arabia, Pakistan and Bangladesh itself (see Eade 1993). Ties with Muslim-majority countries have been encouraged by the Islamization of the Bangladeshi nation-state: a process which can challenge secular Bengali discourses emphasizing political and cultural ties between Muslims and non-Muslims (Hindus, Christian and tribal communities). A focus on Islam has also been encouraged by developments within Britain itself through the development of Islamic discourses in political and community arenas which have been partly promoted by international links with organizations based in Muslim (especially Middle Eastern) countries. The national language (standard Bengali) can also be the basis for an identification with those in the Indian state of West Bengal where the Hindu majority has co-existed relatively harmoniously with a small Muslim minority.

In Tower Hamlets the social and economic problems of the 'inner city', compounded by racial discrimination and physical violence, impact most severely upon Bangladeshis. Recent educational statistics suggest that the disadvantages experienced by the Bangladeshi first generation may well be extending into the second and third generation, albeit expressed in different ways. For example, in 1993 while 56 or 64 per cent of the total number of students entering sixth-form classes were Bangladeshis only 31, i.e. 42 per cent of those proceeding to university, were Bangladeshis (Tower Hamlets Careers Service 1994).

THE YOUNG BANGLADESHIS PROJECT

While we do not wish to deny the problems encountered by Bangladeshis in Tower Hamlets one of the intentions of the project (under the auspices of the Centre for Bangladeshi Studies) was to challenge local stereotypes which portrayed young Bangladeshis as alienated failures. The small band of Bangladeshis at university was targeted and twenty (ten male and ten female) were interviewed by Hasina Zaman, a young Bangladeshi female teacher-training student, during the summer of 1992. Hasina was responsible for selecting those whom she would interview and after getting in touch with her friends and acquaintances she moved on to those who were recommended by her initial contacts. The twenty were aged between 18 and 25, most had been born in Bangladesh and were attending (or were entering) university.

Hasina used an interview schedule which we had jointly constructed and which contained seven sections and eighty questions. The interviews were tape recorded and usually an informal atmosphere prevailed where Hasina felt free to explore issues beyond the confines of the interview schedule questions. Informality and openness was facilitated by the social links already established between Hasina and many of her contacts.

The study engages, therefore, in qualitative research where the interviews go far beyond what most quantitative studies achieve in terms of the depth of feeling and the sense of exploration of complicated issues shown by the young Bengalis. The twenty are not 'representative' in a statistical sense, but their deliberations are part of a more general debate among British Bengalis about belonging (see Adams 1987; Eade 1990; Choudhury 1993). The complexity of that debate will become evident as we focus on that section of the interview schedule which deals with a range of social identities – Bangladeshi, Bengali, Muslim, British, English, Londoner, East Ender, Cockney, black and Asian, and those based on class and gender – as well as the issue of racism and recent events, i.e the Salman Rushdie affair and the Gulf War. Given the constraints of this chapter my account will be confined to the deliberations of those interviewed concerning national, local and religious identities.

NATIONAL AND RELIGIOUS CONSTRUCTIONS OF BELONGING

Although all the twenty young informants were either born in Bangladesh or were the offspring of Bangladeshi migrants they frequently chose to describe themselves as Bengalis rather than as Bangladeshis. Lutfur, for example, who was on a chartered engineering programme after completing a degree in chemical engineering at Brunel University, does not see any sharp distinction between the two and claims that people prefer to describe themselves as Bengalis:

A Bengali? Is that different to being Bangladeshi? I don't know. Bengali, Bangladeshi – what is the difference? Being from Bangladesh will be Bengali – it is the same thing, isn't it? Maybe it is that everyone

150

talks about being Bengali in this area. No one says being Bangladeshi. I don't know why – it is just something you have used from when you are small.

Jahanara, who had been accepted to do a pharmacy degree at the London School of Pharmacy, also could not clearly distinguish between Bengali and Bangladeshi but added that:

> I don't use Bangladeshi probably because I believe I am in a British country and I am more towards British than towards Bangladeshi sort of thing. I don't know. I am a person who is very mixed within both cultures – like Bengali and British but more towards Muslim.

These comments explore the complexities associated with moving between two nation-states and not necessarily conforming to essentialist definitions of national belonging. The term Bengali may provide, in the local context of Tower Hamlets, a better basis for describing the situation of having moved from Bangladesh and for no longer being a 'pure' Bangladeshi. Jahanara cannot describe herself as a Bangladeshi because she no longer lives in that country. Yet although she feels pulled between rival national identities she is also aware of the hybrid nature of her cultural identity: she is both 'Bengali and British'. The new social circumstances in which Jahanara lives are not explicable in simplistic terms. Moreover, the sense of being pulled in different directions by competing constructions of social difference is further deepened by Jahanara's introduction of a third social identity – 'Muslim' – which is even more important to her.

When Kadir, who was undertaking a post-graduate diploma at the London Guildhall University after completing an electronics degree at the University of Bath, comes to discuss the Bengali/Bangladeshi distinction he refers to what we had in mind when framing the question, viz. the difference between Bangladesh and the wider cultural region of Bengal incorporating West Bengal (India).

> Bengali? Bangladeshi? Bangladeshi is someone from, obviously, the east – what was East Pakistan – and a Bengali is someone who speaks the language, I assume. Is that right? But then what does that question mean? That is what I would assume but it is a very open question, isn't it? I know a few people from Calcutta and I have spoken to them – they are very friendly.

Kadir begins by firmly locating 'Bangladeshi' within the nation-state and defining 'Bengali' more generally in terms of language, thereby including Bengali-speakers who live outside Bangladesh in India, Britain and the Middle East, for instance. Yet he immediately becomes aware that the question's opennness can raise problems. The specific problem he addresses here is the issue of how Bangladeshis should interact with other

Bengali-speaking people. Kadir's comment that his acquaintances from Calcutta are 'very friendly' appears to refer to the tangled relationship between Bangladesh and its huge neighbour, India. Although he shares with West Bengalis a common language and cultural heritage the relations between Bangladesh and India have been soured in the past by competing interests. One area of tension has focused on religious differences between Muslim-majority Bangladesh and Hindu-majority India and the position of their respective Hindu and Muslim minorities.

The ways in which people's interpretation of the Bangladeshi/Bengali distinction can be shaped by the history of religious conflict is also indicated by Shahjehan, who had completed a law degree at the University of Kent and was currently taking a higher law degree at the University of London. He refers to the history of the Bengal delta introducing the issue of religion once again:

> I see the difference. Bengal is a region of India before it split into East Pakistan, West Pakistan and India. When it split into East Pakistan part of Bengal was incorporated into India . . . when you talk about being a Bengali it has a sort of Hindu connotation to it, you know, because there used to be a lot of Hindu . . . people living in Bangladesh. . . . After it became East Pakistan a lot of Hindu people moved out so Bangladesh has more of a Muslim connotation to it, you know.

Shahjehan clearly believes that the nation-state of Bangladesh and Islam are intimately related. Farida, who had completed a degree in primary education and language at the University of North London also establishes the same connection:

> Well I don't know about other Bangladeshis but I feel being a Bangladeshi I hold my religion . . . my religion is very important whereas other Bengalis their religion isn't. Islamic religion I am talking about. Other Bengalis are, like, Hindus and they don't consider their religious values as highly as I do . . . I wear *shalwar kameez*[2] at home . . . I eat dried fish. These are Bangladeshi things . . . I think Bengalis wear skirts and all those things because I have met a lot of Bengalis and they are not very into their religion. Being a Bangladeshi when I go home I help my mum, cook and everything . . . I consider my mum's opinions all the time. I consider her feelings and how she has to face the community and stuff like that. I wouldn't do anything to put my mum in a difficult situation. I think that's the main difference between being a Bangladeshi and a Bengali.

Farida appears to distinguish between Bangladeshis, i.e. Bengali Muslims, and 'other Bengalis' who are principally Hindus. Yet rather than talk about historical conflicts in the Bengal delta she is mainly concerned in this extract with explaining differences between the two in terms of the interrelationship between religious observances, domestic duties and family loyalties. Bengali Hindus (presumably from India) living in Britain are less religious in the sense of conforming to her notions of respectable dress and domestic responsibilities – a view which has been noted in other studies of British Bengalis in London and northern England (see Khanum 1994; Lakhmana 1995).

For Husna, a social anthropology graduate from the University of Sussex who was working as a youth and community worker in Tower Hamlets, 'Bangladeshi' referred to both Muslims and non-Muslims in her country of origin. Furthermore, Bangladeshis could also identify themselves as 'Bengalis':

> There are minorities in Bangladesh . . . [and] they are obviously Bangladeshi. Some of them might not want to be but they . . . have Bangladeshi nationality . . . I do describe myself as Bengali because to say Bangladeshi sometimes – it depends on the situation – . . . can be a bit separatist.

Husna appears to see a certain situational advantage in using the term 'Bengali': when she does not want to appear 'separatist', for instance. She may be thinking here of circumstances where she meets those in Britain who have come from Hindu or other minority backgrounds in Bangladesh as well as Hindus who hail from West Bengal.

Another twist to the discussion was added by Faud, an economics student at Staffordshire University, who distinguishes between Sylheti and Bengali and reflects a widespread attachment to the specific area of Bangladesh from which most British Bangladeshis/Bengalis have come:

> I see a difference . . . there is Sylheti and Bengali . . . I'd say Sylheti [is] to do with region. I use the Bangladeshi culture. I am a Sylheti not a Bengali in terms of region. I don't see myself as a Bengali. As a Bangladeshi, yes.

These deliberations reveal differing perceptions of the interdependence between national, regional and religious constructions of belonging, reflecting perhaps a range of opinions among British Bangladeshis generally about these various identities. These young people's understanding of what it means to belong to a nation-state is clearly shaped by political debates and practices in their country of origin, especially those which establish an association between a national (Bengali) culture and Islam. At the same time they engage in national constructions of belonging to Britain and reflect on their experience as Bangladeshis, Bengali and Muslims in a nation-state where they constitute a minority.

PRIORITIZING PARTICULAR IDENTITIES

Despite our attempt to encourage the young Bengalis to consider each identity in turn the extracts above reveal a tendency to bring them together into a composite identity and to discuss their interrelationships. There is also a tendency to rank the identities within a single scale. Jabida, for example, who was going to study political science at the London School of Economics (LSE), describes the relationship between Muslim, Bengali and British identities in the following terms:

> if you had to go on a one to ten scale of who you are, what you are, it comes Muslim, Bengali and then British and then whatever the things that make me up. If you take the top two away that wouldn't be me. If you take the British bit away I think that would still be me. Is that what you mean? . . . But Bangladeshi is the full thing . . . if I was just talking to somebody I would say: 'Yes, I am Bengali'. . . . To somebody who doesn't really know anything about Bangladesh I'd say: 'Yes, I am Bangladeshi. Because we had a war. Because I identify . . . with Bangladesh. Because my parents come from there.' . . . Even though [my culture] is more associated with Indian culture I still see it as Bangladeshi more. I don't see myself as Pakistani. No way . . . because [Pakistanis] look down on Bangladeshis. . . . Maybe I am at the bottom of the heap but I don't really conform to what you see me as. Because you are Bangladeshi you don't have to be a stereotype.

In this lengthy quote Jabida moves imaginatively between South Asia and Britain and draws the various categories together into a composite of levels. She prioritizes her Bangladeshi and Muslim identities over British and other collective constructions. Jabida is eager to tell people who do not know about the origins of Bangladesh how the nation-state was created (after the 1971 war of independence) and she draws on her own family history (her parents migrated from Bangladesh). However, she moves on to locate herself within contemporary Britain and the similarities and differences between herself and those from other ethnic minority backgrounds. Another relationship is established – between 'Indian culture' and Bangladeshis – as well as another unequal division – between British Pakistanis and Bangladeshis. She concludes by suggesting that Bangladeshis are considered inferior (economically perhaps) by British Pakistanis but she refuses to be included in the stereotype, possibly on account of her education.

We have already seen the importance which some of the respondents attach to Islam and their desire to rank Muslim identity over others. Amina, who was studying social policy and administration again at the LSE, begins with constructing a composite identity but immediately asserts the priority of her religious identity over the other identities:

154

. . . if I was to describe myself I would say I am British Bengali Muslim, if you like, but my religion is more important to me than my culture at the end of the day.

Jahanara also supports the prior claims of Islam over other (political and cultural) identities:

If somebody comes up to me and says: 'What are you?' First I would say: 'A Muslim.' Then I would say my national identity because I personally believe, yes, we are British. I am British. I believe I am British because I was – I haven't been born in this country [and am] not necessarily going to stay the rest of my life in this country, but I believe that I am British. Yet I believe in my own identity as Muslim and as a Bengali because once a person has their own identity, their own history, their own family history and everything, they can be a firm person. And their old culture or background, as long as it doesn't contradict towards Islam, they can become [a strong person].

The firm grounding of individual personality is dependent here on a composite social identity where Islam holds pride of place and cultural traditions do not contradict Islamic injunctions. This grounding enables Jahanara to contemplate with equanimity a future where she may remain in Britain or migrate elsewhere.

However, there was no consensus even among this very small number of informants concerning the place of Islam within their lives. Some refused to identify with Islam and preferred to describe themselves in secular nationalist terms although they did not find their position an easy one to explain. Husna responds to the question 'Are you a Muslim?' in the following terms:

Muslim? I have just had an argument with someone about that and I am really confused now. I kept on telling them I was an atheist and they kept on telling me: 'Well, actually you are a Muslim.' I don't know. I don't describe myself as a Muslim. I've described myself to you as Bangladeshi, feeling British, etc., but thoughout my whole interview I have never mentioned the word 'Muslim'. . . . When I talk about Bangladesh I would have mentioned that because that's what a lot of people say about Bangladesh – they say it is a Muslim country. . . . I don't see myself as a Muslim but other people do see me as a Muslim.

This extract poignantly expresses the tensions between an individual's self-definition and the categories used by others to define that particular individual. Husna refuses to identify herself as a Muslim but she is so identified by others presumably on the grounds that she comes from a Muslim family, bears a Muslim name and has ancestral origins within a predominantly Muslim country.

Those who prioritize Islam above all other social identities are sometimes attracted by the idea of an Islamic state and the prospect of living in Muslim countries where Islamic law (*sharia*) prevails. In response to the question: 'Where would you say that you belonged?' some begin by considering the claims of their country of origin but then proceed to discuss the merits of other Muslim countries. Jahanara explains her position in the following terms:

> The answer might not necessarily be Bangladesh. But yes, as I said, I do have a tendency for my mother land. But I would say that and Islam which is . . . the land which became Muslim. . . . I would say a Muslim country where probably the law of *sharia* is established . . . that country is where I belong more than anywhere else. Most of all I feel I might belong more towards Bangladesh because my relatives and everybody is there and my family history is back there.

Others identify with an Islamic community which is not confined within national boundaries. Kadir, for example, refers to his identification with an 'Islamic community as a whole – not just here, everywhere'. Hassan, who was going to study law at the Guildhall University, also identifies with an Islamic community which he describes as a nation:

> In Islam, you see, it does not matter where you come from . . . all Muslims are one *umma* – that means one nation. But I was born in that particular area so I say I come from that area. It doesn't mean I am separated from all the Muslims.

The demands of secular nation-states are transcended, therefore, by an Islamic nation or *umma* whose unity rests, one may surmise, on an Islamic way of life guided by *sharia*.

BRITISH AND RELATED IDENTITIES

The accounts which have been quoted so far make several references to British identity. The interviewees' identification with Britain was raised in a specific question after the discussion of Bangladeshi and Bengali solidarities. The question asked whether they would describe themselves as (a) British, (b) English, (c) Londoner/East Ender/Cockney. Most people embrace the term 'British' but reject 'English' because of its associations with white people and notions of indigenous culture.

The young Bengalis frequently define themselves as British by virtue of citizenship. Azad, for example, who was training as a youth and community worker at Goldsmiths' College, University of London, claims that:

> 'British' I use when I am applying for jobs or applications, or whatever, because my status is a British citizen. I also put a stroke in and put

156

'British/Bengali' so people know that I am not an original British person and I have got an identity as a Bengali.

Azad introduces here the tradition of defining nationalist belonging in terms of origins. This tradition is relativized by his insistence on his composite, hybrid identity (British/Bengali) which co-exists with other people's 'original' (possibly primordialist) construction of national belonging.

Faud also defines his British identity in terms of citizenship and makes a sharp distinction between British and English:

British because I am a British citizen. No matter what the whites say, I am British. Not English but British.

The refusal to identify with the term 'English' appeared to be bound up with assumptions about 'race'. Amina, for example, explains that:

I'm British and a Londoner . . . I don't know why, I just feel to be British you don't actually have to be white. But to be English I always have this feeling you have to be white . . . British people are not necessarily English . . . but to be English you have to be white. The English, I think, would agree although they probably wouldn't say it directly.

Jabida is aware that being British could also be appropriated by white exclusivists:

I have got a British passport. . . . You know, when you think of British sometimes you think somebody who sort of goes about with a Union Jack. You would think that they were really racist in a way but I think it is . . . sometimes dangerous to think they are really racist because . . . they are asserting their British culture . . . they have this thing about being really free and getting loads of communities in and there isn't this caste system at all . . . I would say: 'Yes. British descendant but not British to the bones.'

The experience of racism in Britain is discussed in other sections of the interviews and has clearly encouraged these young Bengalis to be wary of white outsiders. However, Jabida does not see herself as belonging to her country of origin and was even prepared to be proud of Britain – with reservations:

I would be stupid to say Bangladesh because I am not growing up there . . . I can be proud of being British being that I came over from Bangladesh and I did it. Like, I made the best of it, you know. . . . Some people ask me questions about identity – I don't find it really simple. I could say I am Bengali and Muslim and British and all of that but it is really hard because at the end of the day you are enjoying all these things you never have in Bangladesh. . . . I would be lying if I said

157

I am not proud of being in this country but sometimes I think: 'I wish they hadn't fucked up all of us.' Otherwise we would have been this really proud country . . . and we wouldn't have this stupid thing called the Third World and all of that.

The impact of racial discrimination encourages some to identify closely with other black people in Britain. Husna describes herself as a British citizen and rejects the idea of living in Bangladesh but adds:

I don't really identify with white British people but I identify with people who are black and British. There are . . . about three million black British people [now] and I think it is important to accept that there are people who were born in this country and this is all they know . . . I am not English . . . I am not white. I am not European. I've got no European heritage.

A few are insistent that they do not regard any of these terms as applying to them. Salma, a medical student at the Royal London Hospital in Tower Hamlets, looks towards her country of origin and religion:

Which one? I don't think of myself coming from a particular part [of this country]. . . . In my house anyhow – I don't know about other people – the English terminated at that point. You came into your house and Bengali started and also your Arabic. Everything was Bangladesh. Home was like a realm of Bangladesh. It was a second Bangladesh.

Even if she wanted to be British she would not be accepted by those she wanted to identify with:

I belong totally to Bangladesh and if I think I belong half there, then there is something really stupid, something wrong with me mentally, because nobody in England would see me as part of their [country]. No matter what age we come into – we would all be classified as somebody from abroad. It comes to the point where they don't even know that Bangladesh exists. You are just an Asian . . . I don't want to be integrated into the whole system and just become nothing in their sort of pot. I want to retain my identity and possibly go back with it.

Azad expresses his identification with Bangladesh in similar terms:

I'd like to belong to Bangladesh, I'd like to. But because of economic and different issues like that, you know, it is necessary for me to be in England. It is not something that I want but it is something that I have to . . . right now, I don't know. Belonging is something that is catching, holding on to and I don't think the English society holds on to me whereas my Bangladeshi society does because I always want to go back. . . . I belong in Bangladesh but I am here. I don't really belong here.

There is nothing that I don't like about being here but I don't see this country's people actually accepting us which makes you feel uncomfortable in a sense – where you have to fight twice as hard to get something. But when I go back to Bangladesh everything there is mine and everyone around me is my own type of person and no one can say he is white or black.

Although the extracts quoted here are intended to reveal the range of beliefs the interviewees hold about different identities it would be dangerous to suggest that their beliefs are clearcut. There is much heart-searching about where they feel they belonged – in Britain, Bangladesh, another Muslim or an Islamic community. They are keenly aware of their family's ties with their country of origin, their upbringing in London and the claims of different belongings.

The difficulty of deciding where someone belongs is vividly portrayed by Justna:

I know they say: 'Your home is where your heart is' but I don't know where my heart is so that makes it difficult, you know. I know I keep referring back to my childhood but that's the only way I can compare it and allow for it. So I used to say that I could never move to Bangladesh and live there. Maybe to stay there for a couple of months but never to live there. . . . I just want to be left alone, maybe in the country and just do my own thing. I don't even know what my own thing is but I just want to be left alone without any hassle . . . London is my home, you know – the East End. But now I don't think . . . like I said I don't know where my heart is so I can't call home home anymore.

CONCLUSION

The deliberations outlined above of individual Bangladeshis at university were part of a much longer exploration of identity where statuses based upon class, gender and 'race', for example, were also considered. The informants were invited to reflect on the meanings which different categories had for them so that we could undertake an qualitative analysis of the 'imaginary worlds' which they inhabited.

In this account I have focused on their discussions of national and religious identities which take them across different national boundaries and link them to diverse 'homelands'. What emerges is a wide range of opinion about the claims to belonging with which these boundaries and homelands are associated. Even though individuals acknowledge that their social identity is a composite of different elements there is also a recognition that these elements may have competing claims to their allegiance.

Constructions of Islam as a primordial identity can create in individuals an uneasy sense of having to choose between religion and nation. Some reconcile the competing claims by referring to composite, hierarchically ordered identities – as British Bengali Muslims, for example, where Islam is the most important element. They acknowledge the history of their country of origin – Bangladesh – where Islam and nationalism have been closely associated in political discourse. Yet others recognize that their Muslim identity enables them to identify with any nation where *sharia* (Islamic law) is practised. They can look beyond the national frontiers of Britain and Bangladesh to other Muslim nations and to a worldwide *umma* (Muslim community) which transcends existing national boundaries.

Some recognize that attempts to establish an intimate relationship between Islamic and national identities act to exclude non-Muslims in Bangladesh and elsewhere. The relationship becomes even more problematic when they reflect on their position within Britain where Muslims constitute a tiny, controversial minority. Their identity as Bengali Muslims can be challenged by primordial nationalist discourses which strive to forge a bond between 'race' and culture, thereby establishing another exclusion, i.e. all those who can never belong to the 'indigenous' community. Some informants contested such an exclusion by affirming their citizenship as British Bengalis and their commonality with other 'black British people' while others insisted on their desire to return to a Bangladesh where they would not experience racial and religious exclusion.

Competing definitions of belonging made choice difficult, but through highly versatile individual deliberations young Bengalis were able to provide some meaningful order for themselves in response to our questions (Eade and Albrow 1994). An important element in that ordering was their ability to distinguish between collective identities, which were constructed through political and cultural discourses, and the personal significance of these identities. Yet at the same time the consistency of their deliberations must not be overemphasized. There are anxious moments of self-doubt and ambiguity where 'home' – an emotional as well as a political and cultural phenomenon – was not clearly locatable.

What particular light do these conclusions shed on the general discussion of globalization developed in this volume? Answers to this question can be found in the journeys, both physical and imaginary, with which the young Bangladeshis are engaged. Some have moved between nation-states (Bangladesh and Britain) while others who are born in this country can closely identify with their parents' country of origin (Bangladesh) and other nations within the 'Islamic world': worlds which they have never visited but can imagine through the global means of communication. While they are well aware of the powerful ties which bind themselves and others to specific nation-states they recognize that migration across national frontiers can result in the contesting of primordial definitions of national belonging. Hybrid identities, where various elements interweave in complex ten-

160

sions, are created by cultural differences constructed through ethnicized and racialized discourses. These identities are evident to the young Bangladeshis not only in the context of Britain but in their parents' country of origin where different ethnic groups co-exist despite attempts to forge an exclusivist alliance between Islam and Bangladeshi nationalism.

As we have seen their navigation between these divergent physical and imaginary worlds does not necessarily entail an easy passage free from doubt and ambiguity. Global migrants and their descendants may contest official interpretations of belonging to a particular nation-state but they are uneasily aware of the dangers involved in challenging those formulations and struggle with the conflict of loyalties shaped by movement (bodily and imaginary) across national and religious divides. The indeterminacy of translation across geopolitical and cultural boundaries can be seen in the struggle by some of the young Bangladeshis to articulate a response to our questions: a response which does not relapse into the apparent certainties of national and religious recipes which appeal to 'tradition'.

The interviewees' diverse constructions of collective solidarities also suggest that new social ties are emerging from their migrant experience. Their perceptions are a commentary on the development of new social practices which link their everyday lives in a particular locality (Tower Hamlets) to processes taking place within and across national boundaries. An awareness of these national and transnational processes shapes their understanding of locality as they deliberate the meaning of the terms 'East Ender', 'Londoner', 'white', 'black', 'English', 'British', 'European', 'Bengali', 'Bangladeshi' and 'Muslim'.

While recognition is given to the power which traditional definitions of these collectivities exercise upon the social practices of those interviewed, they are also aware of the ways in which those traditional definitions fail both to control and express the changes taking place in their individual perceptions of the world around them. Their deliberations provide us with further glimpses into a world where discourses celebrating the primordial and competing claims of nation, religion, locality, race and class, for example, are subtly challenged by new understandings and practices associated with a more heterogeneous and mobile everyday world. In this world it would seem that the boundaries which encapsulate the 'Muslim community', the 'Bangladeshi community', 'white people' or the 'British' are largely the products of an interpretative tradition shared by academic commentators, political activists, religious leaders and community representatives; those whom these 'experts' claim to represent develop more subtle and open understandings of the world around them.

The ethnoscapes devised by the young Bangladeshis indicate a more complex, fragmented, deeply reflexive world where individuals can develop highly versatile interpretations of collective solidarities. They are frequently much more aware than 'experts' (academics commentators, community leaders and political representatives) of the ambiguities which characterize this complex world. They are attempting to 'make sense' of a situation where the fixities of traditional social groupings are challenged by global mobility and where group solidarities are variably constructed through discourses and practices which are not rooted in some familial, religious or national essence. We have seen indications above that the descendants of global migrants are responding to this mobile world with versatile reformulations of traditional loyalties which reveal the tensions, hierarchical claims and ambiguities involved in identity construction and relations with others across the global city and national frontiers.

NOTES

1 This is a revised version of an article published in *International Sociology* 9 (3): 377–94.
2 *Shalwar kameez*: a tunic and loose-fitting trousers.

10

'TRIBAL ARTS'

A case study of global compression in the Notting Hill Carnival

Patricia Alleyne-Dettmers

INTRODUCTION

The Notting Hill Carnival in London! This has been acclaimed Europe's greatest street festival. Come Bank Holiday August this is the place to be. There one can view *bands* (groups) of *masqueraders, mas players* (costumed dancers) dressed in every imaginable colour *mashing up de Grove* (dancing on the streets of Ladbroke Grove). This moving asymmetrical entity does not simply happen. Behind the dancing masqueraders is a carefully researched system of *themes* (artistic depictions) of the *designers* (creative artists) who make the costumes at carnival time. These themes showcase a diversity of ideas transcending ethnic, geographical and cultural boundaries. These trans-global aesthetic flows run the gamut from masks of secret societies in Africa, powerful African tribal traditions (which is the topic of this case study), *Ramleela* and other holy festivals of South Asia, political awareness themes, like *Haiti! Let Freedom Rain!*, to *Star Trek* and love songs like *Rhapsody in Blue*. Whatever costumed form the artistic agenda chooses to manifest itself in are then re-inscribed to the local setting in London/ Notting Hill.

This carnival celebration, which represents national culture in Trinidad and Tobago (the peripheral cultural village) came to Notting Hill as part of the cultural baggage of economically marginalized Trinidadians who migrated to London – the mother country, the mecca of Western civiliz-ation – to seek better socio-economic conditions. Today this newly evolving aesthetic representation is intricately linked to African-Caribbean people's active engagement in globalizing processes and global flows. On the one hand carnival is confronted with a discourse of dislocation, fragmentation and questions of belonging generated by continuous waves of migrations, across a constantly compressed world, effected through sophisticated communication networks. On the other, it is bound up with these ethnic minorities' need to use that displacement to create other versions of imagined communities (Anderson 1996), a new sense of place, and an identifiable cultural niche in mainstream British society.

Carnival, and its accompanying *mas* art forms, therefore, seems to be a multi-faceted aesthetic canvass that continually projects multiple versions of what constitutes black British identity in general and black British live art in particular. The question is how does this happen? A closer look at the poly-cultural ethnic diversity surrounding the carnival would provide a broader insight into black British nationalism, in terms of this community's innovative artistic capital and how it is channelled as a means of constructing national and other identities.

This chapter raises another set of issues regarding the impact of globalization processes on migration, diaspora and national identity. The African-Caribbean Carnival festival at Notting Hill is examined from the perspective of these peoples' aesthetic cultural representations: i.e. masquerade themes that are *played* (manifested and enacted) in *mas* (costumes) at carnival time. It is part of an ongoing study that examines the processes of cultural transformation in terms of the socio-historical origins of Notting Hill Carnival and how that cultural and highly artistic form renegotiates and adapts itself to fit into its new cultural locale.

At the macro level the research is motivated by an interest in the notion of global compression and its specific impact on the flow of aesthetic ideas, symbols and fashions around the globe. The chapter is also informed by three related processes which underlie the mechanics of global migrations and global flows of the peoples of the African-Caribbean diaspora. These processes include the influence of the ethnoscape and mediascape (Appadurai 1993: 295–310) the socioscape (Albrow 1990) and how these processes impact directly on these peoples' representations of cultural identity in Britain. The data demonstrate that these globalizing influences impact on carnival *mas* art providing it with an easy compressed world (Harvey 1989: 240) and an evolving aesthetic repertoire that violates all fixed ethnic, geographical, cultural and national boundaries. As the case study will demonstrate, because of global compression designers can and do move powerful cultural symbols around the world through their aesthetic representations.

However, global compression in this context does not imply homogenization of places, nor does it simply facilitate easy movement of images and ideas. Instead, these aesthetic flows metamorphose as they dynamically interact with each other internally and externally consequently leading to other new formulations – new historical readings, new constructions of place, time and other identity formulations. Designers reconstitute and reinterpret these different histories and identities in the global, carnival city of Notting Hill. As a result, national hegemonies are publicly dislocated and open, public arenas are constructed, whereby a variety of these national modes are contested. This makes the Notting Hill Carnival the driving

164

force behind an evolving, transnational socio-cultural system in which there is a constant interplay between the compressed globe and the continual need to define and redefine *localness* and to construct a new identifiable locale if only temporarily.

On the micro level, carnival *mas* art is deeply rooted in the traumatic historical experiences of the Caribbean. It is a complex construct that symbolically re-visions varying stages of Caribbean history: from its colonial settlement and slavery, despair and geographical dislocation of the African peoples, through their emancipation, decolonization and finally globalization, manifested in the massive migrations of the African-Caribbean populace to the former power centre in the heart of London. Plural readings of national identity emerge as designers grapple with the fundamental social and political conditions to represent the complexities of that experience.

Recent scholarship on the construction of national identities refers to the creation of imagined communities (Anderson 1986), hybridization or hybrid identities (Gilroy 1993b), and diasporic communities (Hall 1992a). This chapter, however, suggests another perspective for an understanding of national identities by raising four pertinent issues:

(a) the concept of multiple diasporization effected by globalization and its resultant time–space compression;
(b) new forms of fragmentation and disjuncture as a result of multiple diasporization leading to reconciliation, metamorphosis and subsequent reconstruction of place;
(c) aesthetic representation in carnival as a powerful symbol for the re-attainment of territorial power, female power and as a medium for mobilizing the oppressed; and
(d) more importantly, pluralistic readings of national identity that are constantly and openly contested.

This chapter examines national identity as presented on the carnival stage at Notting Hill as a public re-enactment of early colonial migrations from the horrors of the colonial legacy – human oppression and cultural denigration – and how that experience is re-inscribed as an ideological matrix to provide that renewed sense of cultural wholeness that gets played out in a proliferation of masquerade forms on the streets of Notting Hill at carnival time.

GLOBALIZATION: SOME THEORETICAL CONSIDERATIONS

Before turning to the actual case study, it is important to examine some of the key concepts which have been developed in the globalization literature.

In the process the terms 'mediascape', 'ethnoscape' and 'socioscape' will also be clarified.

Giddens focuses on the global flows of peoples and the dissemination of a diversity of ideas, aesthetic symbols, capital and power as well as the cultural networks and geographical linkages that are forged by nation-states as a result of these international flows (Giddens 1990). For Giddens globalization also encompasses the struggles and the transformations effected by these flows. The means by which these ideas become 'stretched across the globe' are described by Giddens as 'disembedding mechanisms' (Giddens 1990) in which local and immediate contexts are removed from their familiar arenas and placed in larger and more global ones. As a result there is a rupture between time and space, referred to by Giddens as 'time–space distanciation' (Giddens 1990: 14) which caters for larger and larger groups of people who live in a world in which social events and social relations at a distance are interlaced with local contextualities (Giddens 1991: 21).

Harvey also highlights 'time–space compression' as one of the principal features of globalization (Harvey 1989: 240). Distance diminishes so that events in one place impact almost immediately on absent others thousands of miles away.

Harvey's postulation complements Appadurai's concepts of the 'mediascape' and 'ethnoscape'. Mediascape refers:

> both to the distribution of the electronic capabilities to produce and disseminate information (newspapers, magazines, television stations, film production studios, etc.) which are now available to a growing number of private and public interests throughout the world; and to the images of the world created by these media.
>
> (Appadurai 1993: 298–9)

The most important feature of these mediascapes is that they provide to world-wide viewers an immediate and complex repository of representations. 'Ethnoscapes', on the other hand, are created by: 'the persons who constitute the shifting world in which we live: tourists, immigrants, refugees, exiles, guestworkers and other moving groups' (Appadurai 1994: 297).

Another novel contribution to the time–space compression debate is Albrow's concept of the socioscape. Albrow describes, first of all, the 'sociosphere' which refers to 'a field of concern or relevance which does not have in any geometrical sense to be spherical' (see p. 51 above). 'Socioscape' describes 'the vision of social formations which are more than the people who occupy them at any one time' (see p. 38 above). People are actively involved in global flows and Albrow draws on the research conducted in Tooting which revealed plural ethnicities with diverse lifestyles and social networks, co-existing in one community without untoward interference with each other, yet maintaining family and religious ties over the globe.

This notion of the 'socioscape' highlights complexity and the multiplicity of social relations. People interpret their world in various ways without making direct connections with each other because of their different perceptual horizons. In the case of the Notting Hill Carnival there are two important question related to these paradigms:

(a) what then is a national identity?
(b) can it be preserved in the light of these globalization processes?

One should not forget that the carnival's most important feature is aesthetic representation through *mas* art. Consequently, processual shaping and re-shaping of time–space relationships deeply affect how identities are represented and located because all identities are symbolically located spatially and temporally. Said describes this process as resulting in 'imaginary geographies' (Said 1990: 81–100).

GLOBAL COMPRESSION:
MULTIPLE DIASPORIZATION AND PLURALISTIC
READINGS OF DIVERSE IDENTITIES

As pointed out earlier in this chapter, the Notting Hill Carnival was brought to Britain by migrant Trinidadians. When one further examines Trinidadian/ Caribbean society it is made up of dislocating, fragmentary and disparate structures. The fragments are the remnants of the colonial legacy of slavery which have left African-Caribbeans riven from each other. This is the earliest notion of a diasporic community. From this fragmentation pluralistic societies evolved comprising diverse ethno-cultural components (Braithwaite 1960; Smith 1965). Because of the ease of travel facilitated by global compression, a new process of diasporization occurs when these African-Caribbeans migrate to the metropolis – in this case London. Bear in mind, however, that these African-Caribbean individuals are products of a society shaped by its own dynamics of internal and external interactions. However, with migration these African-Caribbeans do not find themselves at the top rung of British society. Instead, they are confined to the margins where they have to renegotiate their sense of balance, politically, socially and otherwise given the alien structures of mainstream British society.

In the process of re-mapping their sense of place and their *culture*scapes they are also confronted with other marginalized groups which are equally displaced and also operate on the margins of British society, competing for the same resources, seeking to create an identifiable space, as well as trying to make sense of new locales and other cultural forms. These diverse groups find themselves developing new discourses concerning place, values and identities.

167

The Notting Hill Carnival seems to have provided the forum for these various groups to coalesce and for the shaping of new collectivities. This happened in the late 1950s when one member of the West Indian community was murdered in a race-related incident. The West Indian community and other marginal groups retaliated through what was later to become known as the infamous 'race riot' of Notting Hill. The riot also transfigured the grandeur of England, tarnishing the migrant West Indian image of Britain as the 'Mother Country'. The new African-Caribbean grouping originated as people from different Caribbean islands who had never come together and who probably would never have come together before (in the Caribbean) came together to solidarize and to support each other. They did this by playing *mas* together at Notting Hill thereby laying the foundations for the first version of a black British identity.

In this political context ethnicity and nationalism/national identity emerge in a very special way. What we are looking at is the fragmentary nature of the society, the diversity of groups that proliferated as a result of the colonial legacy, later migration, and later solidarity through threats of racial and political extinction from the dominant power group. With the formation of new collectivities through groups coalescing and subtly falling apart again, a very complex process is taking place – what I have termed *multiple diasporization*. In the course of this process groups impact on and interact with each other and socio-cultural and political symbols are constantly reworked. Ideas collide with each other. Other ideas become redundant, illogical and are discarded. Disjuncture leads to reconciliation and metamorphosis. Consequently, new creative activities, new groupings and new explanations evolve, producing various new identities (Hall 1992b) and relocation or a new sense of place. As Lash and Urry have argued, globalization can affect new local configurations of place as people critically review notions of space (Lash and Urry 1994).

In the carnival context, nationalism is not homogeneous, static or normative. From all the disparate fragments – and the way in which these are continually depicted through carnival themes that are articulated in costumes – we see a processual enactment of this community's quest for national and other identities. There is a constant evocation of the multiple, global configurations left by the various historical antecedents: American-Indian, European, African, Asian, Indian, Chinese and Hispanic. At the same time these global legacies are not static remnants of a long-forgotten past. Instead, they are retrieved and revitalized to create other new forms and even empower old ones to create new accounts and new myths. The new forms appear not only with alternative meanings and values but recast in another form or language all representatives of the African-Caribbean's on-going quest for national and other identities.

The *mas* continually metamorphoses. It changes shape and grows – it is always negotiated and in a constant state of becoming. *Mas* is a powerful symbol within the global system for the attainment of territorial power and it becomes the cultural medium for mobilizing subordinate groups. In this way nationalism becomes a contested reality. It becomes an arena for power politics – in terms of the on-going struggle of the subordinate to become powerful. What the diasporic peoples are doing is giving some temporary specificity to national identity, to nationalism, to define ethnicity and, by extension, culture through the enactment and the dancing costumes on the streets.

Finally, the Notting Hill Carnival has been adopted by this particular multi-ethnic community as the most important public forum where the best of its community's art can be proudly displayed. Thus, we are presented not with the uniformity and homogeneity of national identity, but with the politics underlying different versions of the nation which are continually being contested, formed and reformed.

Culture in this sense can no longer be seen as the expression of a community's identity. Culture also moves away from being fixed and monolithic. It becomes heterogeneous, differentiated and processual, embracing in its definition the defining categories and knowledge associated with the formation of communities. By extension, cultural identities in Britain are no longer fixed categories. They transcend narrow versions of the British nation, becoming ambivalent through multi-dimensionality.

'TRIBAL ARTS'

'Tribal Arts' was Carl Gabriel's 1993 presentation for the Notting Hill Carnival. Gabriel is the designer and bandleader of *Misty Carnival Club.* Why the title 'Tribal Arts'? According to the designer: '*Mas* has to return to remote Africa to become meaningful. That's how I see our arts. I wanted to take it back to its roots.'

'Tribal Arts' was a cyclical presentation of Nature's rhythms. It progressed from Birth to Maturity culminating with Death mirrored through the African face mask taken from several African tribes. Four different regions of Africa were recreated with each face mask symbolically expressing in its orientation a powerful function for the continent it symbolized. This notion of African aesthetic representation was selected not only to emphasize the importance of the face mask in African tribal traditions but as a metaphorical vehicle to dramatize and recreate the real moments of various African historical and socio-political landscapes destroyed through the traumas of colonization.

The first section of the band was a microcosmic vision of the Tutsi tribe. Given the political upheavals associated with contemporary Tutsi life, this section reconstructed pertinent features of the traditional African world view. The masqueraders were dressed in simple costumes that pitted the colours black and white against each other. They had long flowing hair as

169

headpieces. They were led by an individual, taken from another African tribe – the Bakuba tribe (also known as the Kuba) of Central Africa (see Figure 10.1). Bakuba art is one of the most highly developed of all African visual arts. This masquerader wore one of the sophisticated, artistic masks that symbolized the ritual of circumcision – a rite of passage in the Van Gennep sense – marking the movement from birth/childhood to maturity/ adulthood (Van Gennep 1947). Circumcision, in this case, is definitive, marking the child from the adult.

According to the village elders of the Bakuba when the boys come of age they are circumcized. Before the ritual of circumcision begins, the elders responsible for its performance run through the village wearing this mask. A large procession comes into the village to greet the initiates who will eventually move into adulthood.

By rejuvenating this powerful mask in the context of carnival in the global urban centre of London, the designer's pan-Africanist reading of Africa symbolically moves Africa back to take centre stage from where it was tragically mangled in slavery and the Middle Passage Crossing to the Caribbean. The power of the African village is reconstituted as a symbol of recovery to empower members of the black British community, extracting them from their impoverished histories, fostered by colonial subordination and dispossession. It affirms black British identity by asserting their power through their aesthetic representations of black British society.

The second section of the band showcased an ancient extinct mask of the Dula tribe from the forest region of the Republic of Cameroon. It was rejuvenated by the designer because of the notion of extinctness and the appeal of the colours. The principal masquerader wore a mask that looked like an ancient animal head with black, orange and white shapes, similar to something between a zebra and a donkey with horns. The designer developed costumes for the floor members of the band using a similar pattern of triangular shapes found on this mask (see Figure 10.2). By retrieving an extinct mask on the global, carnival stage, we see a re-valorization of the African heritage that provides a psycho-social uplifting of the African-Caribbean peoples. At the same time, these powerful African models seek to redeem the black image through the contemporary carnival art form.

The next dynamic individual was the King of Tribal Arts. Again this was powerful circumcision mask of a secret society somewhat similar to the Ngere Wobe tribe of the Ivory Coast. With this tribe the mask functions as a medium of communication between the living and the dead ancestors. The tribe is also famous for its sculpture, embodying two extremes of stylistic variation: the smooth, refined style of the Dan De and Diomande tribes and the grotesque, cubistic style of the Ngere (or Guere) Wobe tribes of the same region. The artist sought to recapture these dualities in the face mask worn by the King (see Figure 10.3). The actual mask was made of

Figure 10.1 The Bakuba circumcision mask from 'Tribal Arts'

Figure 10.2 The Duala extinct mask from 'Tribal Arts'

Figure 10.3 The Ngere Wobe King's mask from 'Tribal Arts'

fibre-glass, and decorated with retrieved garbage (empty cans and bits of rope). The actual King's costume was a simple construction with moss-green as the predominant colour.

THE WOMEN AS CARNIVAL QUEENS: POWER AND GENDERED AESTHETIC REPRESENTATIONS IN TRIBAL ARTS

Before looking at the Carnival Queens of this band it is important to describe briefly the role of the women in carnival. If women are not involved in wearing a costume, their role seems to be quite a traditional one. In the carnival *mas* camp (the specific locale where the costumes are made), women are responsible for the semi-skilled work, such as costume-decorating and sewing. The division of labour is also such that the women work within the private confines of the house and the men work outside in the yard at the back of the house. The women are expected to plan and to execute their sewing or decorating tasks earnestly and patiently, paying attention to the details of the costumes. There is an element of orderliness here, when the costumes are relatively close to completion. In addition, since most of the would-be masqueraders come into the house to choose a costume, the women are expected to create a working atmosphere that emphasizes a certain correctness of behaviour so as to impress prospective clientele and win masquerader support for the band. In this respect, the women's role is quite a traditional one: linked to the image of 'woman as homemaker'; and it is quite a subordinate one, since all that is really expected of her is to do the lighter work on the costume and to create a good impression on the outside world so as to increase the band membership.

The figure of most importance in a carnival band is the Carnival Queen of the Band. A band may or may not have a King but there is almost always a Queen. Generally she is an elaboration of the theme of the band. In this respect women always have the opportunity to create a situation of power for themselves simply by wearing and articulating the Queen's costume (i.e dancing and enacting it). Depending on what the costume is expected to portray women can confront, resist and even modify assumptions about their role within the wider society. Moreover, since competition is the name of the game, in that the women have to wear the costumes and compete in the various carnival competitions, they can and do negotiate a powerful situation for themselves. In this way any assumptions about women's subordinate position are re-interpreted: a process effected through that very situation of power in which they find themselves.

The first of these power figures in 'Tribal Arts' was the junior Queen of the Band. The artist showcased 'Osyeba' – a funerary figure from the Gabon Republic. In this society art is closely linked to death and its accompanying rituals which placate the dead spirits when they depart this world. The power of this death mask rejuvenated by the artist lay in the very simplicity of the costume. The heart-shaped mask was three feet tall by two and a half feet wide. It was constructed in such a way that the masquerader's head peeped through an aperture cut into the skull. The mask was decorated with leaves and acorns representing the natural beauty of untarnished nature (see Figure 10.4).

On a metaphorical level, through the image of death, this junior Queen's costume (the woman's costume) became a symbolic unmasking of the diasporic people's historical experiences. Death is equated with history and the virtual death/destruction of African culture through black enslavement and a people's loss of a sense of history. However, by capitalizing on the power of the African death mask, that very death becomes a political strategy to re-address the psychological tensions and conflicts that the African-Caribbean people face in their various attempts to come to terms with themselves as blacks, their African past and the Eurocentric West in which they find themselves. It was like holding up a broken mirror to reflect the problems confronting them. Death within the global, plural context of carnival provided the medium for the diasporic peoples to reclaim a sense of territory for themselves.

Because of global compression, therefore, with the playing of African 'Osyeba' a powerful dialectic is seen between timelessness and placelessness that leads to relocation, a reconstruction of place, even mobilization if only in the sense of carnival play. Ironically enough it is a woman who championed that novel aesthetic version of the diasporic peoples.

The most powerful costume was the senior Queen of the Band, depicting the mother of the African village. The mother, the village elder, was choreographed as the life blood and unifier of the village. She helps by giving birth: providing the village with new life. She is then left to give guidance, and to regulate and order life in the village. By the same token, as pointed out earlier, the Carnival Queen is the most important, and the most outstanding figure in the band, since she carries the band. She is an elaboration of the designer's vision for the band.

Again the most prominent feature of that costume was the face mask based on an elder of the village with very prominant features and whose hair was in braids, similar to the Mambuti-type headdress. The braids were weaved from the forehead to the back of the head, tapering off like a cone. The costume was a very basic one. The masquerader wore a simple top made from golden, earthy brown autumn leaves, with highlights of gold. The skirt was made from palm leaves. It was a larger-than-life female figure towering high above all the other masqueraders' heads (see Figure 10.5).

What Gabriel has done with this costume is to allegorize Africa. Africa is presented as a female puppet as if awakened from a deep sleep. It is a

Figure 10.4 'Osyeba': the death mask from 'Tribal Arts'

176

Figure 10.5 The African Mother of the village: Queen of 'Tribal Arts'

dynamic vision of Africa's Renaissance reconstituted in the process of becoming something powerful akin to Prometheus Unbound.

THE AFRICAN HERITAGE RE-INTERPRETED: RECLAIMING TERRITORIAL POWER

A closer examination of 'Tribal Arts' reveals some very interesting processes with respect to the designer's agenda for nationalism in the black British cultural context.

From the perspective of the designer, Africa is not a specific geographical area. Instead it is a vision that Gabriel has in his mind that constitutes a yardstick for black aesthetic achievement and black national identity. Africa becomes an imagined community, which is aesthetically realized when it climaxes as a carnival costume on a masquerader dancing through the streets of Notting Hill. Four different regions of Africa are recreated with the intention of re-evaluating African culture. In this context Africa is meant to recapture African-Caribbean people's alienation, subsequent social estrangement and their attempts to reconcile the paradoxes of their slave heritage in order to interpret and find a place in their social present: in a word, reconstruction.

Because of the deculturation of the African slave, the subsequent myth of the *tabula rasa* and the acculturation of the colonized to the colonizer, black people in the Caribbean were caught up in a web of cultural traditions, languages and models, all of which were alien to them. As a result, black Caribbean peoples frequently linked Africa to non-identity, non-progressiveness, drumming, dancing, superstition, naked and uneducated tribesmen, permanent displacement and hopelessness. These negative images, which are Western-centric versions of the African heritage, conjure up notions of fragmentation, disruption, of being castaway (Walcott 1966), of striving for a sense of direction in a Western world whose people claimed to be the guardians of civilization, intelligence and social prestige.

The geographical and social dislocation from the native land (Africa) and the continual attempts to escape from Western-imposed models led to the problem of defining home. Some African-Caribbeans were nostalgic for an African homeland even though many had never seen or knew much about Africa. By symbolically revitalizing four different regions of Africa Gabriel attempted to construct an African-Caribbean identity by consciously re-ordering through *mas* that other African identity whose progress was continually crippled and censured by European, colonial exploitation.

Despite the fact that Africa is a visionary abstraction, the designer still imagines Africa through the prism of a museum construct. He went to look at various displays of African arts. However, he did not copy them; he produced something akin to what he saw in order to enhance his particular vision of Africa. This in itself is a paradox. On the one hand, he sees the artefacts of the museum heritage as authentic. On the other hand, he is indirectly questioning the culture of authenticity within which museums exhibit artefacts that are totally removed from their original context. Yet this museum culture also provides the artist with a realistic link to enhance his vision of Africa. This preoccupation with authenticity has produced a complex set of aesthetic representations in which the previous African culture is reinterpreted not only as a vehicle of artistic exploration but as a subject to be analysed and explored. As such with *mas* art forms there is a constant interplay between the global and the local. Diverse cultural forms become globalized, yet multiple readings of cultural identities are re-localized so there is a constant tension between the two components.

Africa is also a symbol in the designer's mind. It is not a continent but a concept. It could be one place, many places or multiple readings of familiar geographical places. It is a personal construction of Africa, which becomes a wider cultural product through carnival, in a London urban setting but for the African-Caribbean peoples. What we are seeing is a renegotiation of the coercive removal of the Africans from Africa through the Middle Passage Crossing to Trinidad/the Caribbean. We see a revitalization of African-Caribbean history and a reworking of the cultural denigration of these peoples. Yet at the same time we see the acceptance, the renaissance and the cultural power of that history through its artistic embodiment on the global stage. As a result, black people start to develop a sense of self-assurance and self-respect 'becoming more receptive than ever to issues of ethnic and national consciousness' (Brown 1978).

The African-Caribbean diasporic people thus realize that Africa was not past or present, but something to be confronted if they were ever going to bridge the gap between the homeland, Africa, and the Middle Passage Crossing to the Caribbean. In addition, the reality of the situation is that the designer is also a migrant: a voice from the margins that has moved the carnival from the global carnival village in Trinidad to place it front stage in the metropolitan centre of Notting Hill. The recreated African village heralds the power of marginal groups and assists them in experiencing that sense of power if only for a few hours on the carnival stage. The Western notion of movement from periphery to metropolis becomes meaningless since movement in this context is caught up in a symbolic network of people, ideas and aesthetic representations of these. Not only is there an imaginary vision of Africa but an imaginary movement between geographical spaces because the masks are taken from different regions in Africa and are then renegotiated.

Through this aesthetic, imaginary reconstruction of denigrated African culture powerful symbols belonging to the African continent are moved around the world. Gabriel's playing and dancing of African *mas*, rooted in a rediscovery of Africa and a renaissance of African history, functioned symbolically to give back to black people a sense of a defining history, a sense of roots. In addition, all the predominant costumes of the band tower way above the other masqueraders' heads. This is intentional because these are power figures. Based on their larger-than-life visibility and their capacity to command and attract respect from their over-stated size and their sophisticated levels of craftsmanship, they encapsulated on-going processes of plural versions of reconstructed nationalism of the African-Caribbean peoples.

By the same token there is the notion of ethnic empowerment for the band itself – 'Tribal Arts' won prizes in the Notting Hill Carnival competitions. Winning a carnival prize strengthens the designer's specific vision of authenticity. Thus, because of global compression, aesthetic cultural representation, in this context, reaffirms a sense of history, a sense of time and a new sense of place.

This chapter has closely investigated one carnival theme which forms a part of a complex collage of the diversified aesthetic repertoire of marginal, ethnic groups in Britain. It has also examined the rationale underlying the presentation which has provided important insights into the politics of multiple diasporization and the formation of multiple identities because of the dynamic impact of globalization processes.

ACKNOWLEDGEMENTS

C. Gabriel has kindly consented to the release of the pictures used in this chapter.

BIBLIOGRAPHY

Adams, C. (1987) *Across Seven Seas and Thirteen Rivers: Life Stories of Pioneer Sylheti Settlers in Britain*, London: THAP Books.

Albrow, M. (1987) 'Sociology for one world', *International Sociology* 2: 1–12.

—— (1990) 'Introduction', in M. Albrow and E. King (eds) *Globalization, Knowledge and Society*, London: Sage.

—— (1991) 'Internationalism as a publication project: experience in editing an international sociological journal', *Current Sociology* 39: 101–18.

—— (1993a) 'Globalization', in W. Outhwaite and T. Bottomore (eds) *The Blackwell Dictionary of Twentieth Century Social Thought*, Oxford: B. Blackwell.

—— (1993b) 'The changing British role in European sociology', in B. Nedelmann and P. Sztompka (eds) *Sociology in Europe: In Search of Identity*, Berlin: De Gruyter.

—— (1993c) 'Local ills and global remedies: presentiments for European sociology in the British experience', *Innovation* 6: 135–45.

—— (1996) *The Global Age*, Cambridge: Polity Press.

Albrow, M., Eade, J., Fennell, G. and O'Byrne, D. (1994) *Local/Global Relations in a London Borough*, London: Roehampton Institute.

Alexander, C. (1994) 'Street credibility and identity', working paper to be published in T. Ranger, Y. Samad and O. Stuart (eds) (1996) *Culture, Identity and Politics*, Aldershot: Avebury.

Anderson, B. (1986) *Imagined Communities: Reflections on the Origin and Spread of Nationalism*, London: Verso/New Left Books.

Anderson, N. (1923) *The Hobo*, Chicago: University of Chicago Press.

Anthias, F. (1990) 'Race and class revisited – conceptualising race and racisms', *Sociological Review* 38 (1): 19–42.

Appadurai, A. (1990) 'Disjuncture and difference in the global cultural economy', in M. Featherstone (ed.) *Global Culture: Nationalism, Globalization and Modernity*, London: Sage.

—— (1993) 'The production of locality', paper presented to the Association of Social Anthropologists, University of Oxford.

Archer, M. (1988) *Culture and Agency: The Place of Culture in Social Theory*, Cambridge: Cambridge University Press.

Back, L. (1993) 'Race, identity and nation within an adolescent community in South London', *New Community* 19 (2): 217–33.

Bailey, F. (ed.) (1971) *Gifts and Poison: The Politics of Reputation*, Oxford: B. Blackwell.

Ballard, R. (ed.) (1994) *Desh Pardesh: The South Asian Presence in Britain*, London: C. Hurst and Co.

Banfield, E.C. (1956) *The Moral Basis of a Backward Society*, Glencoe, Ill.: Free Press.

Barker, M. (1981) *The New Racism*, London: Junction Books.

Bell, C. and Newby, H. (1971) *Community Studies*, London: G. Allen and Unwin.

Bertaux-Wiame, I. (1981) 'The life history approach to the study of internal migration', in D. Bertaux (ed.) *Biography and Society: The Life History Approach in the Social Sciences*, London: Sage.

Bhabha, H. (ed.) (1990) *Nation and Narration*, London: Routledge.

—— 'Introduction: narrating the nation and dissemiNation: time, narrative and the margins of the modern nation', in H. Bhabha (ed.) *Nation and Narration*, London: Routledge.

Bhachu, P. (1985) *Twice Migrants: East African Sikh Settlers in Britain*, London and New York: Tavistock.

Bird, J., Curtis, B., Putnam, T., Robertson, G. and Tickner, L. (eds) (1993) *Mapping the Futures: Local Cultures, Global Change*, London: Routledge.

Bird, J. (1993) 'Dystopia on the Thames' in J. Bird *et al.* (eds) *Mapping the Futures: Local Cultures, Global Change*, London: Routledge.

Bott, E. (1957) *Family and Social Network*, London: Tavistock.

Boudon, R. and Bourricaud, F. (1989) *A Critical Dictionary of Sociology*, trans. P. Hamilton, London: Routledge.

Bouquet, M. and Winter, M. (eds) (1987) *Who From Their Labours Rest: Conflict and Practice in Rural Tourism*, Aldershot: Avebury.

Bourke, J. (1994) *Working-class Cultures in Britain 1890–1960*, London: Routledge.

Boyne, R. (1990) 'Culture and the world system', in M. Featherstone (ed.) *Global Culture: Nationalism, Globalization and Modernity*, London: Sage.

Braithwaithe, L. (1960) 'Social stratification and cultural pluralism in the Caribbean', in *Annals of the New York Academy of Sciences*, 83.

Brennan, T., Cooney, E. and Pollins, H. (1954) *Social Change in South-West Wales*, London: Watts & Co.

Brown, A. (1978) *West Indian Poetry*, Boston: G.K. Holt and Co.

Brownhill, S. (1990) *Developing London's Docklands: Another Great Planning Disaster?*, London: P. Chapman Publishing.

Budd, L. and Whimster, S. (eds) (1992) *Global Finance & Urban Living. A Study of Metropolitan Change*, London: Routledge.

Cambridge, A.X. (1992) 'Cultural recognition and identity', in A.X. Cambridge and S. Feuchtwang (eds) *Where You Belong*, Aldershot: Avebury.

Cambridge, A.X. and Feuchtwang, S. (eds) (1992) *Where You Belong*, Aldershot: Avebury.

Carey, S. and Shukur, A. (1985–6) 'A profile of the Bangladeshi community in East London', *New Community* 12 (3): 405–29.

Carlini, G. (ed.) (1995) *Materiali per una Ricerca su 'Poverta' e 'Nuove Poverta' a Genova*, Genova: ECIG.

Carter, E., Donald, J. and Squires, J. (1993) 'Introduction', in E. Carter, J. Donald and J. Squires (eds) *Space and Place: Theories of Identity and Location*, London: Lawrence and Wishart.

Castells, M. (1989) *The Informational City*, Oxford: B. Blackwell.

Census Update (1992) London: Research and Strategy Group, Tower Hamlets.

Choudhury, Y. (1993) *Roots and Tales of the Bangladeshi Settlers*, Birmingham: Sylheti Social History Group.

Centre for Bangladeshi Studies (1994) *Roots and Beyond: Voices from 'Educationally Successful' Bangladeshis*, London: Roehampton Institute and Queen Mary and Westfield College.

Clarke, J. (1979) 'Capital and culture: the post-war working class revisited', in J. Clarke, C. Critcher and R. Johnson (eds) *Working Class Culture: Studies in History and Theory*, London: Hutchinson.

Park, R. and Burgess, E. (1921) *Introduction to the Science of Sociology*, Chicago: University of Chicago Press.

—— (1925) *The City*, Chicago: University of Chicago Press.

Petrella R. (1989) 'La mondialisation de la technologie et de l'economie. Une (hypo)these perspective', *Futuribles*, No.135.

Pieretti G. (1995) 'Affettivita e dipendenza nello studio delle "poverta" urbane estreme', unpublished paper presented at the conference 'Poverta e esclusione sociale: contributi metodologici e concettuali', Genoa.

Qureshi, T. and Toon, I. (1994) 'Race, class and ethnicity in the remaking of "East Enders"', New Ethnicities Unit, University of East London.

Radcliffe-Brown, A.R. (1952) *Structure and Function in Primitive Society*, London: Cohen and West.

Rees, A.D. (1950) *Life in a Welsh Countryside*, Cardiff: University of Wales Press.

Reeves, F. (1983) *British Racial Discourse*, Cambridge: Cambridge University Press.

Rex, J. (1986) *Race and Ethnicity*, Milton Keynes: Open University Press.

Rex, J. and Moore, R. (1967) *Race, Community and Conflict*, London: Oxford University Press.

Rhodes, C. and Nabi, N. (1992) 'Brick Lane: a village economy in the shadow of the city?', in L. Budd and S. Whimster (eds) *Global Finance & Urban Living: A Study of Metropolitan Change*, London: Routledge.

Ritzer, G. (1993) *The McDonaldization of Society*, Thousand Oaks: Pine Forge Press.

Robertson, R. (1992) *Globalization*, London: Sage.

—— (1994) 'Globalisation or glocalisation?', *Journal of International Communication* 1 (1): 33–52.

—— (1995) 'Glocalization: Time–space and homogeneity–heterogeneity', in M. Featherstone, S. Lash and R. Robertson (eds) *Global Modernities*, London: Sage.

Robins, K. (1991) 'Tradition and translation: national culture in its global context', in J. Corner and S. Harvey (eds) *Enterprise and Heritage: Crosscurrents of National Culture*, London: Routledge.

Said, E. (1990) 'Narrative and geography', *New Left Review* 180: 81–100.

Saifullah Khan, V. (ed.) (1979) *Minority Families in Britain*, London: Tavistock.

Samad, Y. (1992) 'Book burning and race relations: political mobilisation of Bradford Muslims', *New Community* 18 (4): 507–19.

Sassen, S. (1991) *The Global City*, Princeton: Princeton University Press.

—— (1994) *Cities in a World Economy*, London and New Delhi: Pine Forge Press.

Scheler, M. (1966) *Der Formalismus in der Ethik und die Materiale Wertethik*, Bern und Munich: Francke.

Schütz, A. (1966) 'Some structures of the life-world', in *Collected Papers Vol.III: Studies in Phenomenological Sociology*, The Hague: Nijhoff.

—— (1967) 'Symbol, reality and society', in *Collected Papers Vol.I: The Problem of Social Reality*, The Hague: Nijhoff.

—— (1970) *Reflections on the Problem of Relevance*, edited by R.M. Zaner, New Haven and London: Yale University Press.

Schwartz, B. (1991) 'Where horses shit a hundred sparrows feed: Docklands and East London during the Thatcher years', in J. Corner and S. Harvey (eds) *Enterprise and Heritage: Crosscurrents of National Culture*, London: Routledge.

Sen A., (1990) 'Se il benessere non e'il nostro bene', supplemento al Sole 24 Ore, No. 296.

—— (1993) 'Capability and well-being', in M.C. Nussbaum and A. Sen (eds) *The Quality of Life*, New York, Clarendon Press.

Shaw, A. (1988) *A Pakistani Community in Britain*, Oxford: Basil Blackwell.

Sheldon, J. (1948) *The Social Medicine of Old Age: Report of an Inquiry in Wolverhampton*, Oxford: Oxford University Press.

Simmel, G. (1908) *Soziologie*, Leipzig: Duncker und Humboldt.

Smith, M. (1965) *The Plural Society in the British West Indies*, Berkeley, Los Angeles and London: University of California Press.

Solomos, J. (1989) *Race and Racism in Contemporary Britain*, London: Macmillan.

Stacey, M. (1960) *Tradition and Change: A Study of Banbury*, Oxford: Oxford University Press.

—— (1969) 'The myth of community studies', *British Journal of Sociology* 20: 134–47.

Suttles, G. (1973) *The Social Construction of Communities*, Chicago: University of Chicago Press.

Taucer U. (1995) 'Il sapere: un antidoto al virus della poverta', in G. Carlini (ed.) *Materiali per una Ricerca su 'Poverta' e 'Nuove Poverta' a Genova*, Genoa: ECIG.

Thompson, E.P. (1963) *The Making of the English Working Class*, London: Victor Gollancz.

Thompson, J.B. (1990) *Ideology and Modern Culture: Critical Social Theory in the Era of Mass Communication*, Cambridge: Polity.

Thrasher, F. (1927) *The Gang*, Chicago: University of Chicago Press.

Tower Hamlets Careers Service (1994) *Schools Destination Survey*.

Townsend, P. (1957) *The Family Life of Old People: An Inquiry in East London*, London: Routledge & Kegan Paul.

—— (1993) *The International Analysis of Poverty*, Hemel Hempstead: Harvester Wheatsheaf.

Tunstall, J. (1962) *The Fishermen*, London: MacGibbon and Kee.

Van Gennep, A. (1947) *Manuel de Folklore Contemporain*, Vol. 1, Paris: Picard.

Walcott, D. (1966) *The Castaway*, London: Jonathan Cape.

Waldenfels, B. (1985) *In den Netzen der Lebenswelt*, Frankfurt: Suhrkamp.

Wallman, S. (ed.) (1979) *Ethnicity at Work*, London: Tavistock.

Warner, W.L. and Low, J.O. (1947)) *The Social System of the Modern Factory*, New Haven, Conn.: Yale University Press.

Warner, W.L. and Lunt, P.S. (1941) *The Social Life of a Modern Community'*, New Haven, Conn.: Yale University Press.

Warner, W.L. and Srole, L. (1945) *The Social System of American Ethnic Groups*, New Haven, Conn.: Yale University Press.

Waters M. (1995) *Globalization*, London: Routledge 1995.

Watson, J.L. (1977) 'Introduction: immigration, ethnicity and class in Britain', in J.L. Watson (ed.) *Between Two Cultures: Migrants and Minorities in Britain*, Oxford: B. Blackwell.

Weber, M. (1978) *Economy and Society*, Berkeley: University of California Press.

Wemyss, G. (1992) 'The politics of multiculturalism and equal opportunities in a college of education', unpublished MA dissertation, University of Sussex.

Werbner, P. (1985) 'The organization of giving and ethnic elites', *Ethnic and Racial Studies* 8(3): 368–88.

—— (1990) *The Migration Process: Capital, Gifts and Offerings among British Pakistanis*, Oxford: Berg Publishers.

—— (1991) 'The fiction of unity in ethnic politics: aspects of representation and the state among British Pakistanis', in P. Werbner and M. Anwar (eds) *Black and Ethnic Leaderships: The Cultural Dimensions of Political Action*, London: Routledge.

Werbner, P. and Anwar, M. (eds) (1991) *Black and Ethnic Leaderships: The Cultural Dimensions of Political Action*, London: Routledge.

Wiese, L. von (1933) *System der Soziologie*, Munich und Leipzig: Duncker und Humboldt.

Williams, R. (1984) *The Long Revolution*, Harmondsworth: Penguin Books.
—— (1976) *Keywords: A Vocabulary of Culture and Society*, London: Fontana/Croom Helm.
Williams, W.M. (1956) *The Sociology of an English Village: Gosforth*, London: Routledge.
Willis, P. (1977) *Learning to Labour: How Working Class Kids Get Working Class Jobs*, Farnborough: Saxon House.
Wirth, L. (1928) *The Ghetto*, Chicago: University of Chicago Press.
—— (1938) 'Urbanism as a way of life', *American Journal of Sociology* 44: 1–24.
Wylie, L. (1957) *Village in the Vaucluse*, Oxford: Oxford University Press.
Young, M. and Willmott, P. (1957) *Family and Kinship in East London*, London: Routledge & Kegan Paul.
Zorbaugh, H. (1929) *The Gold Coast and the Slum*, Chicago: University of Chicago Press.

INDEX

191

KING ALFRED'S COLLEGE
LIBRARY